Please Don't Remove MarGreat's Glasses

By

Josh Baker

*T*his book is dedicated to my wonderful daughter, Morgan Sophia, whose bedtime laughter is my greatest inspiration. I will always cherish the many rambunctious MarGreat adventures we have shared.

Acknowledgments

I would like to personally thank the following people whose contributions and support made this book possible:

To the three dearest to me: Wendi, Alec, and Morgan, thank you for your patience and support, and for enduring the distraction of this project for the past fourteen months.

Special thanks to Deborah Lenik for her encouragement over the years, grammatical expertise and honest opinion.

The final form and readability of this work is the result of Katrina Beaver's editorial prowess. Thank you for aiding in my readers enjoyment. Your compassionate cleanup and feedback were crucial to the book's completion.

Heartfelt appreciation to the United States Conference of Catholic Bishops for granting permission to quote the New American Bible, Revised Edition. Special thanks to Colin O'Brien for his swift and kindly assistance.

Thank you Tracy Sullivan, and all at Xulon Press for this opportunity, and your support.

Special thanks to Fr. John Janze, Deacon Tony Patronite, my CRHP Team 21 brothers, and the community of St. Thomas More Parish in Irvine, California.

Prologue

*T*he aching in Timothy's head bloomed with a pain so severe it interrupted his dream and ripped him from unconsciousness. Disoriented and groggy, fear set in. "This can't be good," he told himself. An incessant, sharp beeping cut his ears with its serrated tone. Over and over the horrible beeping pierced his skull. He winced, unable to open his eyes. His face felt taut and restricted, then suddenly he was acutely aware of how uncomfortably sweaty his entire body was. Above the periodic tones, a nervous Hispanic voice pleaded in the distance, "Socorro, Socorro!" The voice called out far from where Timothy lay, eventually seeming to give up.

Gradually, he forced his eyes open. As his pupils painfully adjusted to the bright lights, he heard sheepish footsteps approach. A short older man holding a mop cautiously leaned over his bed. Trembling, the stranger's eyes studied the situation, and he then made an earnest sign of the cross before retreating. "Socorro!" the man yelled just once more from outside the room, then nothing.

Timothy's eyes studied the room, trying to maintain focus. He realized he was in some sort of hospital. The walls were dingy; the horrible beeping equipment nearby appeared outdated and yellowed. While struggling to stay awake, it dawned on him that there were tubes and a mask affixed to his face. Feeling claustrophobic, he reached up to free his mouth and nose from the restrictive apparatus, but his arms stopped. His arms were secured to the side of the bed with straps. As he fought clumsily to escape his binds, he noticed how pink and blotchy the skin up and down his arms looked. Timothy examined his mangled forearms, the remnants of an amateur skull tattoo barely recognizable below the welted skin. It was all coming back to him now. His hands trembled in the straps as he slowly rotated his palms upwards, revealing pink scar tissue that began at the base of his fingers and traveled well past his wrists. A sharp cleft vertically divided each of his palms. Yes, now he remembered. The collection of blemishes formed a roadmap of who Timothy Clement was and how he ended up here.

Timothy turned his palms back down and a tear rolled down his cheek. A familiar feeling came over him - aloneness. He meditated a while on the sensation, and his situation. His thoughts meandered back in time, reflecting on his childhood. He half smiled, recalling how he used to imagine that a stay in the hospital would be a treat. He had fantasized about how the nurses would wait on him hand and foot while he relaxed in a mechanical bed watching television. All of his friends and family would come by, concerned about his wellbeing and bring flowers and gifts. But here he was, all grown up and no one was coming for him.

He tried several more times to free his arms but failed. He rested again, then stiffened his hand and meticulously worked his fingers in and around one of the knots. At last, he felt his finger in a loop and tugged desperately until he heard a loud rip. His hand darted immediately to his face and yanked off the mask. He gasped loudly. He grabbed his collar and ripped the front of his hospital gown to his stomach. Ineptly, he pulled away the ripped material until he found what he was looking for. It was still there! His finger gently stroked the rose tattoo on his chest. His mother's name, "Eunice" elegantly embroidered around the bud. Below, his sister's names "VICTORIA" and "ELIZABETH" were stenciled in all capital letters next to respective thorns on the flower's stem. Further down the stem there appeared a larger, gnarled thorn bearing his own name, "Timothy". A single rose pedal lie painted underneath on the flesh ground. Upon the fallen rose pedal were a teardrop and the name "Stephen" written in gentle handwritten script.

"Sorry Mom." Timothy whispered, his finger resting on the fallen rose pedal. His eyes welled up, and then more tears tumbled down his cheeks. He sobbed deeply. His heart was heavy and his head felt light. His vision so obscured by his weeping, he could not make out the face of the tall man who entered the room. Timothy thought he recognized a trace of a smile on the man's face through his tears, but he couldn't be sure. Before determining if he knew the man, everything faded to blackness and he lost consciousness.

Part I

Thrown Away

I lie down and I fall asleep,
[and] I will wake up, for the LORD sustains me. – Psalm 3:6

Chapter 1

Seven years earlier.

*T*he small hand-drawn, not to scale, map on the back of the party invitation did not do justice to the entry road and guard shack leading to Alabaster Estates. Vibrations from the impressive cobblestone road buzzed Abby's tires as her BMW snaked its way up.

"Visiting?" The man stationed in the guard shack asked formally from behind his thick glasses. His eyes left hers to inspect the gift box strapped into the passenger seat.

"I'm here for the Timothy Clement birthday bash," the young lady announced proudly. "My name is Abby Anderson. I'm on the list." The guard flipped through the contents of his clipboard holding a frown. Abby could see large bunches of balloons billowing in the wind beyond the tall hedges in the distance as she waited impatiently.

"Nope, don't see you on the list. Lots of girls listed, but no Abby."

This perturbed Abby. "Abby Anderson I said! Both my names begin with the letter 'A' so I am probably at the top of the list." Abby let out an exasperated sigh. "You do know your ABCs don't you?"

The man never changed his tone, but began to search from the top page again. "I've got an Abigail Anderson, but no Abby Anderson."

"You have got to be joking! That IS me!" Abby dug into the small black purse lying on the passenger seat and removed her driver's license. "See!"

The guard took the license, examined it for a moment, then removed his glasses and squinted at Abby. He then put his glasses back on and studied the license again. "I suppose. This photo does not look exactly like you. You may want to get an updated one."

Abby snatched the license from the guard and glared ahead waiting for the guard to let her through the gate. A moment later the gate began to slowly open.

"It's always a good idea to get an updated license when you change hairstyles or put on a few pounds." The guard barely got the words out when Abby's tires squealed and her car jetted through the gate.

"Jerk." Abby muttered under her breath.

Once she made her way to the estate and parked, Abby spent a few moments touching up her makeup and making kissy faces at herself in her mirror. She eventually grabbed her purse, adjusted her cleavage, and proceeded to the party. This was a big deal for her. She and Timothy had spent the past year exchanging flirtatious messages while he took a year off to 'find himself' in Paris. Both of their families were peppered with well-groomed success stories so it seemed a perfect match to her. Wealth, status among the elite and having reasonably attractive features were important, but the family name Clement was simply irresistible to her. She imagined how pleased her family would be if she were to marry a Clement boy.

"Your invitation, dear." The doorman smiled and held out his gloved hand. Abby proudly handed him the heavy French style invitation, strategically covering the party hat wearing cartoon character lurking at its top edge. The amateur drawing was immature to her and ruined the overall elegance of the invitation. Timothy Clement, the birthday boy, was known for his amusing drawings featuring the alter-ego of his kid brother, Stevie. Realistically, Timothy was not a very good artist. He was rather awful really. His comics consisted mostly of crudely sketched figures, rivaling something an eight year old might produce. "Please come right in and make yourself at home." Gesturing to the floral garden he added, "Mister Clement is currently entertaining guests just beyond the gazebo." A waiter stood nearby offering a tray with refreshments.

"Thank you." Abby chirped, taking a Champaign flute. She took a sip and weighed the glass in her hands, mentally gauging its value.

After high school Abby went off to the University of Virginia to study music theory like her father. Her entire family had a natural aptitude for music. By age seventeen, Abby had developed remarkable skills as a pianist, representing her family name on an international level. While competing in Paris she met Timothy and the two hit it off.

Rambunctious collegiate hoots and hollers bounded as Abby turned the corner. Several dozen young adults dressed in sloppy formal wear did their best to show they were not yet adults. For every tactless presentation of the female physique there was a matching half-tucked in shirt and loose necktie. Abby felt right at home.

"Abby!" Timothy called out from the rattan couch he was sharing with two young girls. She presented herself before him and smiled. He remained seated with both arms around his companions. After an awkward pause he abruptly sprung up to properly greet his guest. "Wow, you look great!" he said as he embraced her.

"Thanks, you too!" She handed him the small gift box.

"Oh, Thanks. Can I get you a little something?" Timothy asked holding up his red plastic cup.

"Um, no I'm good" Abby flashed her Champaign flute with a sly smile hoping he'd remember the bottle the two shared in Paris. He didn't. Instead he started to open the gift box.

Abby quickly put her hands on top of the box. "Oh, not now. That's a surprise for later."

Right then Timothy's father and younger brother Stephen approached. His father put his arm around Timothy's shoulder and squeezed him tight. "Hey birthday boy, I think we're just about ready to cut cake."

"Let's eat some cake!" Stephen urged, yanking on Timothy's tie.

His father continued. "Think you can pull yourself away from all these beautiful young ladies for a bit?" He winked at Abby.

"Sure Dad." Timothy held up his hands to Abby, and he was led away.

Abby tried not to let her disappointment show. This wasn't exactly the reunion she was hoping for. Furthermore, she was suddenly aware of all the catty stares directed her way. Bagging a Clement boy wasn't going to be easy.

An older girl came up to Abby wearing a plastic smile. "Try to not take it so seriously sweetie, he's just not capable." Abby gave a quizzical look as the girl extended her hand. "I'm Elizabeth, Tim's sister.

Abby lit up, the more family connections the better. "Oh, hi! I met Tim's other sister Victoria in Paris." Timothy's older sister Victoria was the piano coach of a nine year old Canadian prodigy. Abby was envious of her glamorous profession because it presented exciting adventures around the globe. The reality was that although Victoria was well paid, the hectic demands of her job kept her from finding a husband and she was very lonely; lonely, and increasingly bitter as the years passed.

Elizabeth pursed her lips, unimpressed. "She's off somewhere in Asia and couldn't make it today – shocker!" Elizabeth paused and leaned in closer to Abby. "Listen, if it's a serious relationship you're looking for, then you're barking up the wrong tree."

Abby laughed nervously as she waved her hand. "Oh, you know how boys are."

"I know how my brother is. He's like an alley cat." As Elizabeth spoke Abby smiled uncomfortably not sure how to respond. "Don't say I didn't warn you." Elizabeth gave another insincere smile then wandered off.

Across the yard, Timothy's father and younger brother Stephen escorted him between the spread of rented tables filled with guests. Leaning in, his father said, "Your mother would have really enjoyed this." Timothy nodded then looked at his brother and smiled.

Timothy had a special relationship with his mother. His mother accepted him along with his faults since he was constantly trying to stay in his father's good graces. He was clearly her favorite and it created friction growing up. His older sisters called him, "Mamma's Boy" and his father found every opportunity to remind him he was weak. The afternoon of his mother's funeral, his father proclaimed in front of all those paying respects, that the umbilical cord had finally been cut. The time for Timothy to become a man had arrived. That was just over five years ago, but the sting remained fresh.

His mother battled cancer for the good part of a year, but its rapid conquest got the best of her. Timothy was the only one by her side when she passed away. The doctor's prognosis granted her at least another year, but one day while Timothy and Stephen swam in their backyard they heard their mother call from the upstairs window, "Timothy, can you please come here – alone." Timothy could sense fear in her voice. With his father and sisters away, it was difficult persuading eight year old Stephen to stay in the pool. Stephen shared an equal fondness for their mother and could also tell something was amiss. Eventually, the threat of a smack to the head kept Stephen waiting in the water.

Timothy made his way up the spiral staircase and approached the open door to his parent's room. He was frightened to find her curled up on the ground. "Mom, you okay?" He asked but she didn't answer. It was clear she wasn't. "I'll call 9-1-1!"

She held up her hand in protest. "Sit with me." She whispered and Timothy reluctantly sat down next to her. On the ground were pictures of the family and a Bible. Then he noticed the spots of blood on the front of her shirt and in the corner of her mouth. "Don't be afraid, Timmy." She said gently. "It seems The Lord is calling me home earlier than we thought."

"Mom, hang on, let me get a doctor." Timothy begged with tears in his eyes.

She shook her head. "I need you to listen to me. There is no more time. It's out of the doctor's hands." Timothy threw himself upon her and held tight while sobbing. "It will be okay son, don't be sad." She reassured him.

"No Mom. No!" He pleaded with her.

"Shhh. . . quiet now, I don't want to frighten your brother." Instinctively, she rocked him lovingly just as when he was younger. "Settle down." She whispered softly as she stroked his hair. Timothy continued to sob. "I need you to do something for me."

"What?" Timothy said barely above a whisper.

"I need you to promise you'll do it." She paused, waiting for him to commit. "No matter what, you'll do it for me. Promise."

Timothy sat up and looked at her. "I promise. What do you want me to do?"

His mother coughed while she removed an ornate patron saint necklace from her neck. The beautiful gold necklace was one of her most precious belongings. "I got this shortly after your brother was born." She slipped the necklace over Timothy's head. "This is Saint Anthony of Padua. Have you heard of him?" Timothy shook his head. "He was a good man who lived long ago. He helps find people who are lost, like your father." She began to cough hard and wheeze. "Promise me you will look after your brother and keep him on the path to righteousness. He looks up to you." She slumped forward and coughed roughly.

"Sure, I promise, Mom." Timothy rubbed her back as she coughed. It all seemed like a dream to him. He couldn't believe this was happening. He thought about his brother waiting for him in the backyard and about the saint necklace. Then he realized she was no longer coughing. She was no longer with him.

Timothy's father gave him a hearty slap on the back of his neck. The time had come for the unavoidable charismatic toast to the birthday boy. "Many of you are well acquainted with the escapades my son Timothy has been on over the past year."

"It's Tim. Nobody calls me Timothy. Geez Dad!"

"Oh yeah Tim-o-thy" Stephen teased.

His father ignored the interruption. "In fact, I'm pretty sure some of you here are directly responsible for his little Paris diversion." The crowd laughed at his jesting tone. "No hard feelings, I can live with that knowing that in the fall Timothy will be beginning his studies at Yale." The guests let out a collective howl. Timothy's father smiled while pointing to the Yale Law Alumni pin on his chest. "We've got a fellow bulldog in the making!" They howled louder this time. "So I impart these words of wisdom on my freshly nineteen year old son: Get what you can in this dog-eat-dog world, because when you die they bury you and the worms eat you!" A few people clapped, but the rest waited to see if it was a joke. "If you aren't leading, you're following. If you aren't taking you're getting taken."

Timothy was uncomfortable with his father's one-dimensional chest puffing and finally intervened, "Okay Dad, I get it. Don't worry I'll get to school soon enough and conquer the world." The guests laughed.

Just then Timothy's two best friends, Fitch and Carlos, began chanting, "Miami, Miami, Miami!" Timothy's father raised his eyebrows inquisitively.

"It's just for six weeks Dad. We're staying with Fitch's cousin Bruno. I was going to tell you later." The guests burst into laughter. Timothy was glad it came out in this setting. He had wrestled with how to tell his father for over a week. "We're leaving next week. I'll be back well before orientation."

His father tried not to show his disappointment in front of everyone, but it seeped out from behind his forced smile. "What about our Annapolis cruise next month? You've never missed it." For the past three years Timothy's Uncle David treated the whole family to a summer Annapolis pilgrimage on his schooner. Timothy's father always had a great time bonding with his brother and the kids.

"Oh man, you're not coming?" Timothy's younger brother Stephen complained.

"You guys are perfectly capable of having a good time without me. Besides, there'll be more room for you and more food!" Everyone laughed.

Timothy's father let out a reluctant chuckle. "You hear that Stephen, more food for us? That is a very consoling!"

"It's a dog-eat-dog world out there Dad, you gotta grab what you can!" Everyone cracked up at Timothy's boomerang advice, even his father. "Fitch's cousin is letting us put in some hours at his import firm. It'll give me an edge."

"Very well son, enjoy Miami." Fitch and Carlos cheered obnoxiously as soon as the words left his father's lips. An army of servers appeared distributing cake to the guests. The music came back on and everyone went back to celebrating.

Abby waited another hour before approaching Timothy. She hoped he had respected her wishes and hadn't yet opened the present. "Timothy." She called out to him but he was too busy trying to release himself from Fitch's headlock to notice her. Those two imbeciles Fitch and Carlos were constantly around him and it irritated her.

Timothy's younger brother Stephen walked up and stood beside Abby. He watched the boys wrestle, giggling incessantly. Abby glanced over and realized it was Timothy's brother but wasn't sure if meeting the rest of the family was even worth it after the run in with Elizabeth. Then she noticed something funny about his face, something familiar. "Oh my gosh, it's you!" Stephen looked over at Abby apprehensively as she dug through her purse. "I thought you looked familiar." Abby then pulled out the party invitation. "A-ha! See, that's you!" She tapped the tip of her index finger on the hand drawn party-goer celebrating in the margin.

"Yeah sure, of course!" Stephen smiled proudly. "Tim draws me all the time. Stevie the Great!"

"Stevie the Great - that is so cool!" Abby suddenly had an appreciation for the art she had hidden under her thumb earlier. "You're lucky to have a big brother like Tim." Despite Elizabeth's warning, Abby was swooning over Timothy once again.

Stephen smiled. "Yeah, he is pretty cool."

As Abby and Stephen talked, Carlos held up an unflattering comic Timothy had drawn of Fitch sitting on a toilet and cackled, "It looks just like you man!" Fitch tightened the headlock. Carlos stopped laughing at Timothy and Fitch as soon as he noticed Abby's presence. "Dudes, it's her! Broadway girl!" He pulled headphones from his front pocket and put them in his ears. He then pressed play on a small portable music player and began singing in a girl's voice, "Oh the time in Paris was so beau-ti-ful to me. Oh, ooooohhh, yeah!" Carlos pranced around like a love-struck teenage girl attracting the attention of the other guests.

Abby looked down at Timothy who was laughing as hard as the others. She couldn't believe she had been such a fool. She had spent the past week writing and recording a personal birthday song for Timothy. She transferred it to a high-end music player engraved with his name as a gift. She had waited patiently to play it for him in private. Now her presentation was ruined by this unsophisticated man-child mocking the sentiment, pawing the gift with his grubby hands. All the while, the boy of her dreams guffawed carelessly from the sidelines. "Timothy Clement, you are the most rotten person I've ever met." Abby burst into tears and fled the party.

Timothy thought about running after her, but that seemed too hard a task in front of his friends. And besides, what would the other girls at the party think – that he was taken? That was definitely not an option. He blew it off. "Stupid girls, what can you do?" Fitch and Carlos couldn't high-five him enough.

Chapter 2

The following week dragged on mercilessly. By his departure date, Timothy had successfully avoided any spontaneous father-son talks. He made minimal eye contact, offered brief two-word responses and ate his meals in private. He was up and dressed at five in the morning although his flight didn't leave until noon. He'd figured the morning would be less complicated at Fitch's place. He began writing a note to his father detailing Fitch's cousin Bruno's address and his flight information. The sense that his father wouldn't just let him sneak off to Miami without more words of wisdom lurked. As it turned out, it was an accurate presumption.

"Hey sport. Heading out early?" His father's voice bellowed through the morning silence startling Timothy. Pen ink slashed erratically across the note as he jumped.

"Uh, yeah. You're up early." Timothy looked down at the messy note and decided it was beyond repair. He crumpled it up and began again. "Here's where we are staying." He sloppily scribbled the address down along with his flight itinerary. ". . .and our flight times." He passed the paper to his father.

His father squinted at the paper. "How am I supposed to read this?" Timothy laughed which made his father happy. It was a welcomed departure from the week-long drought of interaction. "Listen, I want you to enjoy yourself on this trip. Just be-"

"Be safe, I know Dad!"

"Yes, be safe. You can still have a great time, just be smart about it." His father could see Timothy was not in the mood for a lecture. He knew it was this very kind of discussion that drove a wedge between the two of them. He opted to lighten the conversation. "I'm just saying don't go breaking too many hearts Don Juan!" Timothy laughed. "I know how these things work. I was once a hormonally charged young man too you know."

"Oh man, just stop." Timothy was turning red. "It's for work experience."

"Does Fitch's cousin run a bikini inspection service?"

Timothy was both amused and terribly embarrassed by the comment. "No, I told you it's-"

"It's right there down on the shore, right?" The two of them laughed like school buddies. "It's good to have fun son. You're a healthy young man, and you should be out there having a good time."

Timothy was still laughing and shaking his head. "Don't worry, I plan on having plenty of fun Dad."

Timothy's father placed his arm around him. "When you get back we'll have a beer and you can tell me all about it."

"A beer, seriously?" Timothy's mouth hung open. "I'm not even twenty-one!"

"Rules are made to be broken. You're old enough." His father raised an eyebrow. "And besides, you've been hiding that stash of empties behind the barbeque pit since winter. I think you can share a brew with your old man."

Timothy's stomach sank. "Oh, that. . ."

"Don't worry about it son. I understand." An expression of reflection overcame his father's face. "There are different kinds of people in this world. There are folks like us who seek adventure responsibly. Rules and regulations do not constrain us, but around every corner there are simple-minded prudes trying to prevent us from truly enjoying life to the fullest." His eyes peered intently at Timothy, punctuating the lesson. "You're only breaking the rules if you get caught. Otherwise it's considered resourcefulness."

This unexpected nugget of wisdom was a surprising relief to Timothy. Anchored in the promise he made to his mother, he battled daily to do what was right although he desired what was easy. His Mother's superstitious morality had long been a hindrance. "Thanks dad, that is good to know."

Chapter 3

*T*he boys erupted into catcalls as Fitch's older cousin Bruno's tiny red sports car glided into the airport loading zone. They didn't seem to mind the fact that it could barely hold them and their luggage. A red convertible is very cool - that's the thing that matters. "Hey boys, need a ride?" Bruno purred soaking up the adoration. After a number of strategic attempts, they finally got everything to fit and were on their way.

Bruno's pad was a short ride from the airport. Balmy weather and magnificent tropical views paved the way. All kinds of people were out cruising and enjoying the sun. "Man, this is so great!" Timothy blurted out causing an arrogant smirk to blossom on Bruno's face.

Just off the main strip, the car turned into a private track of homes and journeyed all the way to the end of the road. "We're here guys." Bruno said causally, almost disinterested, as they pulled up to the spacious beach house. It was clearly the most luxurious estate in the community with the best view of the ocean. The boys were pleased to say the least.

"That's where I'll be spending my time." Carlos announced, pointing to a gazebo covered hot tub. "Mixing it up with the ladies!" The others laughed then scampered out to explore the grounds of the Spanish style home. There was plenty to explore.

Bruno told them they could go and do anything they liked, but there were three rules. First, don't track sand into the house. Second, don't pee in the pool. Last, and most important, Bruno's office was off-limits. It seemed easy enough to the boys. They explored the grounds for the good part of an hour, eventually deciding on who would take which room. Bruno then suggested they go to a local restaurant where he knew the chef. There was no arguing, everyone was starving. Bruno promised that after dinner they'd have some serious fun downtown.

Timothy, Fitch and Carlos spent the remainder of the weekend sleeping until noon, lounging at the pool, eating, and then hitting the clubs all night long. In their amazement, it was easy to get in while accompanied by Bruno. No cover charge, free drinks and never carded. Bruno wore machismo-infused fashions and ALWAYS had on sunglasses. His presence intimidated the men while his hot-shot pheromones attracted the women. Carlos, Fitch and Timothy were more than happy to ride his coattails and catch scraps.

The boys developed a system. They'd follow Bruno around until he stopped nearby a group of young women. Carlos, the smooth one, would hit them with an irresistible line. If they didn't run for cover, Fitch would move in and ask if the boys could buy them some drinks. Once drinks arrived, Timothy started doodling juvenile comics on the napkins. Their reaction would give them an indication if they had any chance to seal the deal. The more the girls liked the comics, the better their chances. It worked smoothly, except for Carlos getting sick on the second night and throwing up at the table.

The trio was woken up early Monday morning by the sounds of two men yelling. It sounded more like one man yelling while the other pleaded. The three got up independently, running into each other in the main hallway. Bruno emerged from his office, face red and sweaty. "Go back to your rooms, this doesn't concern you!" He announced with an intensity they hadn't seen in him before. The trio backpedaled – no questions asked.

None of them could really fall back asleep after the bizarre wake up call. Timothy pulled out his sketch pad to pass the time and drew a caricature of Bruno holding up a large beer stein full of money. He accentuated his large bug-eyed sunglasses and bushy chest hair. Off to the side he drew "Stevie the Great" puking at the club. Then he closed his eyes and wondered how his brother and dad were doing out on his uncle's boat. He sort of wished he could have gone.

An hour later, Bruno knocked loudly on each of their doors. "Rise and shine boys." Bruno hung an Italian suit and leather shoes in each of the boy's doorways. "Enough playing. Eat and get dressed. Today we work." The boys were stunned by the change in schedule. "Get moving, we leave in exactly one hour." Bruno came up to Timothy and grabbed the St. Anthony medallion hanging from Timothy's neck and examined it closer. "What the heck is this?"

With all eyes on him, Timothy felt self-conscious. "Nothing, just something my mom gave me."

Bruno nodded tilting the oval piece to get a better view, "How much you want for it?"

"Sorry, not for sale." Timothy pulled back and the pennant slipped from Bruno's hands.

Sighing, Bruno pulled out his billfold and began peeling off bills. "C'mon, everything has a price. I like it. It's got that little old guy on it and looks all official and stuff. Chicks love that kind of stuff."

Timothy shook his head. "I told you it's from my mom. Didn't you ever get anything from your mom before? It's not for sale."

The corner of Bruno's lip tightened as he put his money away. "I never met my mom." He looked at his watch. "Less than an hour boys, get ready!" Then he left the room.

The boys remained mostly quiet during the ride downtown. Bruno's serious shift had killed their party mood. As they traveled further, the tropical sights melted into pawn shops and neon check-cashing signs. Instead of seeing sexy co-eds like they had grown accustomed to, all they saw were desperate and dilapidated souls wandering skittishly. Bruno pulled up to a gas pump at Frank's Service Station. Immediately, a ruddy, leather-faced man hobbled over to the car and began to fill up the tank. "Nice to see you Bruno. It's on the house of course!" The man said nervously.

"That's a nice gesture, but you know I only deal in cash Frankie." Bruno stepped out of the car. "I thought you and I had a scheduled service yesterday. What happened?"

"Oh, I'm sorry about that. It's just been kind of-"

"You should be sorry." Bruno interrupted. "That was very rude of you." The two stood silent for a moment. Bruno went over and yanked the gas nozzle from his tank and handed it to Frankie. "I don't want your gas. I want the money you owe." And then Bruno truly freaked out the boys by removing his sunglasses and getting right up in Frankie's face.

"I'll get you the money." Frankie stammered, his eyes darting over at the boys.

"I know you will. You have until Sunday."

Frankie swallowed hard and tried to change the subject. "Are these your nephews or something?" Bruno put on his glasses and nodded slightly. "You want some candy bars and sodas for the road?"

"No." Bruno moved to get back in the car.

Frankie headed toward the cashier station and yelled back, "Seriously, I've got all kinds of stuff here. Hold on." He rummaged around the small booth then emerged with a bag stuffed with snacks and drinks. "Here, take these."

Bruno sighed, then took the bag and tossed it to the boys. He pulled out his billfold but Frankie protested, "No, it's on the house."

Bruno pulled out a couple of singles and tossed them toward Frankie. They fluttered to the ground. "No, you see I pay my debts." He then dug into his pocket and pulled out a handful of change. Looking at the boys he said, "Geez, look at all these pennies. What good are pennies? You can't buy anything with a penny!" The boys laughed awkwardly, none wanting to be louder than the next. Bruno picked out a few pennies and flicked them carelessly at Frankie. "Useless!" He flicked several more pennies at Frankie who just took the abuse. "There, I'm paid in full." Frankie looked deflated. "I'll see you on Sunday." Frankie nodded sullenly as Bruno pulled away.

"Who was that guy?" Fitch asked.

"Nobody" Bruno grumbled. They continued a few blocks further up the street to, 'Apollo Business Center' a run-down strip mall. Bruno parked out front a tattered coin-operated laundry. "Time to get to work."

The boys were stunned. The strip mall was the last place they expected to stop. "Seriously?" Fitch asked.

Bruno whistled and motioned impatiently for the boys to exit the car. As they approached the storefront, a heavyset man wearing dark sunglasses opened the door and held it for them. Inside there were aisles of rusty washers, dryers and vending machines. Bruno went up to an industrial size dryer in the back corner and banged on it three times. After a pause, the entire length of wall swiveled open revealing a hidden corridor. Bruno looked over his shoulder suspiciously. "After me." The group passed through the doorway and the large door slammed behind them.

Inside there was yet another very large man with sunglasses standing between a full-length steel door on his left and an industrial dryer on his right. Above the industrial dryer's circular door hung a sign reading, "Suckers".

"Good day Mister Bruno." The man said in a raspy voice as he cracked opened the steel door. Immediately the pungent odor of tobacco filled the small space. As the boys followed Bruno through the steel door, they realized that he was involved in an elaborate illegal gambling den in the middle of a skid-row strip mall. They were impressed.

There were dozens of men and women shooting dice and playing cards. "Guys, check it out!" Timothy said pointing to a roulette table.

Bruno quickly reined them in. "Be cool. Don't speak to nobody unless I tell you to. Understand?" The boys nodded. "I gotta take care of some business so I've got a little project for you in the meantime." Bruno led them to a side area with dozens of locked metal boxes. "Take these." He handed Timothy a hefty key ring. "Each one of these boxes has a corresponding key. Match it, open the box and then check for slides."

"Slides?" Timothy asked.

Bruno took back the keys and went over to the first box which had 'X19' imprinted on it. He jostled the set of keys for a moment then thrust the matching key into the lock and opened the box. Inside were hundreds of dice sets in velvet lined cases. "Here's what you do." Bruno opened the first set of dice. Removing a die, he brought it close to his eye and ran his fingers along its edges. "All straight, that's what you want. No smooth edges." Bruno tossed the keys to Timothy. "If you find any with smooth edges pull them out."

Timothy took in the large number to inspect. "That's a lot of dice."

"Between the three of you it shouldn't take long." Bruno looked at his watch. "Get cracking. I'll be back in one hour." Just as he was about to go he turned around. "One more thing, keep it down back here. You should be invisible." And with that he slipped away.

The boys divided up the boxes between the three of them and got started. "I honestly wasn't expecting any of this." Timothy remarked.

"Me neither. We are so lucky!" Carlos hissed in an excited whisper. "High rollers man!"

Timothy turned to Fitch, "You said he dealt in imports. Did you know about all this?"

"He deals in imports too. This stuff is just on the side." Fitch thought about the details Bruno had divulged about his work over the years and couldn't decide if it added up. "I think."

A half hour into caressing dice, a provocatively dressed girl wearing a cigarette dispensing belt came over. "Hey boys, care for a smoke?"

Fitch and Carlos just shook their heads while their eyes feasted on her curves. Timothy smiled and said, "Sorry, don't smoke." The longer he studied her the more her allure faded. She was hiding her age and exhaustion behind caked makeup and each second that went by it became more apparent.

The girl giggled. "I'm Maggie, but everyone calls me Mag. I got more than just smokes. I can hook you up." She reached into her waistband pulled out a small bag of white powder. "How about it?"

Timothy had tried it only once before. A long evening of partying that ended with Fitch dropping his irregular beating heart off at the ER. He wasn't interested in a repeat of that. "I'm a runner, it doesn't agree with me." He shook his head at the girl.

She seemed surprised, almost offended, by the refusal. "Suit yourself." As she walked away, Timothy noticed her broad hips and wondered if she had children at home.

Fitch whispered, "Mag? More like old hag. What a freak!" The comment made Timothy cut off any further speculation of her home life. "Looks like she's her own best customer." Fitch's face twisted in disgust.

"Yeah, a real freak." Timothy agreed.

Before they could refocus on dice inspections, there was a loud commotion in the game room followed by cheering. The boys went over to investigate. Bruno addressed the crowd from the entry way. "Looks like we have a sucker who wants to play!" Everyone roared with laughter. "We all know the rules. The house always wins. If you owe the house and still come back, you're probably a what?"

The crowd yelled, "Sucker!"

Bruno pointed to the round industrial dryer door. "There is only one way in for suckers." The hooting continued until a middle-aged man eventually crawled through the round opening and tumbled into the makeshift casino. As soon as he hit the ground the crowd yelled, "Sucker!" The man appeared thoroughly humiliated. The boys realized that he had crawled through the dryer door opposite the steel door entrance they had used.

Bruno fanned colored chips in his hands. "What do you think folks, should we extend further credit to this gent?" The crowd clapped. "It's your lucky day!" Bruno scattered the chips on the ground and the man desperately picked them up. Bruno smirked and shook his head. Then he caught sight of the boys and made his way over to them. "I thought I told you- be invisible." He forcibly moved Fitch's head in order to break his stare.

Fitch pulled away then looked again at the man. "That was crazy!"

"That's part of doing business." Bruno looked at Carlos and Timothy. "Where are we at with the dice?"

"Uh, well. . ." Timothy looked at Carlos then the boxes. They ineptly strained to assess their progress.

Bruno closed the opened bins. "Enough work for today. Let's eat." The boys readily agreed. As they exited the gambling den they all stared at the Sucker entrance. "There's one born every second." Bruno laughed.

That evening they ate at yet another upscale restaurant run by a man who cowered as soon as he saw Bruno. The boys quickly caught on to the trend. Bruno always treated because it was always on the house. Bruno excused himself during the meal and was gone a very long time. When he returned to the table his sleeve was soaking wet. "Time to go boys." The trio motioned to their half-eaten meals in protest, but that just seemed to infuriate Bruno. "Now!" He barked.

In the car ride back to the house Bruno was unusually talkative. "Now that you are my associates I should lay out some rules. Think of it as a verbal employee handbook." He chuckled while the boys listened astutely, hanging on his every word. "This is an election year. That means hard times for my employers. Two of our closest competitors have been run out of town. The only reason we're still in business is because we've got a little insurance policy. Some of our best patrons happen to work down at the civic center. That doesn't mean that we won't be shut down, only that we have delayed it a bit." Bruno's finger bobbled as it pointed at the boys. "You guys are gonna help set up a new shop. Nobody knows you. No records." He smiled, "And you'll earn plenty of money for college." The boys reacted positively to the mention of money. They'd all been wondering when they'd get paid and how much. "You did well today. Here's a little something." He tried to keep the car steady as he pulled money out of his billfold and passed out wads of cash to each of the boys.

"Dang, this is some serious cash!" Carlos rejoiced. Timothy and Fitch counted the bills in disbelief.

"Now in order for you to be effective in your new jobs you are going to need some training." Bruno continued. "You need to learn all the games. Dice, Cards, the Wheel of fools. You need to know how to play them and how to cheat at them."

Fitch interrupted, "You want us to cheat the house?"

"No dummy." Bruno smacked Fitch who was sitting in the passenger's seat. "You can't catch a cheater unless you know what he's up to." Fitch nodded while rubbing his head. "These losers are desperate. Desperate! They'll do anything to win and won't stop until they do. You gotta know what to look for."

Timothy spoke up, "So can you show us tonight?"

Bruno shook his head. "No, it takes time. You need to pay attention and really learn it. Besides, only Fitch and Carlos are going to train for now. I need your skills for a special job."

"What special job?" Fitch asked.

"It has to do with the importing side of business." Fitch made a 'didn't I tell you!' motion to Carlos. "You two start training on dice tomorrow with Xavier."

The car pulled into the driveway and Bruno cut the engine. "One last thing." The boys listened. "This is work, don't forget it. No messing around on the job. No girls, drugs, drinking or gambling while on the clock. It will not be tolerated, understand?" The boys unequivocally agreed to the terms. "Follow the rules, stick to the plan and we'll all score big."

After entering the house Bruno played a waiting phone message. 'Hey sport, its Dad. Just wanted to check in and see how it was going before we take off to Uncle David's.' In the background Timothy's younger brother Stephen shouted hello. 'I'm sure you are out having a good time. We'll be back in a week. Take care and be safe.' The machine beeped.

"Be safe." Fitch and Carlos laughed as Bruno mocked the parental tone. Timothy felt a pang of longing but shrugged it off and joined in the laughter. He convinced himself that he didn't need anything from his father at the moment.

Chapter 4

*T*raining began Tuesday morning. Bruno drove Fitch and Carlos to the coin-op laundry right after breakfast while Timothy stayed behind. Bruno hadn't let Timothy know yet what his special project was, but Timothy had grand ideas. Maybe he'd be in charge of counting all the money. He fantasized about dividing up large towers of cash behind a bullet-proof window. Or maybe, he thought, he would be in charge of hiring beautiful girls to strut around the new casino. Maybe that was his special talent. At the clubs he could always pick out the best of them. After a few moments he finished speculating, and instead laid down on the couch and turned on the television.

Eventually, Bruno made his way back to the house holding a plastic toolbox and a thick two-foot by three-foot gray envelope. He came in and immediately turned off the television. "Didn't I say we were working today?"

"I was just watching a little TV while I was waiting for you."

"You think Fitch and Carlos are lounging around watching TV?" Bruno asked. "You think the guy over at the hardware store is watching TV?" Timothy slowly got up from the couch and waited for Bruno to finish. "Have you even showered?" Timothy nodded. "Get your head in the game. It's work time."

Bruno pointed to the left out milk, cereal and used bowl on the kitchen table. "Do you leave messes like this in your mother's house?" Timothy scampered to clean up the items, too intimidated to let him know his mom was no longer with him. He cleared the table in record time. Bruno put the envelope and toolbox down then went to get himself a drink.

Timothy stared at the items, teeming with curiosity, but he didn't dare touch them. Bruno's training was effective. "What's this stuff?" Timothy asked, but Bruno ignored him as he rummaged through the fridge looking for a drink. Finally settling on orange juice, Bruno closed the fridge and sat down at the table. Timothy asked again, "So, what's all this stuff?"

"You do all those stupid little comics right?" Bruno asked flatly.

"Well, it's just kind of a-"

"You're really not very good." Bruno interrupted. "I mean you shouldn't plan on making a career of it. My niece can draw better than you." Timothy just nodded. "But you're good enough for this." Bruno pulled out several sheets of thick paper from the gray envelope along with a series of stacked black and white photographs.

Timothy reached for the stack of blurry, poorly lit photos. "What is this?" Bruno swatted his hand away.

Opening the toolbox, Bruno removed two sets of drawing pencils, one with red labels and another with blue. Bruno put a blank page in front of Timothy and slid one of the photographs beside it. "See this?"

Timothy squinted at what looked like a pumpkin. "Is that a gourd or a melon of some sort?" Timothy held up the photo closer to his face. "It's at a weird angle and covered in shadows. "

"Can you draw it like it was straight at you? You know, normal like?" Bruno asked.

Timothy's nose crinkled as he looked again at the photo. "That's a pot or a jar or something, right?" Bruno nodded. "Now I see, there are markings along the bottom".

"Bingo!" Bruno chimed. "Can you draw it exactly with all the markings and stuff?"

"I can try."

Bruno removed a pencil from the blue pack and put it in Timothy's hand. "Okay, let's see how you do."

Timothy touched the pencil to the paper and paused, "What exactly is this? I should know what it is I'm trying to draw."

Tapping the photo with his thick finger, Bruno said, "This, this is what you are drawing. And make it look like its facing us."

The details were obviously not for sharing, and so Timothy began blindly drawing. He carefully sketched the object, adjusting its position in his mind; predicting the appearance of the pattern along the object's unseen edge. He added some shading for depth and started to draw the background as well.

"No, no, no. Nothing but the jar." Bruno instructed. Timothy made a mental note – it was a jar! "It's looking good. Better than those lame cartoons of yours."

A few more strokes and Timothy put down the pencil. "Why don't you get your niece to do this if she is so good?" Timothy asked snidely.

"Cause she can't do this." Bruno removed a different pencil from the red labeled pack. Handing it to Timothy he said, "I want you to turn this into something else."

"What?"

"I want you to use the part of your brain that makes those idiot comics and change this into something else."

As he studied the sketch, Timothy tried to mentally juggle the geometric shapes and come up with something. "I've got it." He feverishly added to the sketch for several minutes until a portrait of a lion emerged.

Taking the paper and holding it up to the light, Bruno smiled. "This is great! You're going to work out perfectly." He removed the remaining ten photos from the gray envelope. "Do the same kind of thing. Sketch the main subject facing forward, no background, with those" Bruno pointed to the blue labeled pencils. "And change it into something new with those. "He pointed at the red labeled pencils. "Got it?" Timothy nodded. "Great, I'm going to take a nap."

So much for the work ethic Timothy thought to himself. "When are we going to pick up Fitch and Carlos?" he asked. Bruno sloppily replied while yawning and walking away. Timothy had no idea what he said and didn't care enough to repeat the question.

Figuring out what was in each photograph proved to be a challenge. Most of the objects were barely lit, or over exposed. The photos were taken with a very cheap camera lens, they lacked any sharp detail. There were four more vases, along with three bowls, two statues and a textile banner of some sort. He worked into the afternoon transforming most of them into animal portraits. There were lions, baboons, hippos and one tractor. When he finished putting the final red-label touches on them, he was tired. This was more work than they'd done all summer.

At two-thirty Timothy heard Bruno's alarm go off. Shortly thereafter Bruno was at the table examining Timothy's work. "Very good!" He exclaimed as he sifted through the sheets of paper. Then he stopped at the tractor. "What is this?" Bruno chuckled. "And you were doing so well." Bruno rummaged through the toolbox and took out a bottle of clear fluid and a rag. "Don't worry, it's not a total loss." Bruno poured some fluid onto the rag and began to wipe the tractor picture with it.

"Wait, what are you doing?" Timothy protested.

Bruno's swipes across the canvas provided the answer. Little by little, all of the red-label drawing disappeared, revealing the original intact sketch of a round stone seal. "Let this dry for fifteen minutes and you can try again. Maybe a beetle, huh?"

Insects would be a refreshing change from the wildlife theme, Timothy thought to himself. "Who are these for?"

"I'm a matchmaker of sorts." Bruno began. "Someone has something a bit less than legal to sell. . ." He held up the stack of photos. "And I see to it that the right buyer gets the opportunity to acquire such items. Both parties wish to exist anonymously and they both have plentiful resources to retain my services." Bruno smiled thinking how sophisticated he was, even though it was just the age-old deed of fencing stolen goods.

"Why not just show the photos?" It was a logical question.

"I guarantee my clients anonymity. These photos give away too much." Bruno flipped through the stack stopping at a vase sitting on a decorative rug. "It would be easy to figure out the location this was taken just from that rug. Someone will recognize it." He flipped to the photo of the textile banner. "He's holding it up to a mirror; you can clearly see the snake ring on his finger and that he's wearing snake-skin boots." He tapped on a boot in the bottom shadows. "Snakeman."

Ideas of where all these items came from flooded Timothy's imagination. An old abandoned storage unit perhaps? Maybe Bruno was involved in a museum heist? That would be crazy! "Where were these pictures taken?"

Bruno chuckled. "You're getting way ahead of yourself. Just stick to drawing the sketches and let me worry about the rest."

"Oh, c'mon. You can tell me!" Timothy begged, but Bruno didn't budge.

Bruno collected up the photos and motioned for Timothy to follow him to the backyard. He stopped at the barbeque pit. "This is the important part." He fired up the gas flame and meticulously fed each original photo into the pit making sure they were destroyed. "Use the poker. Never assume it all got charred. Keep poking until it's nothing but ash." Then Bruno put down the poker and removed his billfold. He passed Timothy a large wad of cash. "Keep up the good work and there's more where that came from." Timothy couldn't believe his good fortune.

And that's how it was for the next three days. A new envelope with a dozen or so photos would arrive and Timothy would sketch and re-sketch them. He was surprised at how much he grew to enjoy the task; taking much pride in his work. Nonetheless, he still wished he could have learned dice and cards like Carlos and Fitch. It seemed more glamorous. In the evenings Timothy would show the boys his drawings for the day. They could never guess the original sketch and that always made Bruno happy. Just one week in, and Miami was treating the boys very well it seemed.

Chapter 5

S aturday evening the boys barbequed steak-kabobs in the pit out back. They felt like big shots. After dinner, Bruno pulled out his billfold. Like well-trained dogs, the three boys sat quiet and attentive as Bruno made his way around to each handing out cash. The stack of bills was crisp and weighty to the boys who were more accustomed to handling their funds with ATM or charge cards. "Don't spend it all in one place." Bruno quipped.

Timothy held the stack of bills firmly in his hand. He squared it up, flipped the edges then folded it, marveling at its bulk. "Man, I've never seen so much money at one time!"

"I have." Carlos bragged. "When my uncle bought my aunt's car he paid all cash."

Silently, Fitch pulled out a small pocket notebook and recorded the payment. He was the most fiscally responsible of the bunch.

A few minutes later a car horn sounded out front. Bruno announced, "You boys are on your own for the rest of the weekend." He laid his car keys on the table. "If you guys want to go anywhere, Fitch is the only one allowed to drive. I'll be back late tomorrow night." The boys passed excited glances among themselves. "But remember, Monday is back to work. Be ready for it." And at that he left.

Once the sound of Bruno's ride had trailed off into the night, the boys began celebrating. "Can you believe this?" Carlos shouted. "We've got wheels, cash and the whole weekend to party!" Timothy and Fitch howled along. "I got an idea. Let's put on our work suits and go out. That would be so cool."

Fitch's face lit up. "Yeah, chicks dig those suits."

Carlos laughed. "As long as you don't barf all over us."

Fitch ignored the jab. "Did you ever notice how Mag always runs her fingers along my coat buttons?" Fitch bobbed his eyebrows quickly.

Timothy's face soured as Carlos high-fived Fitch. "No I never noticed, cause I'm always stuck here making stupid drawings. I don't even wear my suit! Just once I wish I could get in on the real action." Carlos and Fitch rubbed their eyes mockingly. "Some friends you are, you never even taught me how to play cards!"

Carlos went to get dressed while Fitch consoled Timothy. "Don't sweat it, we'll teach you everything we know this weekend. It's easy." He turned toward the hallway, "Isn't that right Fitch? Easy!" A muffled response in the affirmative came from down the hallway. "So get dressed, we've got girls to meet."

There were only two clubs in town that the boys felt they could get into without Bruno's company: Corky's and The Shack. Of the two, the boys preferred The Shack, which was a dump, but hosted younger clientele. However, the most important consideration was how scared the owner was of Bruno. The Shack fit the bill. Tonight they felt extra confident wearing their slick suits and having their pockets lined with cash.

The boys sauntered up to The Shack, but as they approached the bouncer he held up his hand and shook his head. "Sorry children, this is for big boys." The boys protested but he wouldn't hear it. "I'm paid in full. Don't owe Bruno a cent. I'm not about to jeopardize my liquor license for a bunch of freshmen." He turned his back on them. It seemed the loose association with Bruno wasn't always golden.

"What now?" Timothy asked moping back to the car. "Corky's?"

Carlos groaned. "I don't want to drink with someone's grandma tonight."

Just then it hit Fitch. "Oh, I know. Let's do a load of laundry!"

"Yeah, that's a great idea!" Carlos patted him on the back. "Mag will hook us up with refreshments, no hassle, and we can show Tim the finer points of cards."

Timothy cheered loud enough to draw disapproving looks from a passing couple. "It's about time!"

Driving down to the Laundromat at night was an entirely different experience. The streets were poorly lit, accentuating the creepy random misfits slinking about. Fitch drove cautiously, not daring to put Bruno's car in any danger. The parking lot was packed when they arrived at the coin-op laundry. The large doorman ran out and removed an orange cone from a spot up front, then motioned for Fitch to park. The car had perks.

Ten minutes later the boys were inside, drinks in hand, watching the action. Every table was full. An older gentleman wearing an expensive suit was on a roll. Win after win. As the dealer shoved another tall stack of chips his direction Timothy asked Carlos, "How much is that?"

Carlos laughed and said, "More than what's in all of our pockets combined!" Timothy's eyes widened. "Seriously." Carlos assured him.

Just then one of the floor men approached the boys with an outstretched hand. "Putting in some overtime?" he asked Fitch.

Fitch shook his hand. "Nah, we're off the clock."

"You need some chips?" The man asked nonchalantly.

Fitch shook his head but Timothy blurted, "Sure, how much?" and took out his wad of cash.

Before Fitch could intervene, the man peeled off a hundred dollar bill from Timothy's wad and dropped four chips in his hand. "There you go. Enjoy yourselves."

Carlos inched in closer to Timothy. "Dude, Bruno said we weren't allowed to gamble." Carlos took one of the chips from Timothy's hand to inspect up close.

Fitch shook his head. "Yeah, if Bruno finds out, he will be pissed."

"Geez, it's our money isn't it?" Timothy rationalized.

Carlos quickly put the chip back in Timothy's hand. "No, it's YOUR money. I don't know anything about it."

"Don't be so afraid all the time. Rules are made to be broken." Timothy looked around at the different tables trying to select one. "Besides, you promised to teach me how to play. How to play and win."

Carlos shrugged his shoulders, "Alright, but just remember, I warned you."

Carlos and Fitch spent the next hour teaching Timothy the rules of each game. They each gave him their own insider tips on how to beat the odds and score. Timothy tried to join games several times, but the boys stopped him. Insistently, they told him he needed to observe for a while before actually playing. He thought they were foolish for being so overly cautious. "I've got it, really. I'm ready." Timothy flicked two chips on a nearby board and proclaimed, "I'm in."

In a flurry of unexpected transactions, which amazed Carlos and Fitch, Timothy spent the next thirty minutes riding a wave of good fortune. Anytime he'd lose a hand he'd come right back double. He seemed unstoppable. Amidst all the excitement an uncomfortable nagging caution crept up Fitch's spine. "Tim, you've got twice what we walked in here with. Quit while you're ahead."

Fitch's words seemed to snap Timothy out of a trance. His face relaxed a bit like he was sobering up. "You're right. I have doubled my money. It's probably time to go now." Carlos and Fitch nodded, relieved to see Timothy's mania subside. But then Timothy unexpectedly reached out and slid all of his chips onto the board. "But not until I go all in!" he laughed. Carlos and Fitch were stunned, but there was no stopping him now. The bet was made once the chips hit that table. A crowd gathered to see how the wager would go down.

From across the room Mag watched nervously. She had seen many men get chewed up and spit out of the place in just this same fashion. She liked the boys and didn't want to see them end up on the wrong side of the tables, like she herself had years back. Before she could invest too much concern, a mighty celebratory roar blasted from the table. Watching Timothy's ecstatic face, she smiled to herself and figured she just wasn't destined to win.

Carlos and Fitch forced Timothy to cash in. They dragged him and his winnings out of the Laundromat knowing they narrowly escaped disaster. "We taught you a little too well." Carlos proclaimed as they drove out of the parking lot.

"Check this out!" Timothy repeated over and over as he fanned the large wads of cash in his hands.

Carlos laughed heartily about the whole incident, but Fitch remained subdued during the drive back. He knew his cousin would not be happy if word got back. "Listen, Bruno cannot know about this. Understand?" The boys nodded assuredly. "No more gambling."

As the car approached the house Timothy protested, "Why are we going home? The night is young!"

Fitch pulled into the driveway and cut the engine. "I'm tired. We've still got tomorrow." Unenthusiastically, the boys followed Fitch into the house and crashed for the night.

Chapter 6

*I*t was a harsh way to wake up. Fitch was yanked from his bed in one swift motion. Dazed and trying to make sense of it all, his eyes focused, and he saw Bruno's red face before him. "Where is it?" Bruno huffed.

"Where's what?" Fitch blurted out. "What are you doing back so early anyways?"

"The car, where is it?"

Fitch's face twisted quizzically. "It's right where I left it, parked out back."

Bruno shook his head. "No, it's not. Go see for yourself."

Fitch led Bruno out back wholly expecting to see the sports car right where he left it, but it was gone. "It was right here, I swear!"

In his rage, Bruno kicked furiously into the side of the house and growled. "Get your friends up, see if they saw or heard anything."

Fitch hustled back into the house and burst into Carlos's room. He shook his shoulder hard waking him up. "Did you hear anything last night?" Carlos swatted Fitch's hand away and rolled over, covering his head with a pillow. Fitch sighed and went on to Timothy's room. His heart sank when he opened the door and the bed was empty. On the dresser was a sloppy note. Before he could read it Bruno snatched it up and read it to himself. Fitch didn't think Bruno could get any more red or sweaty, but he did.

"You're paying the cab fare little cousin." Bruno said gruffly, and then stormed out of the room.

The cab ride down to the laundry was tense. Bruno was sandwiched between Fitch and Carlos who gazed out of their respective windows to avoid Bruno's scowl. It seemed to take forever to get there.

As they entered the parking lot, they could see Bruno's car parked right up front. Bruno paid the driver and shooed the boys out of the cab. As they approached the entrance, Bruno tried to flatten Fitch's bed-head hair without much success. "You guys look ridiculous. You're an embarrassment."

Standing in their T-shirts and sweat pants, they felt ridiculous. It was as if they were nude without their fancy business suits. "Can we wait out here?" Carlos asked. Bruno prodded them toward the entrance. The answer was clearly no.

Inside, among the stale smoke and alcohol vapor, Bruno spotted Timothy in the back corner. "Oh no." He muttered. Timothy was sitting across from the cashier booth glass, a seat known to Bruno as the sucker seat. Bruno knew recovery from this would be difficult. Timothy looked extremely relieved to see Bruno yet fearful of him at the same time. Bruno ignored Timothy for the moment and spoke to the associate behind the glass. "Hey, what's all this about?"

The man behind the glass spoke. "This gentlemen stated double-or-nothing, and now he owes double."

Bruno wiped his brow with his hand. "Look, this is my associate. Just take what he already lost and let's call it even, huh?"

"You know the rules Bruno. Double means double."

Bruno pulled out his billfold calculating in his mind how much he had given Timothy the night before. "Okay, double of what exactly?"

Without hesitation the man spoke, "Eighty-five large."

Bruno was stunned. "What?"

"Eighty-five. I can't wipe that off the books." The man glanced at Timothy. "He says he's good for it." The man behind the glass suddenly straightened up.

Right then Bruno felt a thud of a tap on his shoulder. Turning around, he came face-to-face with Rex Quinn, his boss' boss. The man was seven feet tall with visible traces of muscle under his sport coat. "Hey Rex, how you been?" Bruno asked nervously. Carlos and Fitch watched, marveling at this man who took the wind out of Bruno's sails.

"I'm surprised at you Bruno." Rex outstretched his cigar laden hand toward Timothy. "Have you forgotten the rules?"

"I just found-"

Rex leaned into Bruno, "No one walks away from eighty-five large. Not even your associate." Hints of cigar smoke danced around his lower lip as he spoke. "You should have trained him better." Rex looked over Carlos and Fitch and shook his head.

Bruno wanted to strangle Timothy for putting him in the position. He knew it would only put him in worse standing with the boss if he did. "He'll pay. He's good for it." Bruno stated frankly. Rex nodded slowly, staring Bruno square in the eyes. Bruno broke his gaze and motioned for Timothy to come with him and the boys.

As they began to exit Rex hollered from behind them, "Oh no, that's not how we do it." Suddenly the whole room became very rowdy. Rex pointed to the clothes dryer sucker exit. "There is only one way out for those who owe the house!" The room responded to the proclamation with raucous howls.

Timothy felt flush. He watched Bruno, Carlos and Fitch back away from him. His eyes met Mag's across the room for an instant, but then she darted away. "Sucker, sucker, sucker!" The room chanted. Timothy inched toward the dryer door never feeling so humiliated in all his life. He glanced over at Carlos and Fitch whose faces showed horror and disbelief. He wished they would turn around or leave, but they didn't. The dryer door took some yanking to open, and the crowd seemed to love watching him struggle with it. Finally, it popped open and he journeyed through the small round opening, landing on his neck and shoulders on the other side. He got up quickly and pulled the round door toward him to dampen the jeers on the other side.

Bruno grabbed Timothy by the collar and led him out to the car. Carlos and Fitch trailed close behind. "I gave you guys' simple rules and you disobeyed me."

Back at the house Bruno took all of Timothy's belongings and stuffed them carelessly into his travel bag. "We're leaving in five minutes." He announced.

"Where to?" Timothy asked.

Bruno paused before speaking, trying to contain his temper. "You, dummy, are catching the next flight home."

Carlos and Fitch began to object but knew it was a lost cause. Fitch asked Timothy, "Do you have any money left?" Timothy reached into his pocket and then shook his head. "Why didn't you quit when you were ahead last night?"

Bruno interrupted, "He wouldn't have to quit if he hadn't started in the first place! Didn't I pay you guys fairly for the week?" The boys looked down shamefully. "We leave in five minutes. Be ready."

Timothy went to his room to retrieve his drawing pad from under the bed. He then grabbed his hanging suit on the way out of the room. "Forget it." Bruno barked, grabbing the suit hanger away from him and tossing it into a mess on the floor.

Twenty minutes later Timothy was at the airport ticketing counter rescheduling his flight home. He wondered what he would do. Letting his family know what happened was out of the question. It would be a devastating, monumental failure, and they'd never let him live it down. "I'm sorry sir; there are no more flights until tomorrow morning." The agent told him. Timothy agreed to take the morning flight, which meant he'd have to spend the night at the airport. He had spent the night in worse places and wasn't worried. He walked over to the automated teller machine and withdrew what little cash remained in his account. Over the next few hours he hatched a plan. He decided that once he got back in town he would rent a low profile motel room until his trip was supposed to end. Just as he was congratulating himself on his creativity, more like convincing himself that the plan was tolerable, two hulking men approached on each side of him. The tattooed gorilla on his left wrapped his enormous arm around Timothy's neck. "Mr. Rex asked us to give you his regards."

"Mr. Rex is like that." The other gorilla spoke with a raspy voice. "He keeps close tabs on all his associates."

Timothy was instantly numb with fear. "I'll get the money." He whispered not wanting to draw attention.

The first man continued, "Don't be gone for too long. First payment is due Friday." The two men patted Timothy on the back and left. Timothy's eyes began to well up, but he fought back the tears with all his strength. He couldn't believe how quickly things had turned sour.

Chapter 7

"No parties." The old woman at the Royal Motor Lodge bell desk said sternly. "Rent is due every Wednesday by noon, no exceptions." Timothy gave her the pro-rated first week's rent along with the signed agreement. The woman's odd smell and unkempt appearance fit the place well. Everything about the motel seemed cheap and barely held together. It was as if the owner exerted the bare minimum of care, marginally adhering to health department and building codes. She passed Timothy an oval power-blue keychain embossed with the number '2742'. Two keys dangled from it. "There's a key to the laundry room on there in case you need it." Timothy just nodded and walked off thinking he'd had enough of laundry rooms for a while.

He lugged his bag to the furthest end of the property and found the room conveniently adjacent to a farm of noisy air conditioners. A wall of hot stale air hit him when he opened the door. Looking around the tiny room for the climate controls, he spied them above the sink. Unfortunately, they were locked behind a thick clear plastic enclosure. A hand-written note hung from it stating air-conditioning was an extra fifty dollars a week. Timothy opted instead to open the window. On his way over to the window he noted the room's sparse amenities, among which was a large coin-operated telephone on a table by the window. Also on the table was another hand-written note declaring that opening the window was prohibited in the interest of safety. Timothy dug into his pocket and counted his money. It would be tight, but he couldn't see meeting his demise by suffocating in this tiny room. He trekked back to the smelly lady and paid her the fifty dollars. The transaction seemed to take forever as she made him sign a whole new agreement.

On his way back he cursed her, calling her every vile name he could think of. The truth was that he was actually mad at himself for getting into this position, but she was an easy target. As he rounded the noisy corner to his room he came face-to-face with the two big gorillas from the airport. The raspy one hissed, "Hey pal, glad to see you're settling in." They looked around at the second-rate digs and exchanged dubious glances. "This is kind of a rough neighborhood for a fancy lad like yourself don't you think?" Timothy froze while his heart slithered up into his throat. "No worries, we're going to make sure nothing happens to our new neighbor." They smiled and walked off toward a waiting car. "Don't forget, we got a date on Friday." They were gone as quickly as they appeared, and their message was clear – get the money.

Timothy's hands shook as he unlocked his motel room door. Once inside he slammed the door shut and locked it tight. He stood at the door for a minute to catch his breath and evaluate the integrity of the dead bolt. He knew it didn't stand a chance against the gorillas. If they wanted him, they'd come in and take him. "I've got to get that money!" Timothy said to himself and went to lie down on the bed. Right then his eye caught sight of a single chip resting on his pillow. He'd barely been there an hour and they'd breached his room! A queasy combination of dread and insecurity cloaked over him, and he slumped down at the small table instead.

Using the complimentary notepad and pen, he began desperately trying to figure out how he could get his first payment. He listed all the money in all of his accounts. Most of it he couldn't touch since they were joint accounts with his father and he would see the withdrawal. He then began to inventory all of his possessions. He thought about selling his television and videogames, but he knew he wouldn't get much for second hand electronics. Besides, everyone would ask where they went. Then he remembered his coin and baseball card collections up in the attic. They had to be worth something. The problem was getting them out of the house unnoticed. He was supposed to be in Miami. There was also the problem of not having any transportation.

He weighed his options. The house was a thirty minute cab ride, but that would seriously cut into his funds. Taking the bus would be cheaper, but there was a higher chance of being spotted by someone while on foot, the bus stop being several blocks away. Right then it occurred to him how exhausted he was. He could no longer think about it. He got undressed and collapsed in the bed and was out.

Chapter 8

*T*uesday morning Timothy awoke to the sound of a car horn outside the motel room. He stumbled over to the window and squinted to see. The gorillas were waiting in their car. They spotted him peering through the window and motioned for him to come out. He quickly put on his pants and went out shirtless to meet them.

"Good morning. You look terrible!" The tattooed gorilla said with a sour face. "Mr. Rex is concerned about you."

Timothy looked around the parking lot; they were the only people out. "I told you I'd get the first payment by Friday. Didn't we go over this last night? Why are you hassling me?" Timothy's nervous voice barely masked his irritation.

The gorillas looked at each other as if to say, 'Can you believe this guy?' Then the raspy one spoke, "Mr. Rex cares about you. He doesn't want anything bad to happen to you."

"Yeah, then who'd make your payments?" his cohort added.

The raspy gorilla continued, "So we're staying close to keep tabs on your general welfare. Get used to it." Timothy nodded his head in submission. Without warning the tone of the conversation turned congenial. "We're going to drive-thru and pick up some breakfast sandwiches, you want anything?"

Timothy was taken aback by the offer. It was the first time he'd been on the receiving end of hospitality since the ordeal began. "No, I'm good." He shook his head and started to walk back to his room kind of freaked out by their kindness. As he heard the engine rev an idea struck him. He turned back around and shouted, "Hey!" just as they began to pull away.

Tattoo hit the brakes. Raspy rolled down his window and stared at Timothy who jogged toward him. "What is it kid?"

The words didn't come out on command as Timothy expected. His heart pounded and his throat was tight. He swallowed hard and tried again. "Actually, I could use a ride somewhere if you don't mind."

The right corner of Raspy's lips contracted and his eyebrow shot up as he measured the request. "Yeah, I guess that would be okay, but you need to put some clothes on before boarding this chariot pal." Timothy jogged back inside to change.

Quickly, he threw on a wrinkled shirt and jeans. All of his clothes were wrinkled since Bruno had carelessly shoved them into the bag. Once dressed, Timothy splashed some water on his face then exited his motel room and hopped into the back seat. Timothy briefly described how to get to his father's house. Then it occurred to him that maybe he'd get better treatment if the gorillas got to know him better. "I'm Tim." He blurted out, hoping to appeal to their humanity.

Wearing a cynical expression, the raspy gorilla twisted to get a look at Tim in the backseat. "You don't say. . ."

"What are your names?" Timothy asked casually. "I mean, if we're going to spend this much time together I should at least know what to call you, right?"

"I suppose you can call us whatever you like kid." The driver interjected.

Timothy smiled, "How about Tattoo and Raspy?"

Tattoo burst out laughing, "I like that, has a good ring to it." He playfully tagged Raspy's shoulder. "Don't you think?"

Raspy turned back facing forward. "Whatever you want kid, just get Mr. Rex his money."

Forty minutes later Timothy and his chauffeurs approached the Alabaster Estates guard shack. "Let me do all the talking please." Timothy requested. The back window rolled down and the guard, seeing it was Timothy, opened the gate without a word.

The car proceeded past the gate and into his father's community. "Glad we let you do the talking kid." Tattoo said smugly.

Timothy guided them back to his track. "You are going to make a left at the stop sign." He was exceptionally paranoid, fearing that someone would see him, even behind the dark tinted glass. His pulse quickened as they rounded the corner; his sketchy eyes canvassed the street. "Slow down a little, but not too slow." His companions didn't seem to care whether or not they drew any attention from the residents. "It's three doors down. Pull over here." The car jerked over to the curb, stopping abruptly next to a green electrical box. The conspicuous parking job made Timothy sick to his stomach. A tap on his hand diverted his attention and he realized it was sweat dripping from his forehead. He dragged his sleeve across his numb face mopping up the moisture. "Do one of you guys have a towel or something?"

The driver spent a moment rummaging through the glove box but came up empty-handed. "Sorry kid."

The early morning air was still crisp. It felt refreshing on Timothy's skin as he cautiously cracked open the car door. Getting the deed done as quickly as possible seemed the best strategy. In an instant, his feet hit the pavement, and he was speed-walking, head down, toward the house.

Reaching the house, he veered over to the side gate. He forcefully pressed up on the latch mechanism then kicked the base of the gate and it swung open. After closing the gate behind him he squatted down by the trash cans to catch his breath. His heart was pounding hard, and he felt lightheaded. He knew his Dad and brother were away sailing with his uncle. Both of his older sisters had places of their own and were most likely working so he should be able to retrieve the loot without detection. Moving on, he continued to the back sliding glass door and prepared to enter. He reached into his pocket and hurriedly yanked out his house keys. In doing so, the motel keychain in the same pocket got hitched and was flung into the air, landing precariously on top of a nearby drain grill. He uncouthly dashed down to snatch the motel keys, but instead his sweaty hands ended up propelling them down into the grate. He tried repeatedly, but there was no way he could fit his hand down there. Time was ticking and he decided to worry about the motel keys later.

The back door had two locks, one ornamental and the other a deadbolt. Timothy had unlocked them hundreds of times in his lifetime; it took him just seconds to get inside. He thought about how odd it felt to be sneaking into his own home. This was the place he spent his whole life and now he was tip-toeing down the hall toward the attic entrance like a prowler. He gave the hanging cord a good tug and-

BEEP. BEEP. BEEP. Each pang of the alarm seemed to reach directly into his chest and wrench his heart. In his haste he had forgotten to disarm the alarm. "So stupid!" he chastised himself and scuttled frantically over to the keypad and punched in the code. All went silent. Only Timothy's heavy panting reverberated in the shadows. "No more messing around" he told himself.

Moments later he was up in the attic tearing through the piled up storage boxes. He came across Christmas decorations, his father's old files and even a trunk of his mother's clothing. A flap of floral material peeked out the side of the sealed trunk. Stroking its texture, he recalled how she would wear that dress so frequently that his father would complain and beg her to buy new clothes. But she loved it, and so she always wore it. Continuing on, he eventually came across a collection of his retired toys and athletic uniforms. The loot he sought had to be close by. There, partially hidden behind the support beam, was his shoebox of baseball cards. Not more than three feet away was a knapsack containing his coin collection. Timothy grabbed the two items and made his way out of the attic, down the stairs, and then through the back door as quick as possible.

He ran around to the side gate, his coins jingling loudly with each step. Just then he remembered the motel keys down in the drain. A venomous string of obscenities seethed from his lips. He wondered if it was worth going back to the grate and trying to fish them out. He couldn't guess how much the smelly motel lady would charge him to replace them. Before he could make up his mind he heard a car pull into the front driveway. Squatting where he stood, he felt as if he were going to pass out. He heard the car door open and then a woman's voice in mid conversation approached the side gate. It was his oldest sister Victoria. Not hearing any other voice Timothy figured she was on her cell phone.

She stood on the other side of the fence inches from him. "-I don't know Liz. They said they tried Dad, but he didn't answer. Uncle's boat must be outside the cell coverage zone thingy or whatever. They don't get back until tomorrow. I'm the second person on the list of people to call when the alarm goes off, right after Dad. Besides being older, I'm smarter, prettier and higher on the alarm contact list." She laughed, teasing her younger sister Elizabeth.

The gate was not opening for her. She continued fiddling with the gate latch, getting increasingly frustrated by the obstacle. Victoria wasn't known for patience. Timothy remained still and held his breath. "I'm so dead." He thought to himself. Time played with his head, and the thought occurred to him that getting caught would be humiliating but less stressful than continuing to deal with the situation on his own. He felt a calm come over him for the first time in a day. "I'm just going to come clean." He thought. Taking a deep breath he stood up to face his sister and open the gate, but when the gate swung open she was gone. He heard the front door close shut. "What was I thinking!" he looked out across the front yard, no neighbors were out. This was his best chance.

Timothy walked briskly out to the sidewalk, turned, and then broke into a light jog. With his head down, he held the shoebox and knapsack close against his chest, hoping to deafen the jingling coins. "Just need to make it to the car." He told himself repeatedly. After negotiating what felt like several hundred yards of sidewalk, Timothy raised his head and looked for the car but he didn't see it. He swiveled around, trying to get his bearings. Feeling thoroughly disoriented, he wondered if he had accidentally run off in the wrong direction. Then it caught his eye, the green electrical box where he was dropped off earlier. "They ditched me." The realization set in. He performed a quick three-hundred-sixty degree survey of the street, looking for any plausible exit to the nightmare. Instead of a solution, his eyes detected motion in front of his house. Victoria's car was backing out of the driveway, curving a path that would take her right past him on her way to the main intersection.

He did what came instinctively and dove into his neighbor's prickly hedges, his cargo spilling out. The sharp branches slashed his skin but adrenaline prevented him from feeling any pain. The dial in his brain was cranked to maximum survival. Timothy pulled his extremities in and waited for Victoria to pass.

Victoria's car whizzed by, eventually turning at the end of the block. Timothy extended one leg out of the hedge when he heard another car approaching. Quickly, his leg recoiled. The car pulled up right next to him and he closed his eyes. "What the heck are you doing?" Raspy hissed.

Timothy felt a giant hand extract him from the hedge in one quick tug. He coughed, and then frantically collected up the spilled coins and baseball cards. He never thought he'd be so glad to see those two gorillas. "Where the heck did you go?"

With a matter-of-fact shrug, Tattoo explained, "The drive-thru stops serving breakfast sandwiches at ten." Timothy didn't really care if it was a reasonable answer or not, he just wanted to get out of the neighborhood at this point.

The car pulled away and headed back to the motel. When they arrived, Timothy had them pull up next to the office. "Give me a minute."

Tattoo and Raspy watched him awkwardly walk up to office clenching the knapsack and shoebox against his chest. "Should we have held on to that stuff for him?" Raspy asked.

"No, he's not dumb enough to stiff us." Tattoo was good at sizing up a sucker. He'd seen Timothy's type many times before. Young, spoiled, and scared to death. "We're not going to have many problems with this one."

Raspy shook his head. "That's a shame. I was kind of looking forward to breaking some bones." The two laughed.

A few moments later Timothy emerged from the office holding the shoebox against his chest, but the knapsack was shoved partway into his back pocket, noticeably depleted. "What is this?" Raspy asked bewildered.

Timothy got back into the car. "She charged me a hundred and twenty bucks to replace the keys, can you believe that?"

The gorillas didn't say anything; they just took off toward Timothy's room, skidding into a parking spot. The two jumped out of the car then firmly extracted Timothy from the backseat. They dragged him into his motel room ignoring his protests and pleas. Inside, Raspy gave Timothy a powerful punch to the stomach that sent him to the ground gasping to catch his breath. Raspy placed his leather boot on Timothy's neck holding him down. He pulled the half-empty knapsack from Timothy's pocket and threw it in his face. Some silver dollars clattered out onto the ground. "You think this is some kind of game? Mr. Rex wants that money."

"Frida-" Timothy coughed, saliva drooling from his lips.

Tattoo closed the window shades tighter. "From now on, no one gets paid until Mr. Rex gets paid, understand?" Timothy nodded then coughed heavily. "We'll be visiting you again tomorrow. Don't do anything stupid." Timothy nodded and began to sob which irritated Raspy. "Geez, have some dignity!" Raspy's boot came off of Timothy's neck.

Tattoo opened the motel room door and held it as Raspy exited. Looking back at Timothy he gave him a tip, "Crying won't help you. Use your head kid." The door closed and Timothy breathed a sigh of relief.

He laid on the ground crying for the next twenty minutes. Everything about him ached; his stomach, his muscles and his pride. The musty smell of the carpet only made him more depressed. Never had he stayed in such substandard conditions. "I'm above staying in this rat hole." He told himself. It wasn't even noon, but even so he crawled into the bed and pulled the covers up over his head. He was done for the day.

Chapter 9

Wednesday morning, Timothy was up before the sun. Having slept most of the previous day away in his depressed stupor, he felt refreshed and ready for action. His baseball cards were fastidiously spread out across the motel room floor, categorized by rarity and value. He felt good about the items, as if he had been thrown a life preserver. It had been years since he had looked at them, and he had forgotten how many valuable cards he had accumulated. Every penny counted. His remaining coin collection, consisting mostly of a short stack of silver dollars, was piled up on the cheap table next to the little pile of cash he had remaining. A local telephone book sat beside the cash, flipped open to the 'Coins and Collectibles' section. Timothy had circled the names of two shops within walking distance.

When the sun finally showed up, Timothy called the first coin shop to make sure they would buy the items. It was ironic to him that he had to use his loose change to place a call to a coin shop. Timothy cursed the smelly office lady out loud. He nearly vomited when the proprietor informed him that the current exchange rate on silver dollars was more than ten times their face value. He realized that he had lost well over a thousand dollars by paying for the lost motel keys with silver dollars. That was almost a third of what he needed to come up with by Friday. He wondered if he could persuade the smelly lady to return the coins in exchange for cash. The only problem was that he didn't have enough cash to propose the swap. He called the second shop which featured a large half-page advertisement in the telephone book citing baseball card purchases. The woman who answered the telephone told him that all appraisals and purchases were done after lunch. Timothy began rattling off some of his rare cards, but she obviously wasn't familiar with the hobby. She told him the owner buys a lot of cards and sports memorabilia and to come by after twelve.

Timothy hung up and then planned out his day. He'd leave at eleven-thirty and begin walking over to the card shop. He expected the sale of his baseball card collection to easily cover the silver dollar cash swap and leave plenty remaining to put toward the Friday payment. Once he got the silver dollars back he'd head over to the coin shop, cash them in for the remaining balance of the Friday payment, and then be able to relax for a few days. It was simple.

As he gathered up the cards and coins he caught a draft of his own scent. He was ripe. He tossed the wrinkled clothes in his bag, sniffing each article, until he came across a T-shirt and shorts that were fresh. Timothy turned on the shower and waited for the water sputtering from the crusty shower head to warm up – but it never did. Instead of a regular bar of soap there was a corroded metal box with a hanging switch that dispensed soap granules when you flicked it. There was no indication if it was intended to wash your body or hair; just a generic soap. No matter how much of the powder Timothy put in his hand, it wouldn't lather up. It only transformed into a larger blob of a waxy sludge. He was certain it was just plain old dishwashing granules. He washed himself quickly, doing his best to endure the cold water while hoping none of the soap grains got in his eyes.

As his plan dictated, Timothy packed up the baseball card collection and headed out at eleven-thirty. The walk across town was quiet except for the wind which seemed to blow stronger with each step. As goose bumps lined his arms, he wished he hadn't changed into the thin T-shirt. Stinky beat out freezing every time.

The exchange at the shop lasted longer than Timothy had hoped. The owner and he haggled over the value of every single card. The cards were scattered in a shoebox and that didn't help. He knew the owner was grossly undervaluing the collection, using the shoebox as justification. Unfortunately, Timothy had no choice but to accept, even though he knew he was leaving thirty percent on the table. Timothy pleaded with the dealer, "Can't you do any better than that? I'm really in a crunch!"

The owner sized him up for a moment. "Tell you what; throw in that necklace and I'll-"

"Forget it! Cash me out." Timothy took the loss.

The wad of cash felt good in Timothy's hand. He didn't sweat being underpaid too much since he knew once he got his hands back on the silver dollars he'd be set. The cards had served their purpose. Besides, it was much easier to walk around without that lousy shoebox.

As he walked along the strip leading up to his motel, he sensed someone was following him. Nervously, he glanced over his shoulder just as Tattoo and Raspy grabbed hold of him and threw him up against a chain-link fence. "What the heck!" he cried out. While Tattoo held him Raspy went through his pockets like a pro, and retrieved the wad of cash. "Hey, what are you doing? That's mine!"

Raspy punched Timothy hard in the stomach while Tattoo allowed him to fall to the pavement. "You mean Mr. Rex's don't you?" Raspy hissed.

"I need that!" Timothy pleaded.

Tattoo squatted down to Timothy's level. "We're just going to keep it safe for you until Friday."

Timothy got up on his knees, eyes wide with desperation, and reached out for the money in Raspy's hand. Raspy immediately pulled the cash outside his reach. "Oh no, not for you Mr. double-or-nothing. We'll never see it again."

Timothy didn't know what to say or do. He was frozen. Tattoo and Raspy backed away. "Two days kid. Don't mess up." Tattoo warned. Then the duo walked across the street to their waiting car and drove off, Timothy still on his knees.

Timothy got up and dusted himself off. "What now?" He asked himself. He didn't have the cash to exchange for the silver dollars. Maybe he could appeal to the smelly woman to sell them for her and split the profits. Maybe. He wandered back toward his room going through the various scenarios in his mind. None of them seemed great. When he reached his motel room he immediately noticed an ugly yellow boot around the door knob blocking the keyhole. 'Rent is due every Wednesday by noon – no exceptions.' The smelly lady's voice echoed in his head. "Ugh, how could I be so stupid?" Timothy yelled at the top of his lungs, not caring who heard him. Now he had no choice but to plead with the smelly lady to assist in the sale of the coins.

Timothy sprinted to the office as fast as he could, springing the door open. An older man was behind the desk this time. He looked at Timothy alarmed with one hand on the telephone. Timothy panted, trying to catch his breath. "Can I help you young man?" The office clerk asked cautiously.

"Where's the-" Timothy bent over to catch his breath and held up his index finger. After a moment he stood upright, still panting heavily, placed his hands on his hips and tried again. "Where is the lady who was here yesterday?"

The old man moved his hand off the telephone. "You mean Lydia?"

"I guess. She was here all week. I need to talk to her."

"Well, she won't be back for two weeks." Timothy covered his face with his hands. "Said she came into some money and decided to take a vacation." Enraged, Timothy kicked a nearby trashcan. "You can't do that in here young man." The old man reached for the telephone and dialed the police. As he reported the disturbance, Timothy waved his hands in defeat and exited the office.

The air outside was noticeably cooler than he remembered. Cooler and moist; rain was on the way. He had no way of getting to his things since they were locked in the room. He was out of money. The police would be arriving any minute. Like a trapped wild animal, Timothy broke into a frantic run toward his father's home. It was a twenty-minute car ride away. This was going to take a while on foot. As he ran, thunder erupted and buckets of water from the sky broke loose, dowsing him. He thought about how the rain felt warm on his numb skin. It was a more pleasant shower than he experienced in his motel room earlier.

Chapter 10

*A*fter jogging for half an hour, Timothy stumbled across the entrance of a storm drain riverbed where he and he father used to go cycling. Water rushed down the center of the canal, but the outskirts were safe. He navigated down the concrete divider and settled into a mild paced walk. His mind floated to a chimerical state as the receptors in his brain numbed. He became weary of the sensation and decided he needed to slow down and process what had happened to him. He'd been so unnerved, so stressed out, that he hadn't stopped to consider the long term consequences of his actions. He wondered how this crisis would play out. He wondered if he would still be going away to college in the fall. Was there any possible way to hide his debt from his family and continue to make payments while in school? It didn't seem likely with the high interest he was accruing. He would have to use his college fund to pay back Mr. Rex. It was the only way. He could apply for financial aid and pay back his loan once he graduated, but it would cost him in other ways. His father would never respect him again. That was the most painful part of the ordeal; knowing that his father would think even lower of him - the weak child - when it was all over.

Timothy followed the storm drain deeper into town. Once the rushing rain water reached an uncomfortable proximity to his stride, he exited the canal and found himself along some railroad tracks. He followed the tracks for a bit, eventually coming across an old switch with two abandoned railcars at the split. Among the various vulgarities spray-painted on the derelict railcars was the phrase, 'Jesus Saves'. Timothy picked up a rock and threw it at the railcar. A high-pitched ping resonated over the storm, echoing briefly throughout the clearing.

A poorly dressed older man with a wiry beard stumbled out of the railcar. "Who's out here!" The man's craggily voice growled above the rainfall. Timothy jumped back, startled by the unexpected presence. The stranger squinted and held his hand to his forehead to shield his eyes from the rain. Once he spotted Timothy, his other hand came out from behind his back holding a broken chair leg. "Whadda you want!" He shouted angrily, the chair leg raised high.

"Nothing, I'm just going home!" Timothy's puny voice cowered to the stranger's forceful growl. He held up his hands instinctively to show he was no threat to the man.

"Got something against using the sidewalk?" The stranger pointed the chair leg toward the nearby highway. "Why are you down here throwing rocks at my place?"

Timothy slowly backed up, tripping over part of the track and falling over. He awkwardly scooted and got back up. "The riverbed is flooded. I'm taking a shortcut."

The stranger put the chair leg down and evaluated Timothy for a moment. "Riverbeds and train tracks? Who you running from boy?"

It was a good question, causing Timothy to hesitate before blurting out, "No one, just trying to get home."

The stranger turned back toward the open rail car. "Too wet out here for my taste. Got some chili cooking, want a bite?"

Chili, the idea detonated in Timothy's head. He hadn't realized how famished he was until hearing the prospect of a hot bowl of chili. "Yes, that would be great. I'm starving." He didn't care if he got beat with the chair leg, it would be worth it.

The stranger waved Timothy over to the vacant railroad car entrance where the glow of a fire enticed them both. "C'mon, it's warmer in there." The invitation suddenly made Timothy aware of how cold he was. He followed the stranger aboard, allowing the man to grab his hand at one point and pull him up into the car. The man's hands were startlingly rough with calluses. "I'm Steve." the man announced casually, as if he hadn't just been threatening Timothy with a chair leg.

"That's my kid brother's name - Stephen." The fire provided a better look at the man's wrinkled face; Timothy marveled that he was interacting with a person so far down the ladder. "I'm Tim." He volunteered reluctantly. "I've never met a hobo before."

Steve laughed. "A hobo, is that what you think I am?"

"Well, you kind of look the part."

Steve looked himself over. "I suppose I'm not as spiffy a dresser as I once was." He pulled one of his pant legs out from his sock. "I'm not a hobo. Hobo's wander aimlessly. I have purpose. I'm a man with a purpose, you hear me?"

Steve's conviction was alarming to Timothy. "I didn't mean any offense by it." He didn't really care what Steve's purpose was, he was simply hungry. "I wouldn't mind a bite of that chili now."

Suspended by an unraveled coat hanger was a single can of store brand chili beans roasting above the makeshift fire pit. "My purpose is to serve my fellow man. I wasn't always a man of purpose, but I am now." Steve reached in with a handkerchief and grabbed the can. He put it up to his lips and then scooped the contents into his mouth using his finger. "Mmm, that's good eating." After a few bites he held the can out for Timothy to take his share. Although hungry and cold, Timothy's pride caused him to hesitate for a moment, just long enough to offend his host. "What? You're too good to break bread at my table?"

Timothy lunged at the can and swiped it away, digging his fingers inside to get at the beans. His hunger outweighed his vanity. The spiced legumes tasted better than any meal he could remember.

"Hold up, save a little for me!" Steve pulled the can out of Timothy's hands and ate some more.

Timothy appeared embarrassed by his mongrel table manners and blushingly wiped debris from his chin while mumbling, "Thanks."

Steve nodded and asked, "So what kind of trouble you in?" Timothy didn't say anything. It was too embarrassing to say it out loud, much less to some stranger. "Look, I've seen it all. Drugs, gangs, stealing. Don't need be ashamed to tell me. Everyone breaks a law now and then."

"Laws were made to be broken right?" Timothy pulled the phrase from his father's repertoire.

Steve grimaced, "Heck no, what are you talking about? That makes no sense. Why have laws at all then." Steve produced a flask from his inside pocket and took a swig. He offered some to Timothy but he declined. "Nobody is perfect. Man just ain't built that way. We're sinners, every last one of us." Timothy rolled his eyes as soon as he heard mention of sin. "It's true".

Timothy shook his head. "That's a bunch of nonsense. My mom used to try to sucker me into believing that stuff."

"You should have paid attention to her." Steve shook his finger at Timothy. "It's never too late for redemption."

Timothy stretched out his arms and looked about the dirty rail car. "Yeah, looks like it's working out really great for you."

Steve just smiled. It wasn't the first time he had heard that. "I'm not perfect. Done plenty I ain't proud of, that's for sure. I lost a fine woman along the way. Lost my kids and my career too. I was in a pretty dark place when the Holy Spirit came to me."

Timothy's lip contracted cynically. "Isn't that how it always is? God doesn't show up until you hit rock bottom. Only when everyone else has abandoned you do you find God."

"For some folks, sure."

Steve's affirmative reply encouraged Timothy's rant. "God never comes to a man who has his life together."

Steve could smell a foul odor and wondered if it was coming from Timothy or himself. "Now just a minute, that's not true. God is knocking on your door your whole life, some folks just don't answer. Sometimes it takes losing all distractions to really hear his call." Steve sniffed his armpit. "What about your God fearing friends and neighbors who have been faithfully raised in the church?"

Steve wasn't changing Timothy's mind. "They're either brainwashed from an early age or just too uneducated and weak minded. Life scares them and they can't cope without some supernatural explanation for all this." Timothy waved his hands around. "But there aren't any explanations. People like me understand that you've got to get what you can in this life. I'm doing just fine without your God."

Timothy's vigorous tone didn't dissuade Steve. "So was your own mother weak-minded or was she brainwashed?"

Timothy stood up. "Leave her out of it. I know I look a little messed up right now, but I'm from a very influential family; a family of leaders. We have money to buy all the chili we want. I'm going to law school in the fall. Does that sound like someone who needs to be saved? My father's house, a really nice two-story house with a pool, is not far from here and that's where I'm headed."

Steve smiled. "You should see my father's house."

Timothy shook his head. "Yeah, whatever."

Steve stood up alongside Timothy. "Look around - all this is temporary."

"I hope so." Timothy sighed.

"Anything you own returns to dust in the end. Leading a life of service, not clutching onto material things, is what matters." Timothy scoffed at him openly. "Someday you may see what comfort serving the Lord brings."

"I don't need the Lord for comfort."

"Is that so?" Steve asked. "What brings you comfort then?"

Timothy thought about it for a moment then answered, "Drawing brings me comfort. It helps me get focused and think straight."

Steve nodded. "What kind of drawing?"

"Just some funny pictures of my brother Stephen."

Steve picked up a jagged piece of rock and scratched the inside wall of the railcar with it. A thick white line trailed his hand. "Show me." Steve passed the rock to Timothy. Timothy spent a few minutes drawing "Stevie the Great" on the wall. Stevie was standing on top of a train wearing a conductor's hat while being chased by a flying saucer. "Not bad! Kind of weird, but not bad." Steve remarked.

"He's being chased by aliens."

Steve nodded. "I can see that. Still kind of weird."

Timothy noticed the rain had slowed to a drizzle and so he moved toward the open door. "Drawing is just a hobby. I'm going to make plenty of money someday with my own law firm. As I get bigger I'll hire more people, so don't lecture me on a life of service. How many jobs can you and your spray-painted Jesus railroad car create?" Timothy was surprised at how good it felt to sock it to him bluntly. "Jesus can't help everyone. Sorry you messed up your life, but I'm not like you. I don't need to be saved from anything."

Steve shrugged nonchalantly and smiled. "My life ain't messed up at all. Each day is a blessing."

"You live in this dump!" Timothy reminded him with a laugh.

Steve reached outside the railcar and brought in two plastic bottles filled with rainwater and handed one to Timothy. "I've got a roof over my head. I've got fire, food and clean water on most days. Best of all; I spend my days in service to the Lord. No distractions."

As he took a long drink from the water bottle, Timothy became uncomfortable with this new relationship. "He's not a friend." Timothy told himself. "Not even an acquaintance – just some guy." Nourished and revitalized, Timothy's arrogance returned, and he felt his departure was long overdue. "Thanks, but I have to go now." Timothy hobbled out of the railcar and sloshed through the muddy ground toward the main highway.

From behind him Steve yelled, "God will keep knocking". But Timothy just walked faster not looking back. Then Steve yelled, "When I was hungry you fed me. When I was thirsty you gave me drink. When I was a stranger you took me in!"

Timothy was now thoroughly unsettled. "Freak."

Chapter 11

A s he approached the house he noticed his father's car in the driveway with the back opened up. Stephen and his father were unpacking their gear. For a moment Timothy contemplated not going home just yet, but then it began to rain again and hard. "Tim!" He heard Stephen cry out.

"Shoot." Timothy had rehearsed in his mind waltzing up to the front door and making a casual entrance. Now he was sloshing down the block with his sloppy bag, drenched. Timothy waved and smiled to Stephen who met him half way, grabbing the bag.

"What are you doing back so soon?" Stephen asked with a big smile. He obviously didn't mind the early arrival.

Timothy made his way toward his father who had finished unpacking the last item from the car and stood waiting under the eaves by the front door. "Heck of a day!" Timothy shouted above the rain.

Stephen and his father ushered him in. "What are you wearing? You're soaked!" His father sent Stephen to fetch a towel.

Timothy began talking fast. "Fitch's cousin got sick. Like really sick, and was throwing up all over the place. I didn't want to get sick so I flew back early." Timothy could see the questions forming in his father's eyes, so he kept talking. "Then the airline lost my bag, and when they found it half my stuff was missing. All of my good clothes and stuff."

"Did you file a report?" His father was the king of filing consumer complaints. Nothing less than perfection was tolerable.

Timothy nodded. "Yeah, but they said there's not much they can do."

His father's brow scrunched up. "I know some folks on the board. I'm going to give them a piece of my mind!"

Timothy panicked. "No, no, it's fine Dad. I gave them an earful already. I'm nineteen now. I have to fight my own battles."

This made his father smile. "It's about time."

"So then, I took a cab and it broke down a block from here. Can you believe that?" Timothy could hardly believe the lies coming from his mouth. He couldn't imagine his father and brother would buy any of it, but amazingly they did.

"What a terrible trip!" Stephen exclaimed. "You should have gone sailing with us."

Timothy nodded eagerly in agreement. "Well, I'm going to go take a shower and get on some fresh clothes."

"No arguments here." His father backed away. "Frankly, you look, and smell, like hell."

Warm water, a real bar of soap, shampoo, conditioner, a waiting fuzzy towel; Timothy could not have been happier. He took his time cleansing himself of the past days dreary events. The steam melted away his agony and made him forget all his worries.

Afterwards, Timothy put on his most comfortable sweats and settled down for a nap. It felt good to be clean and be resting in his bed again, listening to the soothing patter of rain outside. He closed his eyes and held on to the saint medallion as he did nearly every night while falling asleep. It reminded him of his mother. Just as he was dozing off he heard a tick at his window. He sat up and listened, maybe it was just the rain. Then again, something distinctly hit his window. He went over and peered through the blinds. There, below his window stood Raspy, soaking wet, holding up two fingers. Timothy understood the message; just two more days to get the money. He couldn't believe Raspy would just stand there enduring the rain without an umbrella. These guys were relentless. Timothy's eyes met Raspy's for a moment before he turned and wandered over to the waiting car by the curb and departed.

Timothy slouched back down in his bed but couldn't seem to fall asleep now. The gorillas had jostled him good. These guys watched his every move. There never seemed to be any privacy, no sanctuary! Timothy thought back to the railroad car; they'd never think to check there. Maybe he should hide out with hobo Steve for a while he thought.

A knock on his door startled Timothy. "Can I come in?" it was Stephen.

"Sure, come on in."

Stephen always liked hanging out in Timothy's room more than in his own. Everything was just cooler when it came to his big brother. "The guys from the cab company stopped and dropped this off." Stephen reached out and handed Timothy a poker chip. "They said you left it in their cab. It's pretty cool! Did you get it in Miami?"

Timothy's throat tightened up. "They talked to you?"

"Yeah, just a little. The guy was big!" Stephen was transfixed on the object. "So how did you get it?"

Seeing Stephen's fascination with the chip turned Timothy's stomach. "It's not mine. They made a mistake."

"Then can I have it?" Stephen asked excitedly.

"No!" Timothy's harsh denial shocked Stephen. "Gambling is nothing you want to get involved with."

Stephen's face contorted with confusion, "Who said anything about gambling? I just want it for my room."

Timothy held the chip behind his back. "No." He stood at the door. "Look, I'm tired. I'm going to lie down for a while."

Stephen ignored him and plopped down on Timothy's bed. "And you know what else?" Stephen spoke in a hushed tone. "He also asked if you left a gun in his cab."

"What?"

"Yeah, he showed me a little black gun along with the poker chip, asked if it was yours too." Stephen held up his hand like a pistol and shot at an imaginary target. "I even got to hold it for a second."

Timothy scolded Stephen the best that he could in a whisper. "Are you crazy?"

Stephen laughed at Timothy's concern. "What's the big deal?"

Timothy's anger made the rounds. First with Stephen, then the gorillas and ultimately came back at himself. How could he let things get so out of control? "If anyone else comes to the door for me, you don't speak with them. You tell them I'm not home and take a message. Better yet, just don't answer the door. Understand?"

Stephen was annoyed that Timothy didn't share his enthusiasm for getting to hold the pistol. "You're just jealous. It was pretty cool to hold it."

"Yeah, I'm really jealous." Timothy yanked Stephen off his bed and pushed him out the door. "See you in the morning."

Timothy shut the door and sunk down to the ground. "I've got to get that money." He whispered while kneading the chip in his hand. They knew where he lived. They put a gun in his little brother's hands. They could be outside his bedroom window at a moment's notice. Timothy decided he would liquidate anything and everything he could in the morning.

Chapter 12

"You sure you don't want to speak with one of our financial advisors before proceeding with the withdrawal Mr. Clement?" The young lady at the bank looked across the teller window with concern. It was bank policy for the tellers to encourage delaying any sizable withdrawal.

Timothy looked behind him anxiously, then back to the teller. "No, thank you."

The teller opened the drawer then hesitated. "Would you prefer a cashier's check? It's safer than cash."

"No." Timothy was trying to contain his impatience. He felt as if the entire bank was watching him. The girl began creating piles of twenty dollar bills. "No, I need one hundred dollar bills please." Timothy instructed.

The girl quickly returned the twenty's to the till. "No problem sir." She began stacking again, this time with one hundred dollar bills. As she piled them she counted the cumulative amount out loud. "One-hundred, two-hundred, three-"

"Please, that's not necessary." Timothy scolded in a hushed tone. "I don't want to announce it to the world."

The girl continued on without a word. She was obviously no stranger to this particular request. When she finished she slid the stacks of bills toward Timothy.

Timothy was shocked by the bulk of it. "Don't you have an envelope or something I can keep it in?"

Without a word she slid it back and packed it in an envelope for him. "Is there anything else I can do for you today Mr. Clement?"

Timothy wished she would stop announcing his name. "Um, do you guys do cash advances on credit cards?"

The girl looked down and bit her lower lip. "We do. However, the current rates are not the most competitive. You may want to consider-"

"Here." Before she could finish her sentence, Timothy slid his credit card across to her.

The teller passed across a pen and paper. "Please write down how much you would like to advance." Timothy jotted down the amount and slid the paper back across.

A few minutes later he was walking out of the bank branch with a thicker envelope in his hands. As relieved as he was in securing his first payment, he was equally distressed knowing that his father would eventually discover the fund withdrawals. Timothy got into his car but paused before staring the engine. Across the street from the bank was the elementary school he attended as a child. He could see the basketball courts where he and his father shot hoops so many times before. Memories of the texture of the basketball on his fingertips, the smell of the blacktop, and the squeaking of rubber-soled shoes came back to him. He realized he'd never again play ball with his father.

Timothy started the car and pulled out of the bank parking lot. Driving through town he felt bits of himself dissipating as he passed more childhood landmarks to which he knew he'd never return. The old Timothy Clement had shelter, security, and was part of a respected family. At a stoplight he cranked the rearview mirror down and checked his reflection. His eyes were sullen and empty. He asked, "Who are you?" The car behind him honked its horn; the light had turned green. Timothy flipped off the driver and continued on.

Back home, Timothy stuffed his backpack with clothing, non-perishable food, a first-aid kit and a toothbrush. He wasn't sure exactly how much time he had until his father figured out the kind of trouble he was in; it was better to preemptively split. As he wrestled to get one last sweatshirt in, the door to his room swung open. His father began to come in then stopped. "Sorry, should have knocked." Then he looked at the backpack. "Going somewhere?"

Timothy hung the backpack from a hook on the back of his closet door. "Carlos wanted to go camping this weekend since Fitch is still taking care of his cousin."

His father looked stunned. "Gee, you haven't been home but a day and you're planning to leave already?"

Timothy played it off like it was no big deal. "I actually haven't totally decided if I'm going to go yet."

His father was skeptical. "It sure looks like you packed a lot of stuff." Timothy didn't say anything. "It would nice if you'd spend some time with your brother now that you're back. Maybe you can take him with you. If, of course, you decide to go." He motioned to the hanging bag.

"Uh, sure I'll ask. If we go."

Timothy's father dug into his pocket and pulled out the powder-blue motel key ring. "Found these blocking the drain out back. Do you have any idea whose they are?"

Timothy's stomach did a triple flip but he tried not to show it. As blood drained from his head he blurted out. "Oh, those are Fitch's. He lost them at my birthday party." Timothy took the keys from his father and put them in his pocket. "He'll be glad you found them. Thanks!"

Timothy's father looked around the cluttered room. "You kids are growing up so fast."

Timothy smiled; the keys were burning a hole in his pocket. He didn't have time for a sentimental talk. "I'll talk to Stephen about camping later."

His father took the cue, nodded then left.

Chapter 13

*F*ive minutes to three am. In the dead of the night, Timothy turned his alarm off before the hour struck. It wasn't necessary; he failed to even fall asleep. He was too wired with adrenaline. It was a crazy idea that had crept into his mind the day before. Why scrap along making payments to Mr. Rex when he could take what he had and start a new life? He knew it was crazy. He flip-flopped on the idea several times while lying in the darkness. Ultimately, he couldn't see being both a slave to Mr. Rex and losing face with his family. He might as well just disappear and keep the money. He'd avoid the painful scrutiny from his father and older sisters at least.

Ever so carefully, in the pitch black of his room, Timothy inched up to the corner of his window and checked the street. To his relief he didn't see any unexpected vehicles parked. Earlier that night he had stashed his mountain bike on the side yard along with his backpack for an easy escape. All he had to do now was leave. He looked at the shadows around his room and thought about how it would be the last time he'd be there. He remembered the race car wallpaper from when he was a boy. His mother persuaded his father in earnest to allow it. His father thought it was too childish, but Timothy loved it. He could almost visualize the car patters in the shadows now. He decided it was best to leave quickly before regret caught up to him. Timothy stuffed the large envelope of cash in his waistband then snuck downstairs and out back.

Timothy had planned out taking an unconventional path to the guard shack and then out to the main road. He would keep to the shadows as much as possible until he got to the rail car. He figured Steve would let him stay the night, and he even packed a few cans of chili as a peace offering. From there he'd have to play it by ear. He knew the plan was anemic, but it was too late to worry about. He dashed out of the side gate and pedaled through his neighbor's side yard, kicking up mulch. He began his dash to the guard shack exit, zigzagging through bushes and flower beds. His heart pounded. He felt as if some thug would jump out and accost him at any moment. The backpack straps strained against his shoulders as he stood on his pedals for traction.

Timothy burst past the guard shack and feverishly crossed the main road to cut through a park. Off the pavement his wheels bounced as he tried to avoid obstacles in the darkness. Suddenly, he was thrown from the bicycle as the front tire made contact with a hard object, landing flat on his back in the dark grass. He gasped for air but could not get his breath. After an initial rush of panic, he rolled on to his stomach then propped himself up on his knees. His lungs finally began to work and he sucked in a deep breath of air. He coughed hard and saliva dripped from his mouth. He stood up and checked for damage; there was none that he could see. It was another two blocks to the storm drain entrance, he had to keep moving. He got back on the bicycle and rode some more.

Every fifty feet Timothy's imagination produced the sound of phantom cars in close pursuit. He'd look back, but there was never anyone there. Finally he approached the storm drain entrance. From there it was only another mile along the cement bank. As he lifted his bicycle tire over the embankment he noticed that he no longer had the envelope of cash in his waistband. His heart sank and he felt faint. He searched the ground where he stood, but it was not there. "The park." He muttered to himself. He realized that it must have fallen out when he took the spill back at the park. He started back immediately. In the interest of making up the lost time, he sped along the open road. After the first block he heard what was definitely a real car coming up behind him fast. He veered off the road and down an alley skidding behind a parked truck and stopping cold. He ducked down and waited until the car passed him. He remained hunched down another minute to make sure it wasn't turning back; it did not return. Timothy rolled out from behind the truck and continued back to the park.

As he approached the park he scanned the dark shadows for the envelope. Its light cream color reflected the moonlight, guiding him to it. He rushed over, scooped it up, wiped off the condensation then examined the package for damage. Satisfied that it hadn't been torn open or water damaged, he stuffed the envelope back in his waistband. Right then he heard a distant pop, like that of a power breaker tripping. He looked around to see if anyone was watching, but he was all alone.

Timothy re-launched his trek in double-time, flying through the streets then hopping down into the storm drain. Once he had ventured all the way down to the cement base he slowed down and coasted, catching his breath and enjoying the night sky. He was confident that no one could see him so far below street level. The air was cool and cut through his sweaty clothes sparking the moisture. Sometime during the night his saint necklace had slipped out from under his shirt, and the pendant was now resting reversed on his back. He reached behind his neck and pulled it to the front, tucking it back into his shirt. The cold medallion shocked his skin, but felt refreshing.

The stretch through the riverbed, which should have been the easiest part of his escape, was surprisingly disorienting. Timothy kept glancing up at the top edges of the canal expecting to see the trees that border the train tracks but all he saw was night sky. After traveling for a very long time, he figured he must have overshot his exit. He pulled his bike up to the top and exited the cement river bank. There were abundant trees just beyond the top lip of the canal barrier. They were just far enough back that he hadn't seen them from below. Two gravel paths emerged out of adjoining packets of trees a short way down. Timothy figured one of them, if not both, must lead to Steve's abandoned rail car. Because fatigue was settling in, he opted to follow the nearest ingress into the greenery.

It was extremely dark so he had to go slowly over the slippery gravel to avoid the debris on the path. His intuition told him he was going the right way until the path widened a bit and an opening appeared on his left jetting into the darkness. He stopped to examine the opening and spotted a set of shadowy lines on the ground; they were tracks. It seemed a good indication that he should go that way, but he didn't. It just didn't feel right. Instead he got back on his bicycle and kept going straight. Less than five minutes later, the faint glimmer of Steve's campfire caught Timothy's eye. As he advanced, the large rectangular silhouette of the rail car emerged from the dark shadows. The large spray-painted 'Jesus Saves' declaration on the side confirmed he had made it safely to his destination.

Timothy propped the bicycle up against the side of the large steel wheel assembly. He didn't want to alarm Steve and be hit with a chair leg so he went up to the opening and yelled up, "Steve, It's me Tim." There was no response. "Steve, you there?" He held still for a moment but again, no reply. Timothy climbed up into the open railcar and went directly to the fire to warm his numb hands. He then turned around to look for Steve. In the back shadows of the railcar he spotted Steve sleeping on the ground. Timothy walked softy back toward him then knelt down beside him. He shook his shoulder to wake him up but Steve kept sleeping. Timothy figured it might be better to just let him sleep, and he'd impose his stay in the morning. Worst case, if Steve woke up, he'd recognize Timothy and wouldn't harm him. Timothy began to rise up from beside Steve and felt wetness. His hand was slick and sticky. He wiped it on his pants. He hoped Steve didn't have a bed wetting problem. Timothy turned around wanting to warm himself a bit more by the fire. He walked back to the fire and extended his hands. It was then he noticed they were speckled red with blood. He hardly had time to panic when he noticed Tattoo and Raspy hop up into the railcar.

Tattoo immediately gave Timothy a hard kick to the groin causing him to fall over in pain. Raspy ripped the backpack from his shoulders and begin dumping the contents out. A wallet, pack of gum, compact camera, sweat shirt and many granola bars tumbled out. When the last of the various survival items hit the floor, Raspy turned to Tattoo and said, "You owe me a hundred bucks!"

Tattoo produced a bill from his pocket and passed it to Raspy. Then he looked down at Timothy. "I never figured you were the running type."

"The stupid ones always run." Raspy finished going through the backpack then tossed it aside.

Timothy tried to get to his feet but stumbled over. "You killed him!"

Raspy hoisted Timothy up by his neck and slammed him against the metal container wall. "What kind of nitwit plan is this? Rooming with a hobo!"

Timothy coughed, "He's not a hobo."

"What?" Raspy shook his head. "You really are stupid kid." Tattoo came up and began going through Timothy's pockets while he was restrained, tossing the contents carelessly on the ground.

Tattoo stopped and held up the power-blue motel key ring. "Stupid and a liar?"

Timothy stammered, "N-no, I swear I just found them."

Tattoo socked Timothy hard in the stomach nearly causing him to faint. In punching Timothy, Tattoo felt the envelope and pulled up Timothy's shirt. "Bingo." He removed the envelope and Raspy let Timothy fall to the ground. Tattoo ripped open the envelope and thumbed through the cash estimating its value. "Running is going to cost you an extra thirty percent."

Timothy began to protest but Raspy cut him off. "Did you really think we wouldn't know? We know everything you do, every second of the day kid."

"I can't pay any more. That's all I have!"

Outside the railcar door came a voice. "Can one of you give me a hand here?" Timothy recognized the voice immediately. It was Bruno. Tattoo rushed over and assisted Bruno up into the cabin. Bruno looked around while fanning his nose. "Whoa, what a dump!" Tattoo passed the money envelope to him.

Surprisingly, Timothy had no fear. He didn't have anything left to lose, and being killed by these goons would put him out of his misery. "That's it. You guys have everything. I've got nothing left for you."

"Is that so?" Bruno took a handkerchief from his pocket and walked over to Steve's body. Using the handkerchief, he picked up the nearby pistol and held it up. "Here's a pistol with your kid brother's fingerprints all over it that says different."

Raspy turned to Tattoo, "Shame seeing a young kid like that get put away for hobocide."

Tattoo raised his eyebrow. "Hobocide? Is that even a real word?"

Timothy could not believe his foolish behavior had now placed his brother in jeopardy. "No, no, no, that's not necessary." Timothy pleaded. "I'll do whatever you want. I'll get a job and pay Mr. Rex the rest, I promise. Just leave Stephen out of this."

"That's exactly what I thought you'd say." Bruno's voice was like ice. Bruno passed the handkerchief wrapped pistol over to Raspy. "File this."

Raspy glanced at Timothy. "It'll be in good hands."

Bruno smiled widely, raised his arms up and announced, "It's your lucky day kid! The gods are smiling down on you it seems." Timothy just stared at him; he would do anything at this point to keep Stephen safe. "I've got a little problem I think you can help me with."

"What?" Timothy asked.

"Our friend, the photographer. . ." Bruno pretended to hold up a camera, "Say Cheese!" He made a shutter sound. "Has gone missing. The last set of pictures never showed up and my calls go unanswered." Bruno leaned in close to Timothy and whispered, "Probably better anyway, your two bozo friends can't draw half as well as you." Bruno then backed off and continued in a bellowing voice. "Mr. Rex is not happy about it. We've got hungry buyers on the line and no catalogue, so to speak."

Timothy reached for the compact camera in the pile of his personal effects. "I can do that."

Bruno kicked the camera away. "No need for photos when you can make the sketches right on the spot."

"What do you mean?"

"You like to gamble big, right? So here's the deal: Mr. Rex will wipe the slate clean. All of it." Bruno waved the money envelope. "You'll even get this back. You just have to go in, sketch the last set of items and then get out."

Timothy couldn't see how this job was worth forgiving his debt. "What's the catch?"

Bruno smiled. "The Peruvian authorities don't look too favorably on antiquities smuggling. You'd be our third associate to penetrate the dig site."

"Peruvian, as in Peru?"

"You don't even want to know what goes on in a Peruvian prison." Bruno added. "I won't lie, the Feds on the mainland are highly interested in our business. If you blow it and get caught, you're on your own. Mention any of us, and your family dies."

Timothy thought it over. He didn't really have much of a choice. "Okay, what do I do?"

"You have a passport?" Timothy nodded. "Great, go back to you house and stay there for the next three days." Bruno passed the envelope of cash to Timothy. "While you're waiting, go back to the bank and deposit this."

Timothy reached for the envelope reluctantly. "Just like that?"

"Just like that." Bruno smiled. "Oh, just one more question, does your brother have a passport too?"

"What?" Timothy felt completely trapped. They were quicker, smarter and knew his every move. "I said leave him out of it."

"Sorry, can't do that. Mr. Rex says he comes with you on the job or all bets are off."

Sweat poured from Timothy's brow. "I need more time."

Raspy held up the bagged pistol. "Time for what? It shouldn't be a problem getting away, since you're already going camping and all. It really would be nice for you to spend some time with your brother now that you're home." Raspy quoted Timothy's father which freaked him out even more.

They had him. Timothy knew there was no leverage from any angle. He had to do it, and Stephen had to come along. He buried his face in his hands and sighed. "Okay, I'm in."

Tattoo shoved Timothy's items back into the backpack and passed it to him. "Here kid."

"A car will be out front of your house at five a.m. Sunday morning to pick you up. There better be two of you waiting." Bruno looked over at Steve's lifeless body. "What a waste of a life."

Timothy felt sorry for Steve. Even in death he couldn't catch a break. "He was a man with a purpose." Timothy heard himself blurt out.

Bruno just laughed. "And you'd know? This kid is crazy!"

Tattoo checked his watch while Raspy began removing all evidence of their visit from the crime scene. Raspy directed his penlight around the dark corners of the cabin looking for any remaining incriminating debris. That's when he caught sight of Timothy's "Stevie the Great" drawing midway up the interior wall. "C'mon! What am I supposed to do with this boss?"

Bruno looked it over. "Got any gasoline in the trunk?" Raspy nodded. "You know what to do." Bruno jumped down out of the railcar door and disappeared into the night.

Tattoo then escorted Timothy to the backseat of his car and told him to stay put. As Timothy waited, he heard the sound of gasoline being sloshed about inside the railcar. He smelled the fumes and wondered how long it would be before Steve's family would find out he was gone – if at all.

Raspy and Tattoo emerged from the railcar pouring a trail of gasoline on the ground that led up to their vehicle. Timothy was alarmed up until they joined him inside the car.

Tattoo rolled down his window and held out a cigarette lighter. "Should we say something?"

Raspy grimaced. "This again? You gotta be kidding me!"

"Everyone deserves a few words." Tattoo looked at Timothy in the backseat. "Isn't that right?" Timothy nodded. "Great, so say a few words for the hobo."

"He wasn't a hobo."

"That's a good start." Tattoo encouraged Timothy.

Raspy tapped his watch, "We don't have time for this."

Timothy rolled down his window not entirely sure what to say. He could hear his father's voice in the back of his head telling him that Steve's existence ended once and for all in that clammy railcar. At the same time he could recall Steve's gravelly voice preaching salvation earnestly. "Um, Steve was a good man. He had some bad breaks but-"

Unexpectedly, Raspy chucked his lighter into the fuel trail and flames sprung to life and began crawling up to the open railcar door. "Okay, enough! Let's get going."

Tattoo pulled away somberly. Timothy turned around and watched out the back window as flames quickly consumed the entire railcar. The voraciousness of the flames was overwhelming. He kept his eyes on the glowing beast and dark smoke plumes until they were well out of reach.

No one spoke at all during the ride back. The sky had softened up and dawn peeked out from beyond the horizon. Timothy stared out the window and reviewed his situation. Maybe it wasn't so bad. He had his money back. He had the opportunity to wipe out his debt to Mr. Rex. It was just one job, in and out. Even still, he wasn't completely naïve. The compensation was ridiculously steep in comparison to the work. Bruno obviously wasn't disclosing the full scope of risk to him. Timothy didn't mind gambling his own neck, but bringing Stephen into the situation raised the stakes to a sickening level.

Once at the house, Tattoo removed Timothy's bike and backpack from the trunk and dumped them on the sidewalk. Without a word, he and Raspy drove off. Timothy snuck back in the house, trying not to make any noise. He crept upstairs and into the bathroom. Behind the closed door, he examined his bloody hands, turning his palms up. He could not believe this blood belonged to the man who fed him just a few days ago. Suddenly he was repulsed and couldn't stand being in the soiled clothing another moment. He stripped down to his underwear and then scrubbed his hands and forearms with soap and water. After drying himself thoroughly he wrapped the dirty clothes up in a bath towel and stuck the bundle under his arm. It was too early to shower, the hand washing would have to do for now. Timothy flushed the toilet for show, and then ventured down to his room. Once inside he shoved the money envelope along with the bloody, muddy clothes under his bed, then crawled under the covers and closed his eyes. "Is this really happening?" He asked himself. With that thought he fell hard asleep.

Chapter 14

Despite being out most of the night, Timothy was up at eight o'clock and felt invigorated. Maybe it was the structure of a dictated plan or perhaps just the adrenaline. Either way, he preferred it to sneaking in the shadows. After taking an extra lengthy shower, he went downstairs and cooked up an elaborate pancake breakfast for the family. The aroma seduced Stephen out of his slumber and he hobbled down the stairs rubbing his eyes. "That smells so good!"

"Hope you are hungry." Timothy proudly heaped a tall stack of pancakes and eggs on a plate and put it on the table for his little brother. "Orange juice?" Timothy held up a glass. Stephen nodded then began to devour the food. Timothy filled the glass with orange juice and gave it to Timothy. "So listen, me, Carlos and some other guys are going camping, and well, since I'm back early, I thought maybe you might want to go with us."

Stephen's head popped upright and his eyes widened. "Seriously?"

"Yeah, I think it would be fun."

Stephen took another big bite and then washed it down with a swig of orange juice. "Awesome! Are we leaving Tuesday or Wednesday?"

"We're leaving Monday morning, early."

Stephen stopped eating. "No we're not!"

"Yes we are. That's the plan."

"What about Mom's birthday?" Stephen could tell that it had completely slipped Timothy's mind. "We haven't missed visiting her on her birthday even once since she- ya know."

Timothy's right hand went to his forehead and pushed back his hair. How could he have forgotten? "I know." It was all he could manage to say. Timothy's mind was devoid of any suitable explanation as to why they should miss their mother's birthday. The thought of being in transit to Peru instead of honoring their mother saddened Timothy, but he knew there would be no reasoning with Bruno. "The problem is that everything is already paid for."

"Never mind, I'll stay here."

"Hold on, let me finish." Timothy was tap dancing like a used car salesman. He needed Stephen to come with him, and he needed him to come willingly. "I was already planning for us to visit Mom tomorrow. It's just one day early."

Stephen shook his head. "I'm helping Phil's brother move all day tomorrow."

"Tell you what, when we get back we'll go and visit her first thing. I promise." Timothy could see Stephen weighing the idea. "We'll bring her the best bunch of flowers yet! She'd be glad that we are camping together anyway."

That did the trick. "Okay, I guess that works, but we need to visit her the minute we get back."

Timothy nodded. "Yeah, absolutely!"

With Stephen at ease, and inhaling his food again, Timothy pulled out a piece of paper and began drawing "Stevie the Great". Stephen watched with interest as his likeness appeared poking out of a tent. Then Timothy added a frightened bear running away. Finally he added the word 'Scram!' in block letters along the bottom.

Stephen laughed. "This is going to be fun. I haven't been camping in a long time!" Timothy smiled back, hoping that it would.

Their father came downstairs and was markedly pleased that his two sons were bonding. "Hey, how are my guys?" The two mumbled and nodded. He turned to Timothy, "So did you tell Stephen about camping?"

Stephen answered enthusiastically, "It's going to be great!"

Their father smiled broadly. "I'm so glad to see you guys spend some time together."

"Hey Dad, can you take me to get a new backpack today?" Stephen asked.

Timothy thought about his own abused bag. "Actually, I could use a new one as well."

Their father nodded and said, "Sure, why don't the three of us head over to the sporting goods shop after breakfast?" He then grabbed a plate and began stacking. "Wow, thanks for making breakfast Timothy. This is great!"

It's not that Timothy didn't want to go with them; he just needed some time alone in the house to locate the passports. "You guys go ahead. I've got some stuff to do. Stephen can pick mine out."

"Pink okay with you?" Stephen teased.

"With polka-dots!" his father added.

Timothy laughed. "Just make sure it has lots of pockets." The three of them laughed. Timothy thought about how great it felt to be back home, sharing a laugh with them. He wondered how long it would be until he would be able to do that again.

After breakfast, Stephen and his father headed out shopping. Timothy waited until he heard their car pull away, and then began his hunt. Passports belonged to a group of items which his father classified as important. Important things, unfortunately, were always tucked away in hard to find places. His father had numerous files labeled 'Important' in his library, but as Timothy learned while looking for his birth certificate once before, important things never resided in the important files. They would be hidden in the least obvious places like books or hidden desk compartments. Locating the passports would surely be a challenge.

Timothy began in the library. He combed through his father's various favorites, but found nothing but a yellowing obituary clipping from his mother's funeral. He moved on to the desk contents and checked every drawer. He checked beneath his father's desk globe. He checked a collection of banker's boxes stacked against the far wall, but only found ageing case files.

Timothy checked his watch. He wasn't sure how long Stephen and his father would be gone. Time was burning up. Timothy went to his father's room and rummaged through his father's dresser drawers. Nothing of use turned up there either. As the moments passed he felt sweat beads form on his brow. It occurred to him that he hadn't checked the files marked, 'Important' yet. Desperate, he figured it was worth a try. Timothy raced back to the library and located the three 'Important' accordion files. Upon opening the first one he was presented with a stack of passports. He felt foolish for not checking these files first. Timothy took Stephen's, and his own, and then rushed upstairs to get the money envelope. He had been messing around for too long; he'd barely have time to get to the bank before it closed.

Timothy drove a bit more recklessly than he should have, opting to blow through a few yellow lights. It was all worth it to him. Twenty minutes later he had completed his deposits and could relax. By Monday evening the account balances would be updated and his only problem would be intercepting the statements in the mail; that would be the easy part.

Chapter 15

The following day Timothy prepared for the trip. Stephen had picked out a pretty good bag for him. It wasn't what he would have chosen himself, but it would do. He was packing both of their bags since Stephen was helping his friend's brother move. Having Stephen out of the house was good, but he wished his father, who every half-hour would corner him and start to chat about nothing in particular, would go find something to do as well. Timothy had no patience for it, which is why he was relieved when his sister Elizabeth showed up. He hadn't seen much of her at all since she began college three years prior. She didn't usually come around, not even during winter or summer breaks. "Hey loser!" She punched him in the arm. "Thought you were soaking up the sun in Miami. What happened, did they kick you off the beach for being too pasty white?"

Timothy played it cool. He always gave Elizabeth the least amount of information possible. He knew she didn't really have any interest in him, she just wanted ammunition. She reveled in cutting him down at every opportunity. He knew from experience that the best way to diffuse her was to bombard her with his own questions. "You look tired. Are you still dating the drummer from that band?"

Elizabeth was mortified. She watched as her father raised an eyebrow suddenly, curious about the conversation. "No! That is ancient history. We weren't even dating."

"Hmph." Timothy acted surprised. "How is school?" He knew Elizabeth's favorite subject was herself. The question would keep her busy for a while.

Elizabeth prefaced every sentence with hand gestures and exaggerated eyes. "So amazing! I am like meeting so many fabulous people." Timothy just nodded. This was the part where he tuned her out. She spent the next twenty minutes talking about her various accomplishments, finally showing off her five-hundred dollar purse that she got for only four-hundred and fifty dollars. "Can you believe that? Margie's mom like totally works at the factory, so I get a discount. Well, I don't know that she works like AT the factory with all the, ya know, laborers and stuff. I think she is like a marketing publicity kind of person or something like that." Elizabeth hung the purse on her shoulder and posed for Timothy like a catalog model. "Hey, why don't I take you to lunch?"

Timothy wasn't particularly keen on the idea, but it would get him out of the house and away from his lurking father. "Sure, sounds fine."

He didn't bother to ask where they should eat since there was only one place Elizabeth liked to dine when in town, Basils. It was on the third floor of her favorite department store, Freedman's. A conspicuously expensive vendor known for their heavy security and over-the-top Christmas light displays. Elizabeth thought it the cornerstone of any respectable mall.

Over lunch Timothy listened to Elizabeth blabber on and on about her shallow life. She complained about how hard it was to find qualified girls to join her sorority, and then moved on to the diminishing quality of spas, finishing up with a faux pledge to lose ten pounds. It was a fishing expedition for compliments on her skeletal frame, but Timothy wouldn't bite. He thought how ill-equipped she would be to handle real problems like his. Not getting the reassurances she hoped for, she changed the subject. "Tomorrow is Mom's birthday."

"I know. Stephen and I are going to visit her grave when we get back from camping."

Elizabeth's eyes lit up. This was an opportunity to show how much better she was than Timothy. "Oh my gosh! I'd expect this from Victoria, but not you."

The substance of what she said would be valid coming from anyone else, but Timothy knew her concern was one dimensional. "I'm sure Mom will be very pleased that you were able to make it when the rest of us couldn't."

"It won't be the same without her favorite!" The potent venom of jealousy had flowed through her veins for so long that she couldn't help herself.

The snide comment only gave Timothy satisfaction. He opted to change the subject. "So what happened with you and the drummer?"

Just like that, Elizabeth's focus shifted at the word, 'you'. "Oh my gosh, stop bringing that up! That was like so long ago!" The waitress approached and set the bill on the table. Elizabeth reached for her purse and dug around. "Dang it, I totally forgot my wallet! Do you mind getting this?"

Timothy pulled out his wallet and thumbed through his cash. Wanting to conserve it for the trip, he pulled out his credit card and placed it on the tray. "No problem sis."

"I don't know what I was thinking!"

The waitress took the tray away. "No worries, it happens." Timothy said just casual enough to irritate Elizabeth. Her snotty little brother was not going to spew some cliché life lesson on her.

"Not to me it doesn't. I must have left it on the counter at home." She hunted around the bag a second time to no avail. "That's a two-hundred-fifty dollar wallet."

The waitress approached the table looking apologetic and leaned into Timothy. "I'm sorry sir, but your card didn't go through. Do you have another I can run?"

Timothy then realized that his deposit would not reflect on the card until Monday night. There was no available credit until then. He quickly took out a wad of twenty dollar bills and handed them to the waitress. "Must be demagnetized. This wallet does that sometimes." He could feel Elizabeth's excitement boring a hole in him, but he refused to look up and give her any additional satisfaction. There was nothing she enjoyed more than lathering up in someone else's salacious faux pas. It was the inadequacies of others that held her judgmental being together. Timothy was sure that if he looked up, there would be a puddle of drool right there on the table. "Keep the change." He told the waitress then stood up and put his wallet back in his pocket. "Ready to head out?" he asked Elizabeth casually.

"Demagnetized? I've never heard of that happening."

"Shoot, if I blew two-hundred-fifty bucks on a wallet I'd expect to not hear about it either." He tapped the wallet though his pants. "This one was a gift from Aunt Carol, and you know how cheap she is." Elizabeth nodded with exaggerated eyes, and then they left.

When they got to the house, Elizabeth pulled up to the curb and left the motor running. "I'm going to let you out here. I need to go back home and find my wallet." Timothy hopped out and waved before going into the house. Elizabeth quickly pulled out her cell phone and called her sister Victoria. "Are you sitting down? You are not going to believe what just happened!" The two jackals devoured their favorite meal; their brother's misfortune.

Chapter 16

At four-fifty-five a.m. Timothy and Stephen were parked out front with their gear. Timothy kept glancing over his shoulder hoping his father wouldn't try to come out and see them off. The television had been blaring from his father's room until late the night before so Timothy figured it was unlikely. Still, he looked back once again. Timothy heard the sound of a car engine down the block and started walking toward it. "Come on." He tugged on Stephen who was still half asleep.

Tattoo and Raspy pulled up a moment later and popped the trunk open. The boys threw their gear in, and then got in the backseat. "Where's Carlos?" Stephen asked immediately.

The car pulled away quickly, sinking them into the leather seats. Timothy answered, "We're going to meet him later." He could see Stephen fixating on the gorillas in the front seat. "These are some friends, Tattoo and Raspy." Tattoo smiled, he liked the nickname. Raspy only stared silently out the passenger window. "This is my brother Stephen." Timothy concluded the introductions.

"How far it is?" Stephen asked.

Timothy wanted to postpone springing the change of plans on Stephen as long as possible. "It's going to be a while. You should probably catch some sleep for now." Stephen slumped down in his seat and shut his eyes. Timothy looked at him and thought about the job ahead. What exactly was he going to tell Stephen when he woke up?

The car sped along the freeway on its way toward the airport. Several minutes into the drive, Timothy looked up and noticed the Grandville exit sign. It was the exit he always took when going to the cemetery. Their mother was less than a mile away. Timothy's heart sank at the missed opportunity. He wished he had paid more attention and planned better. He might have been able to fit in a visit to their mother's grave if he had just been alert. "Sorry Mom, happy birthday." He said to himself as the car sped past.

Twenty minutes later the car merged with a procession of cabs and shuttles that were creeping along the passenger drop off zone. The air smelt of asphalt and fuel. Impatient car horns and whistles woke Stephen from his slumber. He sat up quickly and looked around alarmed. "What's going on? Why are we here?"

The time Timothy was dreading had come. "Relax."

"Why are we at the airport?"

"Just relax!" Timothy urged Stephen. "I'll explain in a minute."

The car stopped in front of the main terminal and the trunk popped open. Raspy turned to the backseat and handed Timothy two tickets. "There'll be a ride waiting for you when you land." He then bobbed his chin toward the curb, urging the boys to get out of the car, before facing forward again.

Timothy exited the car, followed closely by his now thoroughly alarmed brother. "What's going on?" Stephen inquired urgently as Timothy retrieved their gear from the trunk.

Timothy waited until all the gear was unloaded and the car pulled away before answering. "You always say you want to go on an adventure, right?" Timothy began walking into the terminal.

"What are you talking about?" Stephen followed, looking around him at all of the travelers bustling through the terminal. "Was this Dad's idea?"

Once inside the terminal, Timothy stopped at a bench to examine the tickets and determine which way to go. He realized the international terminal was another full section down. "Come on, follow me."

Stephen continued on. "Where are we going?"

"Somewhere exotic, unlike anywhere you've been before!" Timothy handed Stephen his ticket and passport.

Stephen read the ticket. "Peru? Isn't that like in Mexico or something?"

"No stupid. It's in South America."

"Cool!" Stephen socked Timothy in the arm. "Camping in South America sounds fun!"

"It will be an adventure." Timothy said as they entered the security checkpoint and set out on the beginning leg of their so-called adventure.

The first flight headed for Miami, during which Stephen asked no less than a million questions. Timothy answered none of them directly or completely, only adding to Stephens's curiosity. After their brief layover in Miami, they boarded a tiny plane and continued on to Lima for the next five and a half hours.

Stephen slept through most of the first flight, snoring loudly and annoying nearby passengers. The second plane's small cabin put him on edge and he could not fall asleep at all. He stared out the window nervously and ceased asking questions.

In time, twilight shadowed the lush greenery below and they prepared for landing. Stephen closed his eyes and leaned back in his seat, trying to ignore the nonstop vibrations in the small plane's frame. The pilot's request for all passengers to take their seats crackled over the speakers in both Spanish and English. "Finally!" Stephen exclaimed.

The plane descended quickly, bouncing turbulently through the air. Timothy clasped his hands together tightly. He hated bumpy flights, they made him ill. Just as he began to reach for the air sickness bag, Timothy felt the landing gear make contact with the tarmac and he clenched up. He grabbed the bag and just barely got it open in time to avoid a huge mess. He closed up the bag and discreetly slipped it under his seat. Timothy wiped the dripping sweat from his brow and waited for the plane to stop taxiing. Peering out his window into the early evening darkness, Timothy was shocked at how small the airport was.

A few single story buildings and a radio tower were all that greeted them once they climbed down the mobile staircase. The perimeter of the airstrip dissolved into lush jungle just beyond its borders. The air was warm and balmy with the scent of vegetation. Timothy and Stephen followed the other passengers through a rope maze which fed them towards the entrance of the largest building. As they passed through the doors they were disappointed that the air inside was even hotter and stuffier than outside. "No air conditioning, really?" Stephen complained.

"When was the last time you had air conditioning on a camping trip?" Timothy remarked just prior to wiping his face down with the front of his T-shirt. An oval visage of sweat appeared on the shirt. Looking around, Timothy did not see anyone who looked like they could be a contact. He sat down on a bench and waited while Stephen paced.

"This is so cool! I never imagined I'd be in South America when I woke up today." Stephen had quickly rebounded from the travel and was wired with excitement. "How did you talk Dad into this?"

The truth was on the tip of Timothy's tongue, but he simply could not bring himself to dish it out. "I'm nineteen now. I should be able to do more stuff with you."

"So what are we waiting for now?" Stephen was pumped up and ready for action.

Before Timothy could concoct an answer, a young boy about seven years of age approached holding a black slate with the name 'Clement' on it. "Clee-mint?" The boy asked. Timothy nodded and the boy grabbed his hand and began leading him away with Stephen following close behind. The little boy's clothing was scarce and tattered; his body looked three days unwashed.

"Hey kid, what's your name?" Timothy asked the boy.

"Clee-mint."

"No, that's my name. Who are you?" Timothy pointed at the boy urgently.

The boy looked puzzled for a moment then smiled. "Clee-mint."

"Maybe that's his name too?" Stephen suggested.

Timothy playfully tagged the back of Stephen's head. "Don't be stupid."

The boy led them to a bare metal jeep waiting in the parking lot. The vehicle lacked any options or conveniences; truly it was a method of transport only. A gruff teenage boy stuck his head out the driver's window and said, "Get it in!" in broken English. The teenager then gave the boy some coins before he ran off.

As they got in the metal box on wheels, Stephen asked, "Who are these people? When are we going to meet up to Carlos?"

Timothy hung on as the jeep jerked forward and sped away from the airstrip into the greenery. The narrow road was poorly lit as the jeep's weak yellow headlamps forged ahead. "I guess I should tell you. . ."

"Huh? What?"

Timothy now wished he hadn't waited so long to reveal the true nature of their trip. The bumpy dark ride and wind blasting through the jeep cabin forced him to shout if he hoped to be heard. "We're not meeting Carlos!" He yelled above the wind torrent. "It's just you and me this time!"

Stephen suddenly looked very worried. "What do you mean? Does Dad know?" There was neither a hint of approval or excitement in Stephen's voice. "Who knows we're here?"

The jeep slowed as it neared a set of dingy metal sided barracks. "It's just our adventure. No one knows."

Stephen looked around at the primitive lodging. "Tim, I don't think we should be doing this."

"Relax, it will be fun. You gotta bend the rules to have fun sometimes." Timothy's words were not reassuring to Stephen. "It's just for a few days."

Once stopped in front of the barracks, the teenage driver jumped out to meet a guard posted out front. The guard wore military fatigues and a holstered pistol on his hip. Large floodlights lit the area, creating an almost prison-like atmosphere. After doling out bills to the teen, the guard approached the jeep. "Clement brothers?" He asked. Timothy and Stephen nodded, too intimidated to speak. "I am Cabal. Please get out and follow me."

"I don't like this." Stephen whispered to Timothy.

Cabal led them around to the back side of the compound. Along the way they passed a kennel housing a pack of angry watch dogs. Unlike the boys, Cabal was unfazed by the beasts' barks and snarls as he led the brothers around and into one of the sparse rooms on the ground floor. "I REALLY don't like this place!" Stephen said again.

"Relax, don't be such a baby!" Timothy snapped.

The barren plywood floor of the room was cracked and half rotted away. A rusty metal basin sat in the corner next to a metal frame bunk. As the boys looked around in disgust, Cabal did his best to be hospitable given the circumstances. "I trust you will find your stay comfortable." Cabal's satellite telephone chimed. He answered and spoke a moment in Spanish before handing the large device to Timothy.

Timothy held the phone up to his ear. "Hello?"

"Glad to see you made it. I wasn't looking forward to chasing you again." Bruno's egotistical voice echoed from the speaker. "We have a situation. All of the appropriate parties on the ground have been paid, but it seems the air is still hot, if you know what I mean." Timothy did not. "So there's going to be a slight change of plans."

"What kind of change?"

"Don't worry kid, we'll still call it even at the end of the day. You just have a slightly different job to perform. No artwork this time." Bruno's voice was calculated and insincere. Timothy had no doubt this was a premeditated change of plans.

"We had a deal. A set of sketches and then I'm out of here."

"Sheesh, relax kid. This job is even easier, and you'll be on your way home tomorrow night."

Stephen moved in to eavesdrop on the call but Timothy shooed him away. "Okay, sounds good so far. What do I have to do?"

"You know how to drive stick?" Bruno asked.

"Sure, done it lots of times."

"Great. Tomorrow morning you and your brother are going to drive a truck for us. You will make certain that its contents arrive safely at an airfield."

Timothy was relieved. "That's easy. It wasn't a long ride to get here."

"Not that airport; another further North."

"How far?" Timothy asked.

"It's not a straight shot. You'll be switching vehicles, and offloading the cargo twice before you reach the airport. You'll be busy all day." Bruno paused. "And don't ask me about the cargo."

Timothy made an effort to smile in hopes of putting Stephen at ease. "I think it will go smoothly."

"It better." Bruno said flatly before the phone disconnected.

Timothy handed the satellite telephone back to Cabal. Two additional guards appeared. The first opened a rattan chest and removed fresh bedding and tossed it on each bunk. The other delivered two paper plates piled high with chicken, rice and beans. With a pocket knife, he cut free two cans of warm cola that were dangling from his belt loop. "Eat, you will need your strength. You should get some sleep. We'll be fueled up, loaded and ready to go by six a.m."

"Six in the morning?" Stephen asked exasperated.

Timothy motioned for Stephen to keep quiet. "Thank you. We'll be ready."

The guard left the room. "This place is a dump Tim!" Stephen threw his bag up to the top bunk. "And who are these weirdoes anyway? I wish we hadn't come here."

"Where's your sense of adventure?"

"Oh, just shut up already. You know I'm right." Stephen climbed up to the top bunk and settled in. "I can't believe we missed Mom's birthday for this."

Timothy wasn't sure what to say. Nothing he thought of seemed a worthy response. He settled on a good old fashioned apology. "Sorry Stephen. I promise tomorrow will be better." With that, Timothy turned out the light and crawled into his bunk.

"Yeah, whatever." Stephen muttered.

"I promise." Timothy repeated, hoping it would make Stephen feel better, but he remained quiet. Timothy sulked down in his bunk and tried to fall asleep.

Chapter 17

A throaty truck horn blared beyond the thin metal walls of the barracks, awakening Timothy and Stephen from their slumber. "Are you kidding me?" Stephen slurred, barely able to think.

Timothy jolted upright, his body covered in perspiration and his breathing heavy. He removed his damp shirt and mopped his face with the garment. "We better get up." Timothy checked his watch – Six ten.

"Ten more minutes." Stephen groaned then rolled over.

Timothy thought about forcing him to get up but stopped. Letting him rest a bit more was the least he could do for his brother. Timothy put on fresh clothes and washed his face in the rudimentary basin. Eventually he heard Stephen stir then stretch with a long grunt. "Sleep okay?"

"I had this crazy dream that you kidnapped me and took me to a third world ghetto."

"Very funny."

"Dad's not going to think so."

There was an assertive knocking at the door. Timothy turned the knob expecting Cabal, but instead faced a hardened teenage girl wearing a generic security uniform. Her few comely features were barely recognizable, distorted by years of self-reliance. She tossed two brown paper sacks at Timothy. "Eat in the truck. Time to go." Her clinical manor made it was clear she had no misconceptions about ever seeing the brothers again. The two boys stared at her, dumbfounded. She allowed them to gaze upon her for just a moment before shouting, "rápidamente!"

Timothy scrambled to pack both of their bags while Stephen splashed water on his face and tried for flatten his hair. All the while, the girl muttered in Spanish under her breath. "I'm pretty sure I heard 'estúpido' a second ago." Stephen whispered to Timothy.

"Just get ready." Timothy urged.

In moments they were being led to a waiting truck at the far end of the complex. It was a militaristic dark green vehicle with a canopy on the back. As they approached, the vehicle's large unwieldy size became apparent to Stephen. "This thing is huge! You'll never be able to drive this."

"Sure I will." Timothy said with false confidence. Secretly, Timothy hoped there would not be very many drivers on the road at such an early hour. "Have a little faith in me, eh?"

The girl opened the driver's door and retrieved a thick map book and handed it to Timothy. There was a bright yellow line winding up the page. "You follow this path." She said tapping on the yellow line.

Stephen looked over Timothy's shoulder at the map. "Um, can we get one of these in English?" He asked.

Timothy didn't notice until just then that indeed the map was in Spanish. "It can't be that hard to follow a yellow line."

The girl pointed to two circles along the route. "You switch here." Then she flipped the page. The yellow line continued to another circled location. "And then here." She dragged her finger up the page to a small airstrip. "End here." The girl then gave Timothy a hefty sealed envelope.

The moment Timothy took the envelope in his hands he knew what it was. In his misfortune he had become familiar with the sensation of a cash filled envelope. "What's this for?"

"Your-" The girl paused, seeming to search for the English equivalent to her thoughts. "Your persuasion." Timothy nodded and put the fat envelope in his pocket.

Stephen began to meander off toward the back of the truck. "Stop!" The girl yelled and Stephen froze. "Stay out!"

Stephen came back toward Timothy and the girl with his hands up, as if to say, 'what is the big deal?' She paid no attention and began to walk off. "What's back there?" Stephen called out.

She turned back to him. "A dragon's tail you don't want to step on. Stay out." Then she left.

"What the heck is going on Tim?" Stephen asked.

Timothy sighed. "I'll tell you all about it on the plane ride back home. I Promise. Right now, I really need you to just enjoy the adventure."

"Some adventure." Stephen said sarcastically.

The boys got in the truck and began their journey through the primitive, winding roads. It took a few minutes for Timothy to get the hang of negotiating the large truck, but soon it felt second nature. Stephen held the map and announced the turns like a rally co-driver. "L three into R four" he yelled out as they approached a ninety-degree intersection and continued immediately into another junction. "Over crest!" Stephen called out as a small hill appeared round the turn. For the first time since their 'adventure' began, the two boys were having fun.

They broke into the paper bag breakfasts only to discover more rice and beans sandwiched between stale bread. "This is like prison food!" Stephen complained.

"Eat up. I have a feeling we won't get another meal until we fly home tonight."

"What do you mean tonight? Dad's not expecting us back for two more days. Let's have some fun!" Talk of heading home the moment the trip got interesting irritated Stephen.

"We'll see." Timothy was glad Stephen was having a good time, but he just wanted the job to be over and to return home safe.

"We'll see" Stephen mimicked Timothy. "That's just a fancy way of saying, 'no'."

Before he could refute the observation, Timothy noticed flashing police lights in his side mirror. "Oh man, this is not the way things are meant to happen."

"What's wrong?" Stephen barely got the words out before he heard the siren.

"Don't say a word!" Timothy gave Stephen a stern warning as he pulled the truck off onto the shoulder. The policeman cut his siren once the truck was stopped, but the lights remained flickering. The officer approached Timothy's window and banged on it. Timothy rolled it down and waited for the interrogation. The officer's red face dripped sweat, and his breath reeked of alcohol. The officer said nothing. He just stood there looking impatient. Then Timothy remembered the envelope. "My Persuasion." He said to himself. Timothy grabbed a handful of bills and held it out the window. The policeman snatched the cash without counting and lazily wandered back to his patrol car and took off.

Stephen was flabbergasted. "That was totally illegal! We should report that guy!"

"That's how it works in some places."

"It's wrong!"

Timothy laughed. "Would you rather spend the night in a rat infested cage?"

"That's so lame!" Stephen shook his head. "Let's get out of here."

The boys continued on, covering over two hours of snaky dirt roads before reaching the first checkpoint; a government mail sorting facility. The property was surrounded by a chain-link fence with only one road in and out. Timothy wasn't sure exactly where the switch was to take place as he slowly cruised through the gate entrance. The lot seemed rather empty for a government building so Timothy parked in a spot up front. "Friend of yours?" Stephen asked as a greasy haired man wearing a postal uniform approached the truck.

The man walked right up to Timothy's window and pounded on it. "Clement?" He asked. Timothy nodded and the man motioned for Timothy to exit the truck.

No sooner had Timothy and Stephen grabbed their bags and hopped out of the truck, a brown catering van pulled up alongside them. The side doors opened and three men dressed in camouflage fatigues sprang out of the van. With military precision, they began transferring the cargo from the truck to the catering van. Stephen wanted to get a closer look at what was being transferred, but Timothy kept him at bay. "Don't even think about it." Once the switch was completed, the men jumped in the truck and took off.

The postal employee came over to Timothy. "Map." He said. Timothy gave a confused look not understanding. "Where is the map book from the girl?" The worker asked with less patience.

"Oh, sorry." Timothy nudged Stephen. "Give him the map." Stephen removed the map from his bag and passed it to the postal employee.

"Change of plans." The man said as he removed a standard gas station roadmap from his pocket and showed it to Timothy. It too was in Spanish with yellow pen highlighting the new route. "You go here, no stops." The man traced the path, which seemed very short, with his finger directly north.

"I have got to go so bad! Do you have a bathroom in here?" Stephen whined.

The worker looked around, showing paranoia for the first time. "I'll take you. Make it quick."

"I'll go too." Timothy announced.

"One at a time."

Timothy sighed. "Fine, I'll wait."

The postal worker tossed Timothy the keys to the van. "Wait in the van."

Stephen and the postal worker walked away about twenty feet then Stephen turned back and shouted, "I'll bring you some snacks if there's a vending machine inside." The outburst clearly made the postal worker uncomfortable and their pace doubled.

Timothy turned his attention to the van. He fidgeted with the door lock, but it wouldn't open. He felt the sensation of someone standing behind him so he turned. Standing before him was a leathery faced man in his forties wearing tortoise glasses. A camera bag dangled from his shoulder with academic buttons affixed to the strap. "How's the job going?" The man's Australian accent took Timothy by surprise.

"Just making a little pit stop." Timothy said cautiously as he studied the odd man. Something about him was very familiar, but Timothy couldn't place it.

"A little pit stop, eh?"

Timothy's eyes wandered down to the man's snakeskin booted feet. He couldn't remember where he knew him from. Then he saw the ruby snake ring coiled around his finger and it came back to him. "Snakeman." Timothy thought to himself. "You're the guy. The photographer." The man smiled slyly and nodded. "Bruno said-"

"Bruno's an idiot!" The man interrupted. "Did he really think I'd let him undercut me forever?"

Timothy's heart began to pound faster. He looked around, hoping for someone to approach but no one did. "I don't even know anything about that. I'm just trying to pay back Mr. Rex." Timothy said sheepishly.

"If you owe Mr. Rex money, then you're probably both stupid and desperate."

Timothy thought about it. "A little of both I suppose. What do you want?" Timothy glanced around again; still no sign of an ally.

"The keys."

Timothy knew if he gave over the keys he'd never get Stephen out of Peru alive. "I'd like to help you out, but I can't do that."

Timothy heard footsteps approach from behind and turned. A policeman held up his badge. "You're parked illegally." The officer stared at Timothy long enough to make the shakedown clear.

Timothy pulled out the rest of his persuasion cash and gave it to the officer. "This should cover it."

Snakeman laughed and patted the officer on the back. "It's your lucky day mate, you've been bribed twice!"

"Wait a minute. . ." Timothy began.

"You'd be amazed how many extra resources you can afford when you cut out the middle man." Snakeman's eyes narrowed sharply and bled contempt. "I'll be taking those keys now."

Before Timothy could decide his next move, he heard the postal facility door swing open as Stephen and the postal worker exited. He turned and made eye contact with Stephen. "Go!" Timothy yelled and the two retreated back inside.

"You son of a-"

Timothy kicked Snakeman hard in the groin and ran for the building entrance as fast as he had ever run before. Remaining solely focused on Stephen, he desperately jetted across the asphalt foot over foot. Upon reaching the door, he anxiously pushed it open – and then everything went quiet. Suddenly, a ringing shrilled in his head. The door's glass window exploded just as he entered the building. A cool sensation of wetness came over his face and neck. There was no pause to wonder or worry, he just needed to get to Stephen.

"Tim!" Stephen cried out from across the office. "What's going on?" Timothy rushed towards Stephen and his postal worker escort. "What happened to your ear?"

"Go, run! He's coming!"

The two brothers scrambled after the postal worker towards the back room. Timothy reached up and felt his right ear. Nothing seemed amiss. Then he then moved his hand to his left ear. Timothy's grasp was empty with the exception of a few remaining bits of ear flesh. He studied his bloody hand as Stephen pulled him into the back sorting facility. "I think you got shot!"

As soon as Stephen said the words, the front door burst open. Snakeman and the bribed officer were close now. "Get those keys!"

The back area of the sorting facility was a noisy maze of conveyor belts and boxes. Stephen and Timothy tried to keep up with the postal worker but he hopped over and under the sorting equipment like an acrobat. Timothy spotted a large plastic container that looked as though it could fit one person. "Stephen, get into that bin!" Stephen took off toward it.

Suddenly, the crackle of walkie-talkies and shouts filled the room. "Get down! Get down now!" United States federal agents swarmed in from all entrances.

Sprinting full speed across the concrete floor, Snakeman pulled a hunting knife from his belt and set his sights on Timothy. Timothy froze. He and Snakeman locked eyes. Snakeman's crazed glare seemed to have possession over him. Timothy waited helplessly for impact.

Timothy looked away to see if Stephen had made it safely inside the plastic bin but didn't see him anywhere. Then the lights went out. "Stephen!" Timothy shouted in the darkness.

A series of rapid pops and flashes pulsed in the blackness. A deluge of muscle knocked Timothy hard, faced down on to the ground. Timothy braced himself for Snakeman's knife. Instead, Timothy felt his hands yanked behind his back and put into metal restraints. A denim knee held his neck to the floor. "Stephen!" he called out, but the only answer he got was more pressure on his neck. Timothy fought for breath, sucking in the stench of fresh gunfire.

"Someone get the lights!" The man atop Timothy called out.

Timothy was relieved the voice had an American accent. Almost instantly the lights came back on. From his vantage point, Timothy could see Snakeman and the corrupt police officer's bodies resting in a pool of blood a few feet away. "Oh my God!" Timothy gasped. His head instinctively recoiled but didn't get far from under the knee.

"Stay down!" Timothy's oppressor instructed.

"I can't breathe."

The agent removed his knee from Timothy's neck. "Remain still."

Timothy coughed and scanned the room hoping Stephen was not too traumatized by the ambush. Stephen had always sworn he'd never get arrested. He was going to be very angry with Timothy for blemishing his exemplary record. "Where's my brother?" Timothy asked, but he did not receive an answer.

Agents began taking photos of the nearby bodies and placing evidence markers around the scene. Each camera flash made Timothy flinch. While the agent frisked him, Timothy noticed a slow moving trail of blood. He strained to follow it back to its origin but could not see. Timothy turned his face inwards toward the concrete, rotating his head until he was looking in the opposite direction. His heart stopped when he recognized the source of the blood trail as Stephen. His brother's body lay face up no more than three feet from him. "Stephen!" Timothy screamed, but he didn't respond.

"He's gone." The agent said as he pulled Timothy to his feet.

"Stephen!"

The agent walked Timothy out toward the back door. "You two should have never come here." Timothy's neck craned to keep his eyes on Stephen's body.

Another agent held the back door open, and Timothy was escorted outside. "I'm sorry Stephen!" Timothy cried out. They exited the facility and the door slammed shut.

Chapter 18

*T*he double-crossers had been double-crossed. The Feds perched patiently looking for their opportunity to pick apart the carcasses. Timothy didn't care about any of their causes. He only knew that he'd stuck to the plan and Stephen lost his life. Life spat in his face.

Eight hours of interrogations went by in a flash. Timothy divulged nothing. He never entertained turning over the information he had on Bruno or Mr. Rex since he was certain they would kill his family without pause. Right now his family was all he had left to see him through the ordeal, and he couldn't afford to harm them as well. He sat stone-faced and waited for the agents to tire and give up, which they eventually did.

Immigration and Customs Enforcement Special Agent-in-Charge, L. Hosnic, loaded Timothy onto a US bound plane. Timothy peered out the window of the airplane and watched as his brother's body was loaded into the cargo bay below. "Enjoying the view?" Hosnic asked spitefully. "You could prevent that from happening to someone else if you weren't so selfish. We could have offered you protection in exchange for your cooperation."

"You couldn't protect me any more than you protected him." Timothy muttered.

"It wasn't our job to protect him. That was your job."

Timothy leaned back and shut his eyes. For the remainder of the flight, his eyes remained closed and he said nothing. The darkness of his eyelids was the only relief from the hell his life had become.

After arriving back in the states, Timothy was again interrogated but still yielded no useful information. The Feds booked and processed him. Timothy was told he would be appointed an attorney if he could not afford one. He scoffed, "My dad has the best attorney, Ira Kallenbaum. When do I get my phone call anyway? You guys keep denying me my rights!"

The booking agent slid a phone across to Timothy. "Help yourself."

With uncensored desperation, Timothy pounded the telephone and waited for an answer. "Hello, Dad?" He was overcome with relieve. "Yeah, It's Tim." After a moment, a look of confusion took over. He pulled the receiver away from his head and stared at it. "I think we had a bad connection." Timothy dialed again. "Dad?" He spoke cautiously. "What?" Timothy's face oozed abject panic. "It wasn't my fault Dad, I swear!" He pleaded. "I know, but I had to! I didn't have a choice!" Timothy paused. "Dad, you there? Dad?" Timothy dialed the number again but was met with a busy signal.

The agent watched indifferently. He had seen this same interaction hundreds of times. "So is it safe to assume you'll need a court appointed attorney?"

With eyes glazed over, Timothy nodded. "I kept my mouth shut for his sake. Those people would have killed him if I had talked." Tears ran down his cheeks. "He said I'm not his son anymore."

"Change of heart then? You ready to make a statement?"

"No."

The agent shrugged. "Suit yourself."

"I did the right thing for his sake. He'll understand once I am able to tell him my side of the story."

"Good luck with that kid." The agent said disingenuously. "They're fast tracking this one. It's an election year and nothing says foreign relations like recovering stolen Peruvian artifacts. You'll be at trial before the month is up."

Just as the agent had predicted, Timothy's trial date was set for two and a half weeks later in Brooklyn federal court. That was fine with him since he was unable to make bail and was consequently still incarcerated. Just like their father, neither of his sisters would take his calls or help post bail. Even though things looked bleak, he had a persistent feeling that his stay in prison was a temporary outing. He was convinced that his father would work his legal magic and spring him just before the trial. Hard lesson learned, but all would be forgiven. He was a Clement after all, and Clements don't go to jail.

Unfortunately, as the court date drew near there was still no relief from anyone in his family and he wished he had taken the meetings with his court appointed attorney, Marcus Gemp, more seriously. He had provided nothing of use to help his case since not being represented by his father's attorney was never a reality to him. The day before the trial, Timothy requested a meeting with Gemp, but he was in court all day and unavailable.

Timothy lay in his cell that night pondering what type of glance or gesture he would shoot his family in court. It had to be something strong to really stick it to them and make them wish they hadn't been so harsh. He weighed all possibilities from outright obscenities to grueling disappointment paired with a slowly shaking of his head. Their hearts would shrivel with regret for abandoning him, he told himself.

Three things surprised Timothy when his court date arrived. First, Marcus Gemp was a legal genius who fought the case expertly with vigor. He had done his homework and knew more about Timothy, Stephen and the smuggling operation than Timothy himself. Gemp passionately painted a picture to the jury of a naïve schoolboy swallowed up by society's vices. During one of the recesses, he leaned over to Timothy and discreetly told him, "A kid with your record and background – We're looking at probation and some fines. I've represented far worse with no jail time." For the first time, Timothy felt he had an ally he could trust.

The second thing that surprised Timothy was how swift and effectually the prosecution annihilated Gemp's defense strategy. Within minutes, a convincing portrait emerged of an unremorseful felon, so obsessed with greed, that he put his underage brother in harm's way. The prosecutor's skillful artistry of words effortlessly tapped into each member of the jury's fears and private thirst for vengeance. Thick imagery stirred the blue-collar worker's repulsion at Timothy's arrogant lack of work ethic. The deep seeded contempt for thieves that all honest business owners share was tapped. Most damaging though, was the unrestrained rattling of every parents' instinctual obligation to protect their children. As closing arguments were posed, even Timothy himself was convinced he was a threat to society.

The third, and most heartbreaking, thing that surprised Timothy was that despite all of his bedtime rehearsing, not a single member of his family was present at the trial. His eyes darted all over the courtroom, but he didn't see any familiar faces except Special Agent Hosnic.

In the end, he was sort of glad no one showed up. It was humiliating enough hearing the jury foreman declare that his peers had found him guilty of all charges. He couldn't imagine having to face that shame with his family looking on disapprovingly.

It seemed surreal. Timothy kept waiting for Gemp to inform him of a loophole or plea deal they could strike, but no such miracles happened. "We'll appeal." Was the extent of Gemp's reaction.

"Appeal when?" Timothy asked restlessly.

Gemp packed up his folders and checked his watch. "It'll take some time."

"How long?"

Gemp sighed. "Look Tim, I know you are disappointed, but we'll appeal the verdict. Let's get through sentencing and then come up with a strategy."

Sentencing – the word turned Timothy's stomach. "How bad do you think it'll be?"

"Maximum is twenty years."

"Twenty years!" Timothy exclaimed.

"Per count." Gemp put his hand on Timothy's shoulder. "These guys came to make a point. We'll have to wait and see just how big of an example they want to make of you."

Timothy shook his head. "No, this can't be right. I've never even gotten a parking ticket before!"

"And that will be considered when the judge decides sentencing."

Disbelief turned to anger. "This is your fault! You were supposed to defend me! You said no jail time!"

Gemp pulled his hand off Timothy's shoulder. "No, I said I've represented far worse with no jail time. Each case is different. There are no guarantees."

"I want a retrial, with a new lawyer!"

Gemp raised his eyebrows indifferently, unhurt. He was no stranger to these words. "You are welcome to retain any legal counsel you wish. Have them telephone my office and we'll provide your case file."

Just like that, Timothy's only ally turned his heel. No sweat off his back. Without a soul to call friend, a fog of aloneness enveloped Timothy. He was ushered out of the courtroom in shackles and returned to his familiar cell to await sentencing.

The four weeks leading up to his sentencing gave Timothy opportunity to reach out to his family and be denied three more times. The first conversation with his father was morose and detached. His father snubbed his request for legal assistance and told him, "I only have enough strength to grieve for one son. The space reserved to honor Stephen came from purging you from my memories, as if you never existed."

Timothy was not welcomed by his sisters either, who also rejected his pleas for help. Surprising to him, Victoria and Elizabeth were much angrier and hostile. Since they could not assault Timothy physically over the telephone, they constructed gnarled, barbed sentences that left deep welts on his remaining humanity. The girls made sure he understood what an embarrassing disappointment he was, and that he wasn't worthy of the family name he had disgraced. Before concluding their final telephone conversation, Elizabeth told him, "Things will never be the same between us. My little brother Stephen is dead, but I wish it was you." She then slammed the phone down.

Timothy tried a few more times to contact various family members, but all of the telephone numbers he could recall had been disconnected or changed without forwarding information. He reached out by letter, but every last correspondence came back rejected and unopened - nearly every one. An envelope did come back with the word, "Loser!" scribbled on the outside.

Chapter 19

*B*y the time the sentencing hearing arrived, Timothy deflated to the point where he didn't care one way or another what outcome prevailed. If he was released with a fine and probation where would he be able to go? Not home. Not to the shelter of his so called friends, and if he were sentenced to hard time, it was probably a fitting punishment for getting Stephen killed. The only certainty was that his old life as he knew it was over.

"I'm ordering that you be committed to the custody of the United States Bureau of Prisons for the term of fifteen years." Timothy could not believe the judge's announcement. The words sounded as if it were meant for someone else. "You have a right to appeal the jury verdict, and the sentence that the court has just imposed." Stunned, Timothy's whole body went numb. His body jolted when he heard the gavel strike down. "Court will stand adjourned."

Timothy was led out to a waiting bus. The journey to his new home, Jacobson Penitentiary, would be lengthy and lonely. The other lost souls on the bus were mostly quiet except for some young hooligans who treated their situation as a joke. Looking through the metal netting that covered the bus window, Timothy watched the other cars on the road and longed to be free and living his old life, but that time was over.

The few possessions Timothy still owned; his clothes, wallet, necklace and sketch notebook, were taken and filed away. He was processed through an admissions assembly line and given his new name: six-eighteen-four-zero-five. The penitentiary intake officers would only refer to him by his number. He was photographed, washed, fingerprinted and given prisoner clothing. In light of his nearly spotless record, Timothy was classified a low risk inmate. He'd be steered towards other inmates new to the penal system.

As the warden led Timothy to his cell, they passed through the general recreation building. Animalistic yells and catcalls echoed in the cement chamber. At first Timothy didn't realize they were directed at him. Then he felt stares and wanted to leave, but there was nowhere for him to go. When they reached his cell block the warden instructed, "Stand here." Timothy stood perfectly still while the warden and another officer stepped aside to discuss the paperwork.

Out of nowhere, Timothy felt a powerful punch connect with the side of his head. He fell to the ground and continued to get pummeled in the face and body. His attacker was a scrappy kid with pimples and glasses. Before Timothy could defend himself, a swarm of guards reached in and yanked the kid off. "Break it up!" The guards yelled. Timothy felt blood pouring from his nose and reached up to wipe it. "Hands down!" The guard yelled at Timothy.

"I didn't do anything!" Timothy shouted in a voice quivering with fear. "This guy just attacked me for no reason!"

The scrappy kid snarled at Timothy, "Snitch!"

Timothy learned quickly that prison was a place where no one looked out for you but yourself. Before he even made it to his cell, he had gained a reputation as a snitch and a soft one at that.

After getting his face cleaned up, he was taken to his cell. At first Timothy was relieved to see it was empty. But to his disappointment, his cell mate was delivered moments later. An older, truck driver looking man covered with tattoos and scars. "Heard you had a fall." He remarked coolly.

Timothy felt compelled to defend himself. "Some guy jumped me for no reason. Total psycho."

"You calling my brother a psycho?"

A knot formed in Timothy's stomach. "That was your brother?" The man nodded. "Well, he's got some issues."

The cell mate raised an eyebrow and smirked. "Really? Well, brothers can be like that. You got any?"

"Yeah. Um, no."

"Which is it? Do you or don't you?"

Timothy was tired and wanted to lie down on his bunk, but was too afraid. "My brother is dead."

The customary, "Sorry for your loss" wasn't offered by the cell mate. Instead he coldly declared, "Big deal. I've got more dead brothers than I can count. Don't look to T.C. for any sympathy."

"Don't worry, I won't." Timothy said, wondering what T.C. stood for.

"You getting smart with me?" T.C. asked with a stone expression.

"I-I didn't mean nothing by it." Timothy stammered.

T.C. laughed. "Bookie said you were milk toast and he was right!"

"Bookie?"

"The guy who did that to your face. My brother you squealed on! He's down in solitary right now cause of you."

Timothy wasn't sure what to say next. Every word from his mouth seemed to get him deeper in trouble. Still, he couldn't resist defending himself. "I'm no snitch. Your brother didn't have to come at me like that."

"We do that to all the new ones. Only way to tell what they're made of." T.C. unexpectedly punched Timothy in the stomach causing him to double-over and fall to the ground. "That's for squealing, and you are a snitch." The man pulled off Timothy's newly issued shoes and tossed his own worn out pair at him. "Thanks, I think we're even now. From now on you don't see nothing and you don't hear nothing. Anybody asks what happened you just put that dumb face of yours to use and look away." Timothy's eyes welled up. "What's the matter? Gonna cry to your momma?"

"My mom is dead."

"I told you already, I got no sympathy for you, your brother or your mama, so stop crying." T.C. sat down on his bunk. "You ain't gonna last in here being stupid."

Timothy cautiously followed suit and sat on his bunk. "I'm not stupid. I would be in law school right now if-"

"Law school, ha!" T.C. jeered. "What do you know about the law? Not enough to keep yourself out of this place."

"Well, my Dad is"-

"No, I didn't ask you what your pop knows about law. What do YOU know about the law?" Timothy sat dumbfounded. He really didn't know anything more than the fact that law was what his father planned for him to study. "That's what I thought. You don't know nothing! Don't be claiming you are something you ain't in this place. It will get you plenty hurt."

Timothy let out a frustrating sigh. "Alright, you win. I don't know anything."

"Finally, you're making sense. I see guys like you come in here all the time thinking you know everything. That's what young people do." T.C. laughed. "This place will give you a quick education on how much you don't know. The only question is whether you'll learn the hard way or the even harder way."

"What's that mean?"

T.C. raised his shirt and pointed to a skull tattoo on his chest. "You gotta make alliances. A single dog gets ripped to shreds, but a pack of dogs stands a chance."

Timothy studied the primitive skull tattoo until he suddenly felt uncomfortable with how long he was studying T.C.'s chest. "How do you get in?"

"You gotta swear allegiance and do whatever is asked, no questions." T.C. pulled down his shirt. "In return, your time will be a little less miserable."

Timothy could tell there wasn't much of a choice. "Okay, I want in."

T.C. laughed. "You want in?"

"Yeah."

Being able to discriminate against others was T.C.'s favorite guilty pleasure. "It's not open to just anyone. We're selective about our members."

Timothy again referenced his father's repertoire of life accomplishments. "My Dad belongs to a private country club. I'm no stranger to exclusivity."

"Hmmm..." T.C. feigned contemplation. "Tell you what, if you can pass a test, call it an initiation if you will, then you can be a member.

"What do I have to do?"

"Same thing Bookie did to you." T.C. smiled and slowly nodded as he studied the comprehension on Timothy's face.

Timothy slightly sucked in his bottom lip and ran his tongue along the seam of its split. The metallic flavor of blood still resonated in his mouth. "I'm not like a really good fighter or anything."

"You'll learn soon enough in this place!" T.C. chuckled. "You won't get much action. You saw how fast those guards pulled Bookie off you."

Timothy thought about it. "That's true. Okay, where and when?"

"We've got a live one folks!" T.C. jested. "Tomorrow. Could be anytime, so be ready. There will be no second chances."

"Good. I won't disappoint." Timothy extended his hand out. After a pause, T.C. laughed and turned away.

Chapter 20

*T*imothy spent the next day in a continuous jittery state, never knowing when T.C. would call on him to act. Word seemed to have gotten around that Timothy was off limits so he didn't receive harassment, or pleasantries for that matter, from anyone. He felt nearly invisible.

The rigid prison schedule was unlike anything he had experienced. The guards told him where to be and what to do every moment of the day. Timothy couldn't see how T.C. was going to find an opportunity to act while being run around like a robot under the guards' control. Then again, the taste of blood lingering in his mouth reminded him it was absolutely possible.

In the lunch line, Timothy kept his head down and spoke to no one. Once his tray was piled high with slop he looked for the least menacing table to sit at. He would have liked to sit alone, but prison did not afford that luxury. He took an end seat at a nearby table and began to pick at the medieval gruel. It all looked and smelled bad except for a lone biscuit. "I hear you are fixing to be one of the brothers?" A voice from behind him asked as a lanky arm reached in and took Timothy's biscuit like a cobra striking a mouse.

Timothy turned his head and was surprised to see that it was Bookie. He looked around to see who might be watching then slightly nodded his head. "Yeah."

"Two-o-clock" Bookie said in a hushed tone.

Timothy thought for a moment then said, "What if I'm in my cell at two?"

"No. Two-o-clock." Bookie's eyes shifted to a thirty-something Hispanic man sitting to the right and slightly ahead of Timothy. Bookie's eyes came back to Timothy. "Two-o-clock".

Then Timothy understood the reference to the position of his target. "Got it."

"You'll only have a minute; make it count." Bookie left and sat at another table.

Sweat began to ooze from every pore in Timothy's body. Now that the time had arrived he wasn't so sure of himself. He glanced over at the man, clearly older and grossly out of place in prison. The target looked soft and scared; softer and more scared than even Timothy. Something unexpected happened at that moment. Timothy was overcome with compassion for the man he was about to assault. He knew he had to go through with the task if he himself wished to survive his term inside. Timothy found a small amount of comfort in the possibility that in the days to come he'd be coming up behind this man with instructions similar to the same way Bookie had done to him. This is just the way things work inside.

Without over thinking it, Timothy calmly got up, walked over to the target and began to strike him. The man held up his hands to shield himself and cried out in a shrill for help. The surrounding inmates sprung up and encircled the two of them. Timothy swung again and again. "Where are the guards?" He thought to himself. It was taking far too long for them to break it up.

As he continued to wail on the man, he felt a foreign rush of adrenaline that excited and disgusted him at the same time. His hands chilled as they flew through the air. The mixture of sweat and blood on his fingers cooling until each punch made impact. Every strike made Timothy hungry for the next. A barge of pent up frustration was unleashed on this man he had never met.

Timothy felt someone grab his arm as he cocked back for the next blow. "Enough. You're getting his dirty blood all over you." It was T.C.

"Please, Please!" The man cried out, looking upward. His face bloodied and battered.

"Shut up!" T.C. yelled at the man. "You'll get no mercy from us today!"

The man continued. "Please Lord, why?" His trembling hands reached up desperately. "Have mercy on your son Lord!"

Before anyone could react further, the lunchroom was infiltrated by a mob of thrashing guards. Timothy was thrown down and restrained along with T.C. and Bookie. Even Timothy's target was thrown down. Timothy gasped when he finally got a good look at the damage done to the target's face. It was far worse than what Bookie inflicted on him. Timothy's knuckles lost their numbness and a burning set in. He was astounded that such savagery originated from his own hands.

"I'm impressed." T.C.'s voice harnessed Timothy's full attention. "Brother."

Timothy was hauled off to solitary confinement. As far as punishments go, it seemed pretty good. For the first time since he had arrived he didn't have to look over his shoulder. It didn't last though. By the time he really started to enjoy the solitude, the guards moved him back to the cell with T.C.

Timothy entered the cell wearing a smirk and waited for T.C. to shower him with praise. "Welcome back brother."

"So did I do alright?"

T.C. smiled. "I hear that animal got forty-nine stitches in his face. I'd say that is pretty alright."

A warm sense of acceptance overcame Timothy. "Cool. So I'm in then?" T.C. nodded then Timothy clenched his fist and let out a celebratory, "Yes!"

"I could tell when I was watching you knock the snot out of that animal that you were going to fit in." T.C. raised his shirt and pounded on the skull tattoo on his chest.

"He never called out for the guards or nothing so I wasn't able to call him a snitch." Timothy added.

A snarl crossed T.C.'s face. "No, but that animal had the nerve to invoke the Lords name! Can you believe it?"

Timothy laughed. "Just another fool!"

"My pop used to say the only way to judge a man was by the way he uses these." T.C. held up his fists. "The way you handled yourself back there showed me plenty. Felt good didn't it?"

The comment caught Timothy off guard. He had tried to forget that horrible bliss he felt while administering the beating for no other reason than to be accepted. He tried again to stuff it into a deep, deep pocket within his soul. "I told you, I'm not much of a fighter."

"You sure about that?"

Timothy nodded just as the lights went out. "Lights out, see you in the morning."

T.C. continued the conversation. "Talk is cheap. Action is what counts, and everybody now knows what you are. You're a fighter, a real wrecker."

Timothy lay down on his bunk. His knuckles were still stiff and tender. "So, how long until we ask the guy if he wants to be in?" Timothy asked but T.C. just gave out a quizzical grunt. "Will I be the one telling him who his target is?"

"Huh? What are you talking about?" T.C. asked.

"The guy I beat up."

T.C. paused then let out a loud laugh. "Oh, that is rich!" He continued laughing. "Not only can you fight, but you're a comedian too!"

Timothy didn't understand what was so amusing. "Um, yeah."

T.C. laughed harder. "Wouldn't that be something? The first Mexican member of the White Nationalist party! You kill me kid!"

The cackling of T.C.'s voice made Timothy sick. He hadn't put it all together until just then. Not only had he affiliated himself with a group he'd never imagine associating with before, but he had doled out a severe beating on account of their flawed philosophy. Timothy buried his face in his pillow and digested the hardest part of it all; that he had gotten such a rush from beating that innocent stranger. He was horrified that the man's cries for help didn't slow him, but instead flared his savagery. "What have I become?" Timothy asked himself, picturing his father's disappointing gaze from afar.

All of the insults and degrading comments his family had thrown his way echoed in his head. "They're right." He told himself. In that moment, his regret converted entirely to self-loathing.

Chapter 21

As the days passed, T.C. progressively ratcheted up Timothy's exploitation, sending him on increasingly risky errands. The risk if caught was being branded as a trouble maker with the guards. The thought of losing privileges or the opportunity to shave time off his sentence was unbearable to Timothy. It was a tough balancing act to do T.C.'s bidding and stay under the radar. Timothy just wished he could be invisible.

This particular morning was special for Timothy. "Hey T.C., know what today is?" Thoroughly disinterested, T.C. just grunted and continued reading an article on crossbows. "It's my thirty day anniversary!"

T.C. glanced up from his hunting magazine. "Don't expect me to get you nothing fancy."

Timothy recorded a new hash mark for the day in his notebook. "It seems like I've already been here forever."

"Watched pot never boils. If you plan on recording every single day served, you better get yourself a whole bunch more of them notebooks." T.C. remarked as he watched Timothy flip through the remaining blank pages, estimating how many additional days could fit. "It would serve you better to use that paper to write letters or something."

A sigh escaped Timothy's lips. "That would be a waste. Trust me; nobody wants to hear from this guy." Timothy jotted the words, 'Thirty Mark' next to the hash marks.

"Keeping a diary is pointless too." T.C. piled on more unsolicited advice. "Nobody will be interested in reading what happened in here, not even you. Of course that's nothing I need to worry about since I can't read or write."

"Really?" Timothy was amazed. He had never met anyone illiterate before. "Not even a little?"

The disbelief in Timothy's voice irritated T.C. "Words just never made no sense to me. Don't bother, I got other skills."

Timothy printed, 'CAT' in his notebook and held it up. "What does this say?"

T.C. squinted and studied it for a moment then angrily smacked the notebook to the ground. "Didn't you hear me? I said I can't read." He looked down at the notebook which was opened to a 'Stevie the Great' comic. "What the heck is this? You making funny drawings of me?"

"No, not at all!" Timothy quickly corrected T.C. "That's my brother, Stephen."

T.C. glared at Timothy. "You lying to me? I can tell a liar."

"No!"

T.C. bent down and picked up the notebook. He flipped through the dozen or so drawings. "If this ain't me, then how come you ain't ever showed me these before?"

Timothy gulped. "They're private."

"Private!" Years of suppressed hurt and anger erupted from T.C. He ripped out the pages containing the comics and tore them into a mess of small scraps. "I don't want to ever see this again, understand?" T.C. threw what remained of the notebook at Timothy.

The following day while Timothy was flipping through his notebook to see if any of his hash marks were still intact, he stumbled across a single unscathed Stevie the Great comic. Stevie's weak body was pinned to a weight lifting bench by a weightless bar. Timothy smiled and began to tear it out but couldn't bring himself to do it. The memory of Stephen's laugh as he read Timothy's juvenile comics played in his head. "Sorry, Stephen."

The utterance caught T.C.'s attention, and he turned to see what was in Timothy's hands. "What did I tell you about making fun of me?"

"It's not even-" T.C. punched him hard in the mouth. Timothy grabbed his face.

T.C. picked up the notebook and looked at the picture of Stevie. "What's this?"

Timothy felt blood dripping from his mouth then felt what seemed like a large grain of sand on his tongue. He immediately reached up and felt the jagged ridge of his cracked front tooth. "My toof!" He cried out.

A smile came across T.C.'s face as he studied the drawing. "You know, this one is alright. It's kind of funny."

Timothy's fingers fished around in his mouth for any other fragments among the saliva and blood. "Oh man. . ." Timothy groaned.

T.C. went up to the cell bars and yelled, "Guard, get over here!" He looked back at Timothy and said, "Sorry about that."

The guard came up and asked, "What happened to him?" Neither T.C. nor Timothy said a word. The guard shook his head. "Come with me."

A few moments later Timothy found himself in the custody of Nurse Ann, who routinely managed the infirmary. The inmates generally liked her because she had a remarkable memory and could rattle off their individual medical histories, at least the injuries sustained while in custody. It was one of the few times many of them felt noticed. "Have a seat in that chair over there and don't do anything stupid," she instructed Timothy curtly. "It's going to be a few minutes."

"Got some tissue or something?" Timothy slurred.

Nurse Ann gave him a wad of gauze. "Here, keep pressure on and it will stop eventually. I'll be right back." She exited the room.

It was the first time Timothy could remember being alone in a well lit room since he had arrived, but before he could enjoy the luxury of solitude, the sound of a nearby flushing toilet reminded him once again where he was. The restroom door swung open and a man dressed in prisoner threads exited. Timothy longed for a low risk status so he too could do things like use a private restroom.

The stocky figure stopped in front of Timothy and said, "Hello again."

It wasn't until he looked up that Timothy realized who it was. "Oh, h-hi" Timothy sputtered, trying to make the least amount of eye contact with the man he had beaten weeks earlier.

The man smiled warmly. "I want you to know that I forgive you. I understand that this place can make men do things they wouldn't normally do." He sat down across from Timothy. "In the name of seeking protection, some men do terrible things."

"I didn't have a choice. These people would eat me up if I wasn't one of T.C.'s brothers."

"There is always a choice." The man said frankly.

Timothy removed the gauze from his mouth and checked the absorption rate. "Are you telling me you haven't aligned with anyone for protection?"

"I have protection."

"See, you and I are in the same boat." Timothy checked the gauze again. The bleeding seemed to be slowing. "Who are you running with? Do they have you doing all kinds of grunt work like me?"

The man hesitated then answered, "You know who protects me. I called out to him when you and I first met."

Then Timothy remembered the man's cries for help. "Are you kidding me?" The man shook his head confidently while Timothy let out a nervous laugh. "Man, you are such a corny religious nut job! What is wrong with you? So you don't run with any of these guys in here?"

"No."

"Well, if you're going to rely solely on God then you either need to ask him to give you some kind of force field or he could just teach you how to fight. You just-" Timothy stopped and extended his hand. "Sorry, I'm Tim."

The man shook Timothy's hand. "Angelo."

Timothy continued, "You just can't go around advertising weakness and making a target of yourself. You need to learn to fight back."

"I don't fight anymore." Angelo said calmly.

"Why the heck not?" Tim asked, exasperated.

"The Lord says to love your enemies, so that is what I do."

"How can you possibly love your enemies?" Timothy realized his voice had gotten rather loud. He continued in a less intense tone. "That is nonsense! Your enemies want to tear you apart."

Angelo thought about how he could explain himself to Timothy. "All men share the common thread of sin. It is the root of what causes my enemies to, as you say, want to tear me apart."

"Oh, come on! Not every man in the world wants to tear you apart, just the psychos in here. There's a reason these guys are separated from the rest of society. There is no common thread of sin, just crazy and even crazier."

The observation made Angelo laugh. "Semantics. Call it varying degrees of craziness if it makes you feel better, but I think we both know that sin is sin. Man cannot escape his nature. Luckily there is still a way to salvation."

An exhausted look crossed Timothy's face. "I don't believe in all that stuff. Some people are bad, some are good. It's that simple."

"Have you ever heard of a parent teaching their young child how to tell a lie? No. Even so, the day comes in every parent's life when their child looks at them with big eyes and deliberately tells a lie to get something they desire. At that point the parent must teach the child about honesty." Angelo could see the gears in Timothy's head turning. "How many times have you seen small children fight over toys? They'll go right up and take what they want, even if it doesn't belong to them. The kleptomaniac toddler is undaunted by the hysterical fit thrown by his victim. The parent has to stop and teach their child how to coexist with other children; how to share. It does not come naturally. Lust, greed, lying, taking what is not ours; these are all inborn behaviors. Common decency has to be taught because of man's inherent sin."

"Well, I wouldn't say that-" Timothy stopped speaking. He felt he owed Angelo, at minimum, to not argue. "That's fine." Without an argument, Timothy was at a loss for conversation. After a brief awkward pause he asked, "What sin are you in here for anyway?" He wasn't capable of resisting the jab.

Angelo's face drooped. "That is difficult for me to talk about."

"It can't be any worse than the rest of us."

Angelo sat back and decided to share. "My decisions in life have caused my family much shame. I am most repentant for the pain inflicted on them because of my sins." Angelo's eyes welled up. He wiped them quickly and let out a nervous laugh. "It's funny. At the time I thought it to be a very small indiscretion, but it was this little itty-bitty sin that was my undoing."

"Did anyone get hurt?" Timothy asked, secretly hoping he was in the company of an offender who had committed a crime way above his own.

Angelo shook his head. "No one besides my family. I knew that what I was doing was technically wrong, but my ambition was too great to care." Angelo could see the confusion in Timothy's eyes. "I am a doctor. Or, I was a doctor until my license was revoked."

"Is that why you are hanging out here in sickbay?"

"No, I'm diabetic and they don't allow my insulin pump in this place. Nurse Ann administers my injections and regulates me." Angelo's eyes looked distant. "You can't imagine how much I miss that pump." He shook his head to refocus on his story. "Anyway, I was head of a cancer research team- cutting edge stuff. The project was funded by one of the major pharmaceuticals so we had pretty much unlimited access to whatever we needed. Everyone on the team received obscene compensation, myself included. These guys knew that if our method of non-invasive rapid metastasis arrest and reversal was successful it would revolutionize cancer treatment as we know it. Their investment seemed to be paying off. At the very least, initial results seemed unquestionably revolutionary."

Nurse Ann entered the area and looked surprised to see the two men talking. She gave a disapproving look to Timothy then asked Angelo, "Any trouble here?"

"No, just talking."

She hesitated for a moment, staring at Timothy. "I'll be back in five. Holler if you need me."

After she left, Angelo continued on. "The success of the initial trials put a lot of pressure on the team to produce subsequent positive results. You see, the thing was, in order to keep the research progressing we needed access to certain materials. These are not materials you can just pick up at the hardware store. They are rare, expensive and heavily regulated. According to the terms of my agreement with the project sponsor, I can't even tell you what the materials were. Let's just say it was the special sauce that made everything work. The government allows the material for research but they ration it out carefully." Angelo wagged his finger at Timothy. "Rationed, regulated and carefully tracked as I found out. The project sponsor had other research teams like us working on other assignments. It's a small world in this field. Everyone knows, or has worked with, everyone else. I knew through the grapevine that another lab, located three hundred miles passed the state line, had been rationed some of the special sauce. So I persuaded the project director at this other lab, an old friend of mine, to agree to let me have some in exchange for consulting on his own assignment. Seemed like a great idea, but neither of us was actually authorized to make such a deal. I got in my van and drove all night to make the pickup. I'd like to say it was all in the name of helping others, but my ego was doing the driving that night. My thirst for success consumed me."

"So you got busted for trading the sauce?"

"No, I got sanctioned and fined for trading the sauce. I got arrested, lost my medical license and was imprisoned for transporting a dangerous substance illegally across state lines and jeopardizing public safety. The containers which hold the substance are tracked via satellite. The movement triggered an emergency response, and my life has not been the same since."

A puzzled look crossed Timothy's face. "But your research is going to help millions of people!"

"Unfortunately, no. The project was shut down by the Feds that night before we were able to demonstrate consistent repeat trial results. The project sponsor was forced to surrender all project assets to the government and cease any further related research." Angelo's voice got quiet. "Many of my colleagues lost their jobs that day as projects imploded everywhere. My reputation, personal and professional, was destroyed."

"Seems like kind of harsh response to such a small mistake."

Angelo nodded. "I agreed with you at first. Then I realized that the Lord is always righteous and just. This ordeal is a merciful gift to keep my pride from ever raging out of control like that again."

Timothy ignored Angelo's rationalization. "But there's still a chance your treatment might work someday, right? Then it would all be worth it."

Angelo shook his head. "If it does, I won't have anything to do with it. I'm banned indefinitely."

Timothy felt sorry for Angelo. "That is messed up. You were only trying to help people."

"I took a careless risk. Obviously I was wrong." Angelo's head dropped. "So for the next seventeen months I'll ponder my error. Hopefully when I get out my wife will take me back. I'll have a lot of rebuilding to do. I figure in ten years from now I'll be reestablished in a new trade and back on my feet."

Timothy felt sick and removed the gauze from his mouth. "In ten years I'll only be two-thirds done with my sentence."

Nurse Ann returned to the infirmary and took the gauze from Timothy. "Open wide." With a painful grimace she examined his mouth and said, "You won't be enjoying corn on the cob for a while." She threw the mess away in a nearby trashcan. "Another knock like that and you'll be toothless." She stepped back and looked at Timothy. "I know no one wants to be a snitch, but if you want I can have you transferred to another cell."

"No, please don't!" The thought of not being protected by T.C. horrified Timothy.

"Then stop scrapping. The warden is no fan of fighting."

It was happening. Timothy was getting the reputation he desperately wanted to avoid. "I'm not a fighter."

Nurse Ann smirked, unconvinced. "That's hard to believe when you're running with T.C. and his crew."

"Really, I'm nothing like them! I don't even like to fight." Timothy tried to convince her. "I just need allies to survive in here."

"What about him?" Nurse Ann ticked her head toward Angelo. "Do you think he'd back up your story?"

Thick muddy disgrace slowly oozed over Timothy. No matter how hard he tried to stuff it away, the memory of his violent adrenaline rush baked in his mind. "That was just. . ." Timothy searched for some clever string of words and phrases to justify his actions but none would assemble. As the seconds passed, his will to defend himself weakened until it was just a breath on the tip of his lips. "I'm not like them." He whispered shamefully.

Gently, Angelo reached up and put his hand on Timothy's shoulder. "I was there. I saw your eyes."

Timothy's eyes moistened. "This place is crazy. I would never have done that on the outside."

"You've got some time before you'll be back outside, so you may want to work on what's inside." Angelo removed his hand from Timothy's shoulder and turned to Nurse Ann. "I'm ready for my injection when you are."

Chapter 22

*S*even years elapsed, but they felt like twenty. Timothy did his best to lay low and get by. Since beginning his term, no visitors had come for him and no letters had been received. He had become immune to the foul odor of antiseptic mixed with hopelessness that lingered in the air at all times. His left earlobe had healed completely, only its stubby shape gave hint of once being shot at. Holidays were celebrated under close watch in an elementary mess hall, with only the occasional scuffle making them remarkable. He had truly degenerated into nothing more than a number in the penal system. As time passed, Timothy speculated what his friends might be doing on the outside. He was certain that by now most had graduated college, gotten married and had families of their own.

In his forced idle time, he was left to ponder his past decisions and imagine where he might be if he hadn't squandered his opportunities. These thoughts inevitably led to speculation of where Stephen might have been in his life had it not been taken because of Timothy's irresponsible decisions. It was a tortuous mental exercise, but Timothy felt deserving of the pain.

Frequently, as he suffered through the record of his faults, thoughts of Angelo flooded Timothy's mind and gave him some degree of hope. Timothy didn't know where Angelo was or what he was doing, but he was certain it was honorable. Timothy imagined Angelo on the outside earnestly embracing his second chance at life; a chance Timothy knew was well deserved.

A deep voice shouted from across the desk partition. "Six-one-eight-four-zero-five." Timothy approached the commissary desk as he had done every other Sunday for the past seven years and waited for his usual stash of supplies. A mound of plain-wrap toiletries slid toward him. He hesitated without saying a word, until the guard on the other side double-checked his list and then slid three cans of mackerel across. "Owe someone a favor?" The guard asked. Timothy just shrugged his shoulders. Silence had been the safest policy over the years, even when dealing with prison staff. He took the items and waited to be escorted back to his cell.

Canned mackerel, or Mack, was the currency of choice when funding a tattoo inside. Every year on the anniversary of his incarceration, Timothy would get inked to commemorate the occasion. At the end of his first year, he acquired a skull tattoo on his wrist, as was expected by T.C. and associates. By the end of his second year, T.C. was dead and Timothy had gone through multiple cell changes. He decided upon a long-stem rose in honor of his mother. Over the next four years he added thorns to the rose representing his sisters, himself and finally a fallen pedal for his brother Stephen. It seemed logical to add a thorn or another rosebud for his father this year, but Timothy avoided the thought. The pain of his father's rejection was still too pungent, even after so much time had passed.

Back in his cell, Timothy dropped off his supplies while his newest cellmate, Henry, watched with greedy eyes. "Anything good in there you want to share with your celly?" Henry was eighteen, uneducated and without an ounce of class. The feral product of neglectful parents and urban exploitation, Henry's only interest was self-gratification. "How 'bout you give me one of them macks?" Henry punctuated his rude imposition with a staccato laugh, launching spittle from his overbite.

Timothy didn't reply. They both knew it was a preposterous request. It took many hours of custodial work to afford one, let alone three cans of mackerel. Timothy wasn't going to give it away to the guy just for asking. Lacking any comprehension of personal space, Henry reached for, and took one of the cans. Swift as a flung rubber band, Timothy threw Henry to the ground. With a handful of coarse red hair in his left hand, Timothy cocked back his right first readying a strike. "What did I tell you about staying on your side?" Henry just stared up at Timothy, open-mouthed in shock. "Touch my stuff again and I'll break your hand, got it?"

Two sensations overcame Timothy at that moment. The first was the familiar sickening rush of sadistic adrenaline causing his vision to distort with each exasperating spike of anger. Since he had begun serving time, this type of rapid personality shift rendered him out of control several times a year. Over time he had learned how to wrestle back control early in an episode by holding his breath to avoid doing serious damage.

The second sensation, which took him completely by surprise, was a physiological flashback. His muscles contracted exactly as they had when he used to wrestle with Stephen. Stephen was always getting into Timothy's belongings as younger brothers do, and it drove Timothy crazy. They'd frequently argue and wrestle when Timothy's privacy was breached. He'd pin Stephen down in just this same way - minus the fist.

Timothy got off of Henry. Henry scrambled to his feet trembling. "What's your problem, man?"

Timothy pointed squarely at Henry. "Don't touch my stuff." He lingered for a moment for emphasis, and then reunited the three cans of mackerel.

As Henry brooded, Timothy squatted down and slid a column of notebooks out from under his bunk. He reached in a second time and slid another, taller, stack of notebooks out in the open, then repeated the act a third time. All the while he could hear Henry's vacuous mouth breathing behind him. "Why do you keep all those pathetic drawings?" Henry's angst compelled him to ask.

Against his better judgment, Timothy replied, "They remind me of my brother." Timothy's throat swelled and his voice cracked as he spoke.

"He needs to put on some weight!" Henry laughed insensitively. "I've peeked at them when you wasn't around, and no offence, but your brother ain't a very good artist."

"He didn't draw them, I did."

Henry laughed again. "Bull! I've been here near nine months, and I have never seen you draw nothing."

Timothy guardedly opened one of the books and looked into it for a moment before snapping it shut and returning it to its place atop the nearest pile. "It was a long time ago." Timothy then began systematically checking the stacks of notebooks, stopping at each with a green cover and briefly scanning its contents before moving on.

"What are you looking for?" Henry stretched his neck to snoop.

Timothy didn't answer. After scanning a few more, he was suddenly still. His eyes studied a page for a moment, and then he delicately tore it out of the notebook and folded it in half before Henry's craning neck could steal a glimpse. "See these?" Timothy asked as he neatly returned the stacks of notebooks to their original order.

"Yeah." Henry grunted.

"They are part of my stuff. Touch these and I'll also break your hands."

Henry stepped back. "Geez, touchy!" Henry looked at his hands, and then began to pick at his dirty fingernails.

A rattling metal bell sounded in the distance. Timothy hastily gathered up the three cans of mackerel and then moved to the cell entrance and waited silently for the automatic door to unlock. It was time to visit Marco, the block's resident tattoo artist.

Timothy made the appointment each year at the same time. Some guys were constantly revolving through Marco's makeshift tattoo parlor. For Timothy, that seemed to cheapen the act. He didn't want each year's mark to get lost in a sea of trivial flesh appliques.

Not giving or receiving tattoos were entries on the long list of unenforced prison regulations. The guards looked the other way as long as the inmates remained docile. It was an off the books privilege constantly dangled perilously by the guards. The unsaid arrangement with management provided Marco with extra protection from all sides. Marco's Den, the dangling refuge, was respected and protected by inmates and guards alike. Marco was a gifted artist armed with remarkably sophisticated makeshift utensils. Mild in nature, but not shy, inmates from all sects came to him for work without fear of judgment or discrimination. "Feliz aniversairo Senor Clement." Marco said, looking back over his shoulder at Timothy as he scrubbed ink from his hands in his basin. "How is the gardener today?"

Timothy smiled at the greeting. It was one of the few times he genuinely felt welcomed. "It's good to see you. Sorry to disappoint, but no gardening today."

Marco's eyebrows shot up in interest. "There is always room for more thorns. Trust me, I've romanced my share of roses." The two men laughed. "Sit down, relax." Timothy sat down on the edge of the bunk, unfolded the notebook paper he had been carrying and placed it on Marco's work tray. "Oh, what do we have here?" Marco studied the page.

"I want this one on my back."

Marco sighed. "I can put it on your forehead if you want, but I'd be lying if I said it didn't hurt a little that you want to hide my work from your very own eyes."

Timothy couldn't tell if Marco was serious or not. "Lots of guys get tats on their back."

"I put them where they ask, even if I don't agree. To a guy like you, I know each one is very special, and so I look forward to this time of year." Marco wiped his hands one last time and then picked up the paper. It was a sketch of "Stevie the Great's" class picture, complete with a cowlick and an apathetic expression. "What is this?"

"Something my brother and I used to have fun with."

Marco offered, "Then put it next to his rose pedal."

"Well, um. . ." Timothy struggled to find the words. "Can you just put it on my back?"

"Why?"

Timothy calmly took the paper from Marco and studied it. "I just. . ." Timothy's words trailed off to silence. As he looked down at the comic portrait, tears fell from his eyes and trickled upon the paper. The patter of his beads of sorrow seemed as loud as a marching cymbals to Timothy. He turned his face away in shame and covered it with his hand.

Marco gave Timothy a minute to lament. "Let me show you something." Marco removed the top of his inmate uniform exposing an ornamental mosaic of his life. Large black torus linked chains draped from each shoulder, crisscrossing his entire midsection. An open padlock dangled from one of the links, blood dripping from the key hole. Nearly every inch of his skin was decorated. It was too much to take in with just a glance. "See this?" He pointed to a rendition of the Sacred Heart of Jesus occupying the space just left of his sternum. A bursting heart wrapped in barbed wire adorned with fire and a cross. "You can't really tell now, but at first this was just a rosebud wrapped in razor wire." Marco gently traced the memory of the image. "My dad, he was pretty awful to my mom, to all of us really. He had a mean temper like you don't even know."

Marco's eyes closed for a moment. "He took her from us. Then I lost everything when I made him pay for it." Marco sighed and then began to put his inmate attire back on. "Funny thing though, I didn't feel any better afterwards, and I began to hate looking at that rosebud each and every day."

"So you hid it."

"No, I just made it easier to live with." Marco took the drawing from Timothy and looked at it once again. "I once had a guy ask me to write, 'I love tacos' on his arm, and I did it, no questions asked. I knew he'd regret it someday, but it wasn't my business to question him." Marco handed the paper back to Timothy. "No need to rush. Take some time. At least sleep on it. You don't want to regret loving tacos someday. We've got nothing but time amigo."

Timothy gave Marco an understanding nod and departed.

That evening as he lay in bed holding a notebook, Timothy recalled Marco's words. He flipped to a blank page in the back of the notebook and sketched "Stevie the Great". It had been over five years since he had done so, and it felt uncomfortable - as if he didn't deserve to be doing such a thing. His heart burned with sadness and regret. He continued studying the drawing for a while and then an idea was whispered to him from seemingly nowhere. His pencil went up to Stevie's head and drew a bow up top and lengthened the hair. Next, Timothy placed an elongated triangle over Stevie's shirt and pants to make a dress. He drew a pair of simple glasses over the eyes. Timothy crossed out 'Stevie the' then stopped. He looked at 'Great' for a moment, and then printed, "Mar" immediately before it. Timothy smiled, very pleased with the idea. His heart was no longer heavy. "Hello MarGreat, I'm Tim." He said in a relieved tone. "Do you love tacos?"

Timothy held up the drawing as if it were speaking and said, "I hate tacos!" in a trilled voice.

Timothy smiled broadly. "Me too."

Chapter 23

Stevie the ~~Mar~~ Great!

*T*hree weeks had passed since Marco stamped MarGreat upon Timothy's chest. As was the experience each previous year, the scabbing itched and burned miserably. Timothy had been busy fleshing out MarGreat which was a helpful distraction. Droll dialogue flowed effortlessly from her mouth, whereas Stevie had done little more than drool and fart over the years.

"Prisoner six-one-eight-four-zero-five you have a visitor." The guard's voice startled Timothy who was intently drawing an exasperated school teacher towering over MarGreat.

Then guard's words confused Timothy. "A visitor?"

"Let's get going." The door slid open, and Timothy was taken down to the visitation center. He hadn't seen the area since his public defender had come to check up on him a few months into his stretch. It looked the same, gray and dingy. They reached a heavily supervised area with lots of desks, tables and chairs. "Wait here." The guard forcibly sat Timothy down.

Timothy looked around at the different inmates meeting with their visitors. Some were lit up and smiling while others looked miserable. At the desk nearest Timothy, a man sat across from a stern young woman holding a crying baby. The two sat silent while she scowled.

From behind, a familiar voice spoke, "Hello Timothy. It has been some time. I hope you are doing well." It was his public defender Marcus Gemp.

Timothy turned to look. Gemp looked the same, as if no time had passed. "Why are you here?"

Timothy's directness didn't throw Gemp. "I was summoned here today because there is a bit of an occupancy crisis in the county that has worked to your favor."

"I don't understand."

"Mold." Gemp took a seat across from Timothy and opened his files. "The inmates housed in the north tower managed to file a collective Federal complaint against the prison due to a mold infestation. Tests show there is significant growth throughout the facility. Nearly every wall cavity needs to be decontaminated. Consequently, the inmates are being relocated down here during the cleanup." The north tower was home to the prison's more serious offenders as well as solitary confinement.

"Okay. So what?"

"So the warden is thinning out the population of your cell block to make room. Your good behavior has paid off." Gemp removed a court order and passed it to Timothy. "Your sentence has been commuted."

"You mean I'm free?" Timothy asked with reserved excitement as his eyes scanned the document not understanding most of the legal jargon.

"Almost. There are very specific terms to your release. You will be released into the custody of a transitional facility first. There you will be groomed for assimilation back into society."

Timothy nodded, "Sure, I can do that."

"You will receive occupational training for sixty days, after which you will be matched with a partner employer. These are companies who agree to help people like you get back on your feet. After three months of steady employment, you'll undergo an evaluation, and hopefully we can put all this behind you."

"Great!"

Gemp handed Timothy a pen. "Initial the highlighted items and sign at the bottom." Timothy feverishly scribbled his initials down the page and signed his name. Gemp took the page and looked it over and then handed it back. "I need your full legal name on this." Timothy added "-othy" after "Tim" and returned it.

"Does my family know about this?"

Gemp's brow creased. "Every family reacts differently to an inmate's release. We reached out to your family this morning, and they are not quite ready to reunite. It can take time."

Timothy felt his face flushing. "Did they all feel that way?"

"We were only able to reach your sister Victoria and she made it pretty clear that they are not ready."

"What about my Dad, did you talk to him?"

A serious look crept over Gemp's face. "Your father passed away four years ago Tim. I'm sorry." Timothy dazed off in shock. "Cardiac arrest."

"Why didn't anyone tell me?"

"That is up to the family." Gemp glanced at his watch. "A guard will help you gather your personal effects. If you hustle, you might get to check in before sundown."

"This is happening now?"

"Unless you want to stick around." Gemp held up his hands questioningly. Timothy shook his head. "Great, I'll come by the transitional facility tomorrow to check in with you." Gemp stood up, shook Timothy's hand and left.

Timothy was ushered back to his cell to grab his belongings. Henry sprung up from his bunk the instant Timothy stepped back into the cell. "So it is true!"

Timothy ignored Henry. He removed his notebooks but left the rest of his odds and ends.

"Can I have your stuff?" Henry asked excitedly.

"Knock yourself out." It was liberating to not care about the scraps, which had seemed so valuable just hours earlier.

Henry smiled like a kid on Christmas morning. "I guess you won't be able to break my hands this time"

Ignoring Henry, Timothy passed his stack of notebooks to the guard and asked, "Can you please destroy these?" The guard did not take them; instead he removed a large orange plastic bag from his waistband and shook it open. It felt surreal to dispose of them, but each falling notebook was easier to release than the previous. Timothy filled the plastic bag with every one of his notebooks until it bulged. The guard then tied a knot, slung the bag over his shoulder, and they left without a word.

Next Timothy was presented with the clothes he was wearing when he first arrived. Holding the clothes in his hands brought back bad memories. He was apprehensive to put them back on and wear the past again. The female clerk sensed Timothy's hesitancy. "You're right, they probably don't fit right anymore. I'll get you something suitable." She turned around and rummaged through a nearby bin, mumbling to herself, then emerged with a pair of jeans, a grey T-shirt and a belt. "All I got is extra-large so you tie this belt good." She then reached below the counter and pulled out a pair of sneakers and threw it on the pile. "Hope you are an eleven."

Timothy took the items and looked them over. "Thanks."

"Here, I don't want these, take them." Timothy passed over his old clothes.

The woman tossed the items aside and pointed to a nearby restroom door. "You can change in there."

Timothy went into the restroom and dressed himself in the stiff, no-frills clothing. At least two inches of waistband folded onto itself as he cinched the belt tight. Even on the last belt hole the pants were enormous. He pulled the shirt down as far as it would reach to cover his bunched up rungs.

Next, Timothy proceeded to another clerk who slid a box containing his belongings across to him along with a checklist. "Please confirm all items are accounted for and sign." In the box was his old wallet, sunglasses, seventy-two cents in change and his Saint Anthony necklace. Timothy signed the paper then took possession of the items. The necklace felt heavier in his hands than he remembered. He immediately put it around his neck. "Take this, courtesy of the state." The clerk handed him two-hundred and twelve dollars cash secured by a paper ribbon. "Use it wisely." The clerk then pointed over Timothy's shoulder. "Your transportation is waiting just outside the orange doors. Good luck, and please. . . don't come back."

After a moment's hesitation, Timothy walked briskly through the doors and was outside. He saw a van, but instead of heading toward it he stopped to look around, his eyes scanning left and right. The van door opened and a stocky driver in his early thirties called out to him. "Timothy Clement?"

Timothy nodded. "Yeah, it's just Tim." Timothy resumed scanning the area.

"I'm your ride." The driver called out, but Timothy didn't budge. "Expecting someone else?"

"Um. . ." Timothy bit his lower lip and looked around once again. "It's just you?"

"Just me."

Timothy exhaled and walked over to the van and got in. Once buckled, Timothy asked, "How far is this place?"

"About forty-five minutes north of where the steel bridge crosses Jasper creek." The driver started up the van. "I'm not expecting any traffic this time of day."

As they pulled out onto the highway Timothy asked, "Do you mind if we make a quick stop along the way?"

"I'm supposed to drive you straightaway. If you're hungry. . ." The driver opened the glove box and pulled out a half empty paper cup of fries. "You can have some of these."

Timothy held up his hand and shook his head. He hadn't had real fries in years. Although stale, they did smell sort of good, but he couldn't help wonder what else was in that glove box. "No thanks. My sister Elizabeth lives just past that bridge. I was hoping we could just stop in for a minute to say hi."

"Is she cute?" The driver's question was met with a kneejerk look of repulsion from Timothy. The driver chuckled. "No can do. It would just take a minute for me to lose this contract."

Timothy slumped back in his seat and listened to the munching of stale fries for the next seven miles. Eventually the historic bridge came into view and inspired Timothy to reach into his pants pocket and remove the wad of public funds. He counted out one hundred dollars. "I can make it worth your time."

The driver looked over at the cash in Timothy's hand. "I don't know." After contemplating the offer for about one second, the driver reached over and grabbed the cash. Then he reached over again and grabbed the rest of Timothy's money. "Maybe this would make it worth my while."

"That's all I've got!" Timothy protested.

"Do you want to visit your sister or not. It really doesn't matter to me." The driver had obviously entered into this arrangement many times before. Timothy nodded reluctantly then slumped back in his seat again.

Timothy was in a daze for most of the ride. Freedom tasted better than he remembered. As the sun went down, Timothy watched the bridge silhouette fade miles off in the distance. Eventually they passed over the bridge and Timothy gave the driver instructions leading into his sister's neighborhood. "Right there, the green one at the end." Timothy pointed with excitement. "It used to be beige." He added, as if the driver cared.

The driver parked in front of the two-story home. "You've got ten minutes."

For the first time in many years, Timothy found himself flirting with the hope that he might be able to reconcile with his family. He figured he'd begin with Elizabeth, and the rest would fall smoothly into place. After all, he had repaid his debt. Rushing up the driveway to make the most of the ten minutes, Timothy reached the front door and banged on it impatiently. Beyond the decorative glass he could make out an obscured figure approaching. He searched his brain for what to say; he hadn't exactly thought this far in advance. The door swung open and he blurted out, "Elizabeth!"

An older Indian woman stood open-mouthed in shock. After a moment, her nose crinkled and she declared, "We don't want any!" and began to shut the door."

"No, wait!" Timothy pleaded. "Is Elizabeth here?"

The woman held the door momentarily then said, "There is no Elizabeth here."

"But this is her house!"

The woman became irritated with Timothy's assertions. "No, this is my home. I've lived here for five years. Now please, go away!" The door slammed shut.

Timothy stood dumbfounded on the porch, noticing for the first time the name, "Patel" on the mailbox. Up until then he hadn't experienced firsthand evidence that the rest of the world had moved on while he served his time. Deflated, he meandered back to the van, looking back just once more at the property before getting into the vehicle.

"You weren't kidding about your sister." The driver laughed.

"I guess she moved or something." Timothy muttered, not amused.

The driver started the van and pulled away. "Look at the bright side; at least you get to stay at Radiant House. That place is easier than summer camp."

"You've been there before?"

"It's been ten years, but the place looks the same; from the curb at least. I've never feel right about going back inside, like it's a step back." A sorrowful quiet settled over the conversation as the driver's felonious past came to light. "I did some time for dealing. Radiant was real good to me when I got out and had no place to go. They even hooked me up with this job. I owe them a lot, but I won't go in there."

Timothy nodded as he listened. "Good to hear that, because as you could see back there, I've got nobody."

"You'll be fine at Radiant. It's not like some of these other places who just want you so they can get their headcount up. Headcount is everything when you're funded by Uncle Sam. You ever hear of a place called 'Urban First?"

"No."

"It's a place in Old Town. I heard ninety-two percent of its funding goes to the CEO's salary. You can just imagine how crummy the place is with what's left." The driver looked over at Timothy sympathetically.

Timothy shook his head. "My dad once broke down in Old Town. He didn't think he'd make it out alive."

The driver played with the radio. "You like metal?"

"I guess some of it is okay." Timothy could tell he didn't really have a choice.

"This is-" Before the driver could finish his sentence, sharp distorted guitar licks framed with rapid double-kick drums rattled the cab. "My favorite band!" He shouted over the noise. Timothy reached for the volume and turned it slightly down, but the driver immediately turned it back up. "You gotta listen like this man!" Timothy sat back and endured the audio trauma for the next forty miles.

Chapter 24

*E*ven though the modest "Radiant House" sign was small, Timothy felt a sense of relief when it came into view. The moment the van pulled up to the entrance, Timothy sprung from the vehicle and headed up to the door, not looking back. He noticed the van radio behind him quieting and then heard the driver yell for him. Hesitantly, Timothy turned around and headed back to see what he wanted. "Here, take this. I'm feeling charitable today." The driver handed Timothy twelve dollars. Timothy took his former money back and nodded halfheartedly before heading for the door. As the van sped away, Timothy's head throbbed as he tried to acclimate again to normal decibel levels.

The building looked less like a house and more like a lodge nestled in a mountain resort. Timothy tried the knob but it was locked. He noticed a bell on the door frame and pressed it several times; more times than he probably should have. A frazzled female voice seeming to come from nowhere said, "I'll be right down."

After a short wait, the home director, Mary Sims, opened the door for Timothy and greeted him with a big smile. "Welcome to Radiant House!" She gestured for him to come inside.

Mary was a cheerful woman in her mid-forties who, despite having weathered skin, was youthful in every other aspect. "You must be Timothy. I'm Mary Dixon, the house Director." She extended her hand cheerfully.

It had been such a long time since anyone had offered him a civil handshake that Timothy barely knew how to respond to the gesture. He took her small hand in his, barely making contact before withdrawing. "It's just Tim."

"Nice to meet you, Tim." Mary smiled in acknowledgement. "As you can imagine, we are pretty full right now because of the recent environmental developments over at the penitentiary. I honestly can't remember a time when we were this full."

Timothy looked around. "It's a pretty big place."

"Even still, we're doubling up rooms for a while." Mary motioned for Timothy to follow her over to a nearby wooden table. "Please, sit down. Can I get you something to drink?"

Timothy sat down. "No thanks." He traced the lacquered grain of the wood with his fingertip. Furniture possessing aesthetics beyond mere functionality was a foreign luxury to him.

Mary placed a folder tagged with a vertical sticker reading "Clement" on the table, and then flipped it open. She pulled out the recent court order, looked it over then made her most serious facial expression. "I believe in second chances Tim." Mary paused for just a moment to let the idea sink in. "There are times in everyone's life when they need outside help; a friend to get them back on track when things go south. For some people-" Mary glanced back down at the court order.

"The wreckage of their errors is more severe and takes more time and effort to clean up. But I believe every life is salvageable in some way."

Timothy felt inclined to interject before Mary continued much further. "Lady, I appreciate what you're saying, but I'm way past fixing. At this point, I just need to not cause any more damage."

"No." Mary rebutted. "With our help you can live a normal, productive life, but you have to want it for yourself. Do you want it?" Mary studied the dampening of Timothy's eyes then continued in a compassionate whisper. "You've served your time. Don't you want to live again?"

"It doesn't matter what I want." Timothy self-consciously wiped his eyes.

"Of course it matters." Mary strained her neck to see his face. "You've been given a second chance."

With wet swollen eyes Timothy replied, "My brother Stephen is dead because of me. He didn't get a second chance."

"Then don't dishonor his memory by squandering yours."

Mary's words jolted Timothy. His torso thumped at the prospect that there might be a way to somehow atone for his deeds. "You don't understand. My whole family has ditched me. I thought I would be able to finally apologize to my Dad, face to face, but he's dead!" Timothy became angry. "He died four years ago, and no one even told me. Do you hear what I'm saying? It's me; I'm the common denominator."

Wasting no time, Mary pulled out a blue form resembling a contract. "You can't achieve a goal that has not been clearly defined, and you can't expect your life to change if you are not committed." Mary watched Timothy's head bob in agreement. "We start with what I call the pledge and the plan." On the paper she wrote his name on the top blank line. "Do you want to be a better you?" Timothy nodded. "Then proclaim it!"

"I want it." Timothy mumbled.

"Want what?"

Timothy clenched his teeth; this was harder than expected. He relaxed his jaw, closed his eyes and said, "I want to be a better person. I don't want my life to be a total waste." It amazed him to hear what came out of his mouth. He wondered how this woman, a stranger, had managed to tap into his the private recesses of his heart so easily.

"Do you promise to do whatever it takes to achieve that goal? Do you promise to stick to the plan?"

Timothy's voice trembled. "Yes."

"I've got good news Tim. . ." Mary smiled, "I pledge to personally help you achieve that goal." Mary wrote her name on the line below Timothy's. "If you promise to allow me help you." Timothy nodded. "The plan is to teach you a trade so you can support yourself. At the same time you'll be learning other life skills to help you thrive on your own."

"What kind of job training?" Timothy asked. "I'm pretty smart. I was accepted to Yale law school."

The boasting did not impress Mary the way Timothy had hoped. "You'll find that most citizens will not trust you now, especially with important legal transactions. Part of the rebuilding process is taking responsibility for your actions and realizing that there are consequences."

"Even though I messed up, I know right from wrong." Timothy defended himself.

This was always a difficult idea to teach. Mary responded, "Society is not impressed with what, or who you know; they judge you solely on your actions. Right now, your actions tell them to be wary of you."

Timothy scoffed. "Well, that's their problem."

"Actually, it's your problem. The burden is on you to demonstrate that you are a hardworking, trustworthy member of society." Mary got up and took a clipboard down off the wall. "That is an especially hard task if no one is willing to give you another chance to prove it." Sitting back down, she began dragging her index finger down the clipboard, reading intently. Her finger stopped near the end of the page. "Sage Masonry. I spoke to the foreman last week, and they are willing to pick up another apprentice."

"You mean like building stuff?" Timothy said with disapproval.

"It's honest work. It'll pay the bills."

"Yeah but. . ." Timothy searched for the least offensive words. "It's like, you know, manual labor." He finished in a hushed tone.

Mary continued on apathetically. "Like I said, it's good honest work." She wrote Timothy's name on the chart. "Tomorrow I'll go down and discuss my pledge, and your plan with the foreman. He's understands what you are going through better than you can imagine."

"He was in jail too?"

"No, he was a judge." Mary hung the clipboard back up. "He saw too many repeat visitors. Folks who just needed a little guidance to change. He retired and started a masonry business with his brother with the idea of helping out former inmates."

"Wow, I can't believe he would give up a good paying job like that."

"There are things worth more than money." Mary said with a knowing smile. "I'll call him in the morning and tell him all about you."

"Okay." Timothy muttered, still not thrilled about having to do real work.

Mary passed Timothy a numbered key. "Here is the key to your room. It's on the third level. I think you'll find everything you need, but if not, just come see me. Take it easy the rest of the night."

Timothy thanked her and left.

Chapter 25

*I*t had been some time since Timothy had ridden in an elevator, and it brought a juvenile smile to his face. It made him realize how many things he had taken for granted before being locked up. The bell dinged and the doors opened. He walked freely through the hallway without shackles or an escort and marveled at the sensation. It was the same exhilarating feeling he had the first time his father let him take the car out on his own.

As he walked the corridor, Timothy surveyed the door numbers, counting in sequence up toward three hundred sixteen, the number on his key. He reached three hundred fourteen at the end of the hallway and rounded the corner to find his room. Immediately Timothy noticed a pack of cigarettes resting at the base of the door propping it open. The strong odor of tobacco and a haze of smoke emanated from the within. Timothy cautiously opened the door and coughed as his lungs inhaled the stale smoke. "Hello?" He called out. A mini refrigerator and microwave oven served as bookends to a waist-high kitchenette that divided the room, keeping ample distance between the two twin beds on each side.

The toilet flushed in the bathroom and a voice called out from inside, "Sorry, but I just had to go. It will be a while before I'll be able to go again. You can come back." A gangly man with long greasy hair stumbled out of the adjoining bathroom looking guilty of something. "Oh, hey man. I thought-" The man looked around the room. ". . . you were the lab dude."

Timothy looked around the modest room and noticed tissues and fast food wrappers all over the ground on the near side of the island. "I'm Tim."

The man looked Timothy over then said, "People around here call me Hep-C." He smiled at Timothy exposing his grungy teeth.

"Is that for hepcat or something?" Timothy inquired unimpressed.

"They probably didn't tell you downstairs, but I am undergoing treatment for an ongoing Hepatitis-C infection."

"Oh, lovely." Timothy said and began goose-stepping over the trash on his way to the debris-free side of the room.

"Yeah, so I kinda recommend you stay away from my side of the room." Hep waved his hand over his trashy domain. "Don't worry about the kitchen though, I usually order take-out."

Timothy removed his shoes and laid down on the bed. It was so much nicer than his cell bunk. Hep continued to drone on. "Normally it's not this messy, but I haven't been able to pay the cleaning service."

The mention of clean caught Timothy's attention. "Cleaning service?" He asked.

"With all my medical bills and eating out all the time I came up short this month." Hep ended with a loud snort.

"How much?"

"If you wanna pitch in, that's cool. Just give me whatever you can. It's your room too, right?" Hep peered over the island and watched Timothy sit up, pull out his wad of twelve dollars and then remove a five dollar bill and place it on the kitchen counter. "That the best you can do? She's pretty good. Uses bleach and gloves and all the bio-waste stuff you see on TV."

"That is it. I already lost two hundred today."

Hep did an inventory of Timothy's person. "What's that hanging round you neck? Is it fancy? Got any stones in it?"

"It's a saint necklace from my mom, and it's not for sale."

Hep smacked his lips and appraised the item. "If it's sterling then you might get ten or twelve at pawn."

Feeling Hep's covetous stare, Timothy lay back down in his bed and repeated, "I said it's not for sale."

"I'm just saying. . ." Hep continued on, but Timothy ignored him, not wanting to encourage any further conversation. "You don't snore do you?" Hep floated the question hoping to spur further dialog but Timothy said nothing. Hep waited a few minutes then turned out the light and went to bed.

Even though home had changed, Timothy fell quickly into a deep sleep. It was as if a huge rock was lifted from his shoulders, and he was finally able to relax. Throughout the evening, he experienced many vivid dreams yet his body remained motionless. On and off he became covered with sweat and occasionally snored, despite Hep's displeasure. Before sunrise, he emerged from his deep slumber by way of a ticklish sensation on his neck. His eyes fluttered open just in time to see Hep pull away his unclasped necklace. Flashbacks to his sticky handed cellmate Henry filled his mind. Timothy snapped.

In a panic, Hep dropped the necklace on the bed covers and staggered back. "I-I was just gonna clean it for ya." He stammered. Timothy snatched up the precious item, and with it in his fist, began to wail on Hep's face. The two tumbled to the floor and the beating continued amidst Hep's cries. Timothy was completely unleashed, held captive by his rage. Each blow releasing an explosion of endorphins in his brain. He was high on the violence.

The piercing vibrato shriek of an athletic whistle abruptly filled the room, ricocheting off every surface. Timothy's heart froze and he looked around confused. Hep tried to exploit the pause and wriggled away, but Timothy's attention immediately returned with another swing. Again, the shrilling whistle filled the room, this time in short bursts. The lights came on, blinding the men temporarily. "Stop this instant!" A snarling voice commanded. Timothy was disoriented and looked toward the sound but could not make out who it was. "Get off of him, now!"

Timothy's rage cooled down to mere anger as he panted. "He's a thief!" Timothy yelled at the voice. He slowly rose up while wiping saliva from the corners of his mouth.

"This is unacceptable Mr. Clement. Unacceptable!"

Just then Timothy made out the figure and realized it was Mary Dixon scolding him. Shame began to replace his anger. "I'm sorry." He muttered. He looked down at Hep's bloodied face trying to shake the buzzing sting that danced on his knuckles.

Mary pointed out the door. "Take your things downstairs at once!"

Under the unjust scrutiny of Hep's arrogant smirk, Timothy slid his feet into his shoes then reached for his bag. It was then he realized his saint necklace was clenched in his fist the whole time. He uncurled his stiff fingers and removed the item with his other hand. Etched in his palm was a crimson imprint of the medallion and chain. He reattached the clasp and put it around his neck.

"Now please." Mary requested impatiently. Timothy picked up his bag then looked over to the counter for his five-dollar bill.

"That's long gone partner." Hep snickered through his enflamed nose.

Timothy left the room with Mary and headed down to the office. Through the first floor window Timothy watched a sliver of the sun's corona poke above the horizon. It was a privilege he hadn't missed until that moment. As they approached the office Timothy offered another apology which Mary ignored.

Mary appeared more disappointed than angry with the situation. "I know Barry is not the easiest person to live with, but that doesn't make what you did right."

"Barry?"

Mary gave Timothy a look of disbelief. "Your roommate, the one you just beat up back there."

Timothy began to explain, "He told me his name was-"

"I don't care about childish pet names. This is the real world where you are expected to behave in a grown-up way and use your real name." Mary was exasperated. Even after a decade at the home, she hadn't fully mastered patience. "You can't go around punching everyone who slights you either. Why didn't you just report him to me?"

Timothy looked down at his feet. "He was ripping me off, and I got mad."

"Tim, as far as solutions go, has physical violence ever worked out well for you?"

The first thing that came to mind was his initiation in to TC's clan. He contemplated her question and decided that it was necessary to survive in that situation. "Sometimes you gotta do what you gotta do."

Mary looked at him with exhaustion. The glimmer of hope that usually radiated from her eyes had faded away. "You can't expect a new life if you can't let go of your old ways."

Timothy knew she was right. If only he could learn to live correctly he thought. "I'm sorry, it won't happen again."

"I know it won't. I can't afford the liability." With that Mary fetched Timothy's file and put it on her desk. "You can't stay here."

The words stabbed at Timothy's heart. "Please, I promise it won't happen again!" Timothy pleaded. "I won't be any trouble. I can't go back to prison. I have to complete your program. Remember, the pledge and the promise?"

Mary stared at him for a moment and knew he was sincere. "Even if I wanted to give you another chance, I can't keep this under wraps. The news of this incident has probably already spread to every resident by now. The board won't tolerate it."

"Please, I'm begging you!" Timothy appealed in desperation.

Mary hated when men pleaded with her. "There is one thing I can try, but it's not guaranteed." Mary motioned for Timothy to sit down. She then placed a phone call and said, "Hi Ray, got room for one more?" She nodded a few times then thanked the man before hanging up. Then she sat still and stared at Timothy.

"Well?" Timothy couldn't stand the suspense.

"I've held up my end of the pledge. The rest is up to you." Mary studied Timothy, wondering if he really even had a chance. "I was able to get you into another home. The director there owes me a favor."

Timothy let out a huge sigh. "You don't know how thankful I am. Thank you!" Timothy's spirits were soaring once again.

Mary smiled. I small bit of hope crept back into her eyes. "The place is over in Old Town." Mary saw the cheerfulness leave Timothy's face. "Don't get picky on me now. It's this or back to prison, you pick."

"No, I'm thankful. I don't want to go back." Timothy said, sounding more like he was trying to convince himself than thank her.

"The place is called-"

"Urban First." Timothy completed her sentence.

Mary seemed surprised that he knew of it. "Yes, that's right. You'll be able to finish your work study there and meet the court's requirements same as you would here." She glanced at the clock. "Urban First has already sent a driver for you. Your attorney is due at eight. When he gets here I'll inform him of the change."

Timothy nodded with a closed-mouth smile, forcing himself to be gracious. He couldn't understand how he could screw up so badly less than a day into freedom. His spirit was weary, and he figured that maybe he didn't really deserve liberty after all.

"Don't forget the promise you made." Mary reminded him.

Timothy scowled. "You're not even going to be around. What does it matter now?"

Mary looked surprised. "Tim, you didn't make a promise to me, you made a promise to yourself." Mary caught sight of the van pulling up in the parking lot outside the window. "Your ride is here. Best of luck Tim."

Timothy stood up and went out front. He was embarrassed and couldn't leave fast enough. "Let's try this again." he muttered to himself.

Part II

Old Town

Not many of you should become teachers, my brothers, for you realize that we will be judged more strictly. - James 3:1

Chapter 26

*F*or mid-morning, there were far too many sirens and car horns for Timothy's liking. As the van couriered him further into Old Town, the buildings grew taller and packed closer together. The streets narrowed and darkened beneath a shellac of filth. Pedestrians meandered without purpose, oftentimes right down the middle of the street, stopping to stare down the van as it maneuvered around them. The place seemed like a repository for lost souls. Timothy sat on the ripped vinyl bench seat in the back of the van, separated from the driver by a metal screen. An inescapable fragrance of mixed bodily odors hung unpleasantly in the air. The driver wore head-phones and largely ignored Timothy, treating him like cargo on the way to a warehouse. Just about every surface in the back of the van showed signs of defacement with writing and scratches; it was a mobile lexicon of obscenities in at least three languages. Finally, they arrived at Urban First and the side door slid open. Timothy longed for a breath of fresh air, but upon exiting he inhaled a waft of what tasted like airborne carcass. His hand reflexively covered his mouth in disgust.

The driver banged on the side of the van and whistled impatiently before leading Timothy to the entrance. Up until then Timothy had not noticed the driver's pronounced limp. Although Timothy did his best not to stare, the gnarly scar tissue on the back of the driver's calf made his imagination run wild with possible scenarios. After initially speculating a motorcycle crash, Timothy went with the more plausible gunshot wound. The driver never looked back to see if Timothy was following him. He just forged ahead like a machine with an operation to perform.

The home was actually a dilapidated storefront sandwiched between a dry-cleaner and an abandoned check-cashing store. The sidewalk out front was fractured in a hundred places. It was a holding bay for dozens of aimless, broken young men who glared at Timothy as he moved along. He had become immune to intimidating expressions back in prison, and so their stares went unnoticed.

"Home sweet home." Timothy muttered as he entered the gutted marketplace. Foot-wide aisles divided vacant bedrolls and crumpled grocery sacks which occupied nearly every inch of available real estate. A burly man on the far side of the room glanced up as Timothy entered then went back to a conversation he was having on a vintage wall phone. The driver slapped a three-ply form on Timothy's chest then limped back out. Timothy's reflexes lapsed and the paper fluttered down to the ground as he awkwardly failed to catch it. He stooped down and heard the patter of footsteps run up from behind.

"Hey guy." An anemic blonde haired man stood nervously before Timothy, eyes darting to-and-fro. "Looking for a friend?" The man's affected voice quivered as he scratched his elbow.

Before Timothy could respond, the burly man at the far side of the room erupted, "That's it Clyde, get out!"

Clyde held up his hands like he was a victim of unjust prosecution. "What?" His voice now an octave lower.

"Out!" The man pointed sharply at the entrance. Clyde endeavored to casually wander off to a quiet corner but that was not satisfactory. "I'm not playing Clyde, get out!" Clyde continued on as if his hearing malfunctioned. The man's face reddened and he tanked across the room. When he came within arm's reach, Clyde grabbed a bed roll near his feet and sprinted out the front door. The man yelled after him. "Take it; you'll need it because you aren't welcome here anymore!" The man huffed, looking like a sweaty sausage. "Strike three Clyde!"

As Timothy watched the bizarre exchange, his stomach knotted up. The sweaty man wiped his face on his sleeve then walked over and took the three-ply form from Timothy. "I'm Tim. Mary called over from-"

"Yeah, yeah, she's a black hole of payback. She thinks because she saved my life once she has the right to kill me one favor at a time." The man barely glanced at the paper then crumpled it up and jammed it in his pocket. "I'm Alix. Things are really simple here Tim, all you have to do is follow the rules. Leave your baggage at the door because I won't put up with it." Alix pointed in the direction Clyde had run. "Keep your vices out of my shop. The most important thing is to be here for check in every night by five and then check out every morning by nine. I don't really care what you do with your time, but you have got to check in and out every day."

"What about the job training?" Timothy asked.

They were interrupted by the deafening ring of the wall phone across the room. "Hold on." Alix shuffled across the room in a half-jog and sloppily grabbed the phone receiver. "UF Old Town, Alix speaking." Timothy watched Alix pace up and back as he intently listened to the caller on the other end. "Capacity is sixty-seven. We're in the silver bracket with the extra fourteen percent for occupational." Alix listened some more and shook his head. "No, no, no, you people always get it wrong. Every single one of ours qualifies for the extra fourteen percent. That's how we do it." Another minute of affirmative answers, and Alix hung up the phone and then hobbled back to Timothy. "What were we talking about?"

"How does the training work?" Timothy asked eagerly.

Alix grimaced. "It's on the job training. Apprentice stuff."

Timothy's eyebrows lifted. "No classes?"

"I said on the job training, how many ways can that be interpreted! The good news is that you get paid while you learn." Alix watched skepticism flourish across Timothy's face. "Tim, it's a simple arrangement. You go work where I tell you. I get paid. You get paid. We both win."

"You get paid?"

"Only if you check in and out here every day, and show up for work." Alix shook his finger at Timothy. "Don't flake out or your bunk gets reassigned. No work, no bed. Are we clear?"

Timothy only had to play along for a few months. "Yeah, I can do that."

"Good boy." Alix loved the sound of submission.

"So, do I have to do a new plan and pledge thing with you or did Mary just send hers over?"

Alix winced. "Tim, you're in Old Town now. Put on your big boy pants will ya?" Just then a shuttle pulled up out front of the building and sounded its horn. Alix took a clipboard off the wall and thrust it into Timothy's hands. "That shuttle will take you to the plant where you'll spend the day, 'training'." Alix mocked Timothy with air quotes. "You need to sign in and out every day – don't forget!" Timothy quickly signed the clipboard. "And one last thing, don't work too hard. It makes everyone look bad." The courier blasted its horn again and swarms of men began to board. "You better get a move on if you want a seat."

After a crowded fifteen minute ride downtown, Timothy found himself migrating with the flock through the back entrance of Imperial Seven Foundry. Nothing about the cold, cement floored building enticed leisure. Its bare-bones design screamed, "Work!"

Like bidding at auction, the foreman pointed and whistled at various muscular specimens in the line as they paraded through. Those singled out scrambled quickly behind the foreman and waited for their assignment, adorned with expressions of victory. Such glee to perform manual labor puzzled Timothy. Surely there are more opportunities. After a few minutes, the talent pool dwindled to the point where Timothy found himself in the minority of unselected tools. An unexpected pang of desperation shot adrenaline though his veins as he sized up his remaining competition. The other unselected men didn't look that bad to him. In fact, they looked stronger and better equipped for the job which worried him. He needed to work if he was to satisfy the conditions of his release. A final long whistle came from the head shop steward prompting all of the remaining men to halt their march. An anticipatory silence fell over the large open room. A moment later, a gravelly voice announced, "That's it for today boys." Moans and curses erupted from the rejects. In an instant, Timothy understood their desire to perform manual labor. He would do anything they asked, he just wanted to work.

"Hey!" A shout came from Timothy's own mouth, but he didn't recall initiating it. The other grumblings stopped momentarily and all eyes turned to Timothy. "I can do anything you need. I can load, carry, and operate any of this equipment." Timothy pleaded with the foreman but he shook his head. Timothy continued in desperation, "I can sweep, mop, whatever."

The others began cussing at Timothy and telling him they deserved work before him, but he ignored them and never took his pleading gaze off the foreman. His heart lifted when the foreman stepped toward him and began to speak. "You know what you can do for me? Get the hell out of my shop! I told you, we're full today."

"But I-"

"There is no more work. What part of that don't you understand?" The foreman whistled and rounded up the selected crew. Timothy and the other rejects walked solemnly back out to the shuttle.

Chapter 27

*F*or a month straight, it was the same routine: Wake up, microwave a three-day-old bagel in a damp napkin, get clean, hop aboard the shuttle, get rejected by the foreman, then return to Urban First for a verbal slaying by Alix.

"What are you, some kind of moron?" Alix made a practice of 'encouraging' the boomerangs when they landed back each morning. Today he fixated on Timothy, who got the brunt of his uplifting sermon. "What could you have possibly done to make them send you back every day for the past month? Are you stupid, lazy or both?" Alix's own words seemed to work him into frenzy. "You think all this is free?" Spit flew off each word. "If you don't work, neither of us gets paid! You gotta try harder Tim!"

As Alix berated him, Timothy maintained his composure, doing his best to exercise restraint. He couldn't lose control, not this time. "Alix, I offered to do anything they needed. I even offered to clean toilets."

"Clean toilets, are you kidding me?" Alix was suddenly in the throes of a full blown mantrum. "I'm not running a maid service here!"

"I was just trying to-"

"You know what your problem is? You think you're smarter than everyone else." With chest puffed out, Alix slithered goadingly beyond the border of Timothy's personal space. "You probably think you're smarter than me too, huh?"

"No." He said in a husky tone, trying to counter his escalating pulse with deep breaths.

Alix didn't back off; he could smell blood in the water. "I read up on you, Harvard boy." Alix's gaze traced the sweat beads meandering down Timothy's brow. "Daddy got you into law school. Money talks, huh? Without it you didn't stand any more chance than the rest of us slobs."

"That's not true." Timothy's voice quivered. "My LSAT scores were in the top ten-percent. I got in on my own merit."

"Your own merit? How many thousands of dollars did daddy spend on exam prep classes?" Alix stared at Timothy intently, and then an arrogant smile broke out. "Classes, what am I thinking? A rich brat like you had a private tutor didn't you?"

Timothy broke eye contact with Alix and looked at the ground. "Doesn't make a difference."

"Sure it does." Alix scoffed. "Proof is in the pudding. Look at you; you can't even get a job cleaning toilets." Alix laughed and looked to the other rejects to affirm his assessment of Timothy. "Where's your daddy now?"

A surge of hot, unrefined rage boiled in the depths of Timothy's soul causing his vision to bend and distort. His breaths deepened and slowed. A strand of saliva escaped the corner of his mouth but Timothy didn't dare wipe. He didn't trust moving any muscles in this state. His stillness only enhanced Alix's provocation, and Timothy found himself on the receiving end of an obnoxious shove. As Timothy's fists instinctively coiled up, he heard a familiar voice; an unexpected voice that cooled his rage instantly.

"Am I interrupting something?" It was his public defender, Marcus Gemp. As usual, he was dressed to the nines and holding a twenty-five hundred dollar leather attaché case. He and Alix had a long history. Gemp's glaring eyes shriveled Alix down to the hurt little boy he was.

Alix pointed at the wall clock nervously and stammered. "You're a little early ain't you? I wasn't expecting you for another two months."

"I can meet with my client the hard way, or the easy way. You choose." Marcus made a grand wave toward Timothy. "Few things disqualify a flop house from credits faster than obstructing their resident's rights."

Alix glared back at Timothy. "He's all yours."

Gemp propped open the door and motioned for Timothy to follow him outside. "Not exactly the Ritz, huh?" Timothy exited without responding. Gemp led him toward a luxury sedan parked at the curb.

Once outside, Timothy wiped his face on his shirt and shook off his agitation as quickly as possible. He didn't want Gemp's assessment of him to deteriorate any further. "So, why are you here? The mold cleared up, and they want me back?"

"No, actually it's worse than expected. Well, either worse or simply more interested parties involved now. In any case, your circumstances have changed." Gemp pulled a file from his case and removed a pen from his breast pocket. "Evaluation will be today."

"Early?"

"Yes." Gemp nodded as he skimmed the paper in hand. "Have you had any fights since coming to Urban First?"

"No."

Gemp looked up at him square. "Listen Tim, I'll be verifying all this with UF records when we're done here. So, I'll ask again, and think real hard, have you had any fights since you got here?"

"No, none, I swear!" Timothy replied.

Gemp broke his gaze from Timothy and went back to the list. "Have you received any disciplinary action?"

Timothy thought about it for a moment. "Alix yelled at me a few times about being passed over at the foundry, but that's it."

Gemp shook his head. "Doesn't count. Have you ingested any drugs or alcohol since arriving?"

"No. They take a urine sample every week, you can check."

"I will." Gemp replied clinically. "Have you missed any vocational training days?"

Timothy's eyebrows shot up. "Yeah, pretty much all of them."

Gemp looked up stunned. "You're not going to the foundry?"

"I go every day, but they don't pick me."

"Then you have not missed any vocational training."

"But I haven't learned how to do any of the. . . ya know, metal stuff."

"It's still experience." Gemp continued on. "Any illnesses?"

"Nope."

Gemp scribbled some notes on the bottom of the paper then passed it along with the pen across to Timothy. "Sign your full legal name on the 'X' please." Timothy read the words, 'Probation Release' at the top then signed the bottom line and handed it back. "Stay put for a moment, I'll be back." Gemp grabbed his case and re-entered Urban First.

While waiting outside, Timothy looked up at the sky and studied the clouds. Today there was crispness to the wind as it ushered the grey scuffed clouds along; tipping the odds in favor of a rain shower later that night. Timothy contemplated the accuracy of Alix's accusations. The guy was a creep, but if there was one thing he knew, it was the nature of people like Timothy. Timothy wondered if he wasn't as smart as he had been led to believe by his parents. Surely he wouldn't have gotten ensnared in gambling if he were smart. Smart people make money via legitimate means. He wouldn't be lamenting his role in Stephen's death if he were intelligent. Intelligent people are admired by their kid brothers and provide inspiration. As the clouds grew darker, Timothy came to the only conclusion that made sense: he was a fraud. He was a lame contender without the hand of his father guiding him at every step. His father recognized his true nature long ago. Anyone beyond those Urban First doors could attain high test scores with months of one-on-one tutoring and the material pressures of life removed. Even with those advantages, he came up a loser. Timothy figured that his father held on to hope that he would grow out of his ordinariness. Stephen's death dashed those hopes. You can't salvage something from nothing.

Gemp came back outside, putting on his sunglasses as he approached Timothy. "Congratulations!" He announced gleefully. "You are a free man Mr. Clement." Gemp shook Timothy's hand energetically.

"Just like that?" Timothy's stomach fluttered nervously.

Gemp's eyebrows twisted in bewilderment. "Yeah, just like that. It's a new start for you Tim. A new life."

A cold uneasiness came over Timothy as Gemp retrieved his car keys from his pocket. "So, what do I have to do now?"

"Whatever you want. Just don't get in any trouble while you are doing it." Gemp could see Timothy's gears spinning. "Don't worry, you have a care package of sorts. Get in the car and I'll go over it all with you."

After taking one more look at Urban First, Timothy got in the car and could not wait to get out of Old Town. Gemp's immaculate car was beyond luxurious. The sweet scent of soft leather lingered in the cabin, reminding Timothy of his father. "Nice car."

Gemp smiled and nodded in agreement, "She's my baby."

Timothy glanced across and took note of Gemp's perfectly manicured fingers, then looked down at his dirty nails. "Must be nice." The ignition turned over without hesitation, and in moments they were gliding down the gritty street. "What now? What care package were you talking about?"

"You are going to be on your own now. Sure you'll need to check in with your P.O. at regular intervals, but for all intents and purposes, you are a free citizen now." Gemp waited for an enthusiastic smile from Timothy, but it never came. "I've arranged temporary housing for you, along with part-time employment. The rent is very reasonable so the part-time hours should provide an adequate stream of income."

Timothy was only half listening. He was distracted by the direction they were traveling. They were halfway over the central bridge heading deeper into the heart of Old Town. "Where exactly will I be staying?"

"Just about a block past the bridge exit."

Timothy looked down to the end of the blemished bridge in front of them, but could see nothing but old decrepit structures worn by years of use and misuse. "Reasonable rent, I can see why."

Unexpectedly, Gemp slammed on the brakes and swerved to avoid hitting a homeless man. "What the-" Gemp gasped. Before the two could catch their breath, the homeless man was squirting diluted window cleaner all over the windshield and wiping it furiously with old newspaper. The soggy pulp broke into pale blue globs and smeared all over. Gemp laid on the horn and cracked his window just enough to be heard. "No, no, no, stop! I just had this car washed!"

The man smiled broadly, proudly displaying his decayed teeth and said, "Five dollar."

"What are you-"

"Five dollar man!" The man repeated, this time more insistently.

Gemp began to reach for his wallet then Timothy unexpected shouted angrily at the man from across the cabin. "You ruined his car idiot! What the hell is wrong with you?"

Timothy's erratic temper startled Gemp. "It's no big deal." He continued to retrieve his wallet as Timothy's face grew bright crimson. "Relax." Gemp cooed, but Timothy seemed too enraged to hear. Gemp heard the metallic clink of Timothy's belt buckle releasing and instinctively punched the gas, and squealed away. Timothy looked back at the vagrant who had angrily chucked his bottle of window cleaner at them, but it fell short. "Are you crazy? Do you want to spend your first day as a free man getting arrested?"

"That parasite back there is the one who should be arrested. It's people like him that give this city its reputation." Timothy snarled.

Gemp's jittery hand reached for the automatic window button and the whistling wind quieted. "He's just trying to get by. This town can be brutal."

"Right, a rich guy like you would know." Timothy felt foolish for the outburst. Losing control in front of Gemp, his only ally, was disappointing enough, but now he was denigrating the man's compassion; the same compassion that provided the luxurious car ride. Regretfully, he watched the wet, clumpy newspaper pulp flutter on the windshield. "Run the wipers a few cycles and it should clear up." Timothy suggested, but Gemp just continued on, stone faced and silent.

Not much further past the bridge outlet they came upon a modest church surrounded on all sides by a tall chain-link fence, the top of which was fitted with coiled razor wire. Gemp circled around the property to the back then honked his horn impatiently, waiting nervously for someone to open the gates. "Might not look like much, but it's as good a place as any for a fresh start." Gemp honked again then checked the parameter of his car suspiciously.

"A church?" Timothy asked unenthusiastically, to which Gemp nodded affirmatively. "Isn't there supposed to be separation of church and state?"

Before Gemp could correct Timothy, a stocky man with muscular forearms hobbled toward the gate with the aid of a cane and waved. Gemp rolled down his window and shouted, "Brother Jude, it's been too long!"

"Likewise Marcus!" The man shouted back as he wrestled with the padlock.

Gemp turned to Timothy. "Brother Jude is a good friend of mine from a previous life. He has agreed to help you get back on your feet." The gate in front of them swung open. "This is a favor from me, not the state." They pulled forward and searched the parking lot for a spot closest to the church entrance.

"I don't really believe in all this stuff." Timothy mumbled.

Gemp looked at Timothy. "You don't believe in helping out those in need?"

"No, that's not what I meant." Timothy stammered. "I appreciate you helping me out. I just don't think it would be right for me to stay at a church since I'm an atheist."

The two sat silently waiting for Jude to lock the gate and make his way back to them. "Don't ask about the cane." Gemp advised.

Once Jude reached the car, Timothy's door swung wide open. Brother Jude greeted Timothy with a bright, enthusiastic smile, bellowing, "Welcome Tim! Marcus speaks very highly of you."

Timothy wasn't sure what to do at first. It had been a long time since anyone had seemed this glad to see him. He awkwardly slithered out of the car and extended his hand. "Hi, I'm Tim."

"Of course you are!" Jude let out a hearty laugh. "I'm Jude, but most folks call me Brother Jude. Welcome to Saint Anthony!"

"Saint Anthony?"

"Last time I checked." Jude amused himself further.

Timothy reached down into the top of his shirt and fished out his St. Anthony necklace. "My mom gave me this before she died."

Jude got serious and leaned in for a good look. "Very nice. She must have cared for you deeply."

The intimate exchange made Timothy uncomfortable, but he wasn't sure why. Maybe it was the setting, the undeserved hospitality, or being so far downtown, but his skin was crawling. He put the necklace back in his shirt and turned to Gemp. "So the job is here?"

Gemp ignored Timothy and made his way around the car to embrace Jude. "You look good brother!" Gemp complimented the weathered man.

"Of course, what did you expect? I was always the better looking one." Jude jested.

"You might have turned a few more heads, but in the end I got her." Gemp pointed at his luxury sedan.

Jude squinted. "What happened to the windshield?"

"Ah, nothing." Gemp played it down and changed the subject before Jude could inquire further. "I called over to the bakery yesterday to get Tim on staff."

"Oh yeah, how is old man Sutton?"

"I didn't actually speak with him. Apparently, he's retiring this month. I talked to his son who is going to take over. I never even knew he had a son."

Jude shook his head in disbelief. "Retiring. Wow, I never thought I'd see the day. Man, we are getting old."

Gemp scoffed. "*YOU* are getting old, not me."

With a chuckle, Jude pointed out, "You got about four inches of forehead on me buddy, and a pair of specs."

"They're just for driving." Gemp countered, and then removed his glasses. "Even with them off I can still see all the lines in your face."

Timothy had little interest in their reunion. "Do you work at the bakery too? Will I be working with you?" He asked Jude.

Jude raised his eyebrows in surprise. "Me? No, I haven't worked at the bakery in years." He looked over to Gemp nostalgically. "Marcus and I used to throw dough back in the day. They used to call us the 'Dough boys'"

"Some more than others." Gemp pointed to Jude's belly and smiled.

Jude sucked in his gut. "All muscle."

Gemp turned to Timothy and elaborated. "Mr. Sutton, the owner of the bakery, is a good man. He kept the two of us out of trouble in our younger years." Gemp smiled at Jude. "Most of the time."

"Younger years. . . listen to you." Jude smirked.

Gemp continued, "It will be a good place to get your head straight and earn an honest wage in the process."

Jude pointed to Timothy's bag in the car. "Grab your gear. You and I will head over to the bakery as soon as I finish unclogging a drain. In the meantime I'll show you where you'll be staying."

Timothy hadn't set foot in a church since his mother's death. He didn't want to enter one, much less spend the night. The thought completely freak him out. "I'm really staying here?" Timothy asked hesitantly before moving to retrieve his bag from the backseat of Gemp's car.

"Just until you get back on your feet." Jude stated prudently, as if reminding himself of his limited resources.

Timothy took advantage of the out. "I could find somewhere else to stay if space is a problem."

"No, it's fine." Gemp interjected. "There's plenty of room, right Jude?" Jude gave a skeptical nod.

"You should give my spot to someone who is like, more into God and stuff." Timothy slung his bag over his shoulder. "I can just lay low at the Y for a while."

Gemp looked up at the dark clouds above. "Why don't you stay the night and decide in the morning."

"I'll think about it."

"Excellent." Gemp was pacified, but the reality was that Timothy would sooner sleep outside in the rain than step foot into St. Anthony church.

Timothy sat down against the entrance wall. "I'll be waiting here when you are ready to leave for the bakery."

Gemp got back in his car and rolled down the window. Jude approached and said, "It was great to see you Marcus. I'll make sure Tim gets to where he needs to be."

Gemp glanced over to the church and pointed. "Jobs and bunks are important, but don't forget to share the good news with him."

"When the time is right. I've got a backed-up drain to deal with right now." Jude slapped the roof of the car.

"Don't put it off."

Jude nodded and said, "The Holy Spirit will fill his ears and his heart when the Lord sees fit. It's not always on our timetable."

"Well Brother Jude, the Holy Spirit is telling me, to tell you, to not put it off. There is no time for shyness."

Jude shook his head and smiled. "I'm surprised the Holy Spirit is so inpatient. Don't worry, Tim is in good hands."

"I know."

Jude turned and called out, "Hey Tim, mind giving me a hand with the gate?" Timothy sprang into action, taking the keys from Jude and releasing the gate.

As Gemp cruised past, he stuck his hand out the window and waved, saying, "Good luck Tim. God bless."

Tim gave an awkward nod and muttered, "Uh, thanks for. . . everything."

Timothy and Jude stood by and watched Gemp's car disappear down the road. "You know how I feel right about now?" Jude asked solemnly.

Timothy wasn't sure how to answer. "Not really. I know you guys were tight and all-"

"I feel like I don't want to be fixing some clogged drain when we could be enjoying the smell of fresh baked bread!" Jude interjected with playful indignation. "That lousy drain will just have to wait until I get back to mock me." Jude prodded Timothy to the outside of the gate and fastened the lock.

"What are we doing?"

Jude scrounged around in his pocket, and after a bit of squirming, produced a handful of coins which he passed to Timothy. "Here, take these; should be more than enough to get us across the bridge and back."

Only then did Timothy realize they would be taking the bus through Old Town. It was even less appealing after just riding in Gemp's car, but as Timothy studied Jude's bow-legged hobble, it was clear there was no alternative. "Where do we catch it?"

Jude led Timothy across the street and down a block to a row of garment factories at the far end. "We'll pick it up just around that corner." As he pointed to the end, the roar of the bus sounded out of view. "C'mon, let's move!" Jude called out, forgetting it was his limp dictating their pace.

"I got it." Timothy said as he half-jogged ahead and around the corner, waving at the driver to buy some time. As he reached the bench, the bus's hydraulics hissed then the doors sprung open.

Timothy looked back to find Jude hot on his heels, breathing hard. It surprised Timothy that he caught up so easily. Jude bolted past Timothy and up the bus steps. "The young man behind me has the fare." Jude announced as he slid past the driver and took a nearby open seat.

Timothy paid the driver both fares and sat down across the aisle from Jude. "How far over past the bridge is it?" he asked.

Mildly irritated, Jude told Timothy, "Just sit tight. We've got a ways to go." Jude sucked in a deep breath trying to slow his breathing. "Nobody has any patience these days."

Not wanting to appear impatient, Timothy sat silent for the next twenty minutes. The ride gave him time to reflect on how Old Town had become his temporary residence. Nothing was easy, not even gaining his freedom. He knew he'd have to claw his way back to any semblance of a normal life. It was simply the way his life had become. The rhythm of the bus ride induced day-dreams of working hard and being fairly compensated for it. Timothy fantasized about saving up money and eventually getting his own place. He felt a smile beckon his lips but was reluctant to get too excited. The unwelcome specter of doubt had undermined his aspirations more times than not. Its caustic sarcasm echoing just loud enough to remind him that his opportunities had been spent, and he couldn't afford to dream anymore. The weight of failure was exhausting. He craved a few pleasurable thoughts without the fatigue of disappointment eating away at his spirit, but it was never allowed. Timothy rested his numb head against the window and tried to fall asleep.

Timothy's eyes had been shut but a minute when he felt Jude's insistent tapping on his shoulder. "Tim, get up! This is our stop."

The two exited the bus, and were immediately surrounded by the rich scent of fresh baked bread. It was a far departure from the usual foul stenches lingering about Old Town. "Do you smell that?" Timothy asked.

Jude inhaled deeply and smiled. "Heavenly! Come on, it's even better inside." Jude pointed to a nearby storefront adorned with the word, 'Bakery' stenciled on its window. Although the years had cracked and splintered its veneer, the tall authoritative double-doors somehow retained the bakery's dignity, even though the neighborhood had lost its own.

"This place looks pretty old." Timothy remarked as he approached the large double-doors.

Jude held one open and motioned for Timothy to enter first. "There's a lot of history in there. Many young lives have been changed because of this place."

As Timothy entered, his heart sped slightly and his chest lightened. Jude's words replayed in his head, "lives have been changed. . ." Inside, he found black and white floor tiles complimenting an inviting glass display case which ran the full length of the room. The picture-perfect breads and pastries opposite the glass beckoned Timothy toward the counter for a better look. His eyes devoured the many treats, each appearing more delectable than the last. "Look at all these!" he marveled.

Watching Timothy's childlike delight brought a smile to Jude's face. "Pretty amazing, huh? There was a time when I could make almost all of these."

"Really?"

"Mr. Sutton taught us how to bake all kinds of stuff." Jude's forehead crinkled as the memories of came back to him. "I guess, 'taught' is the wrong word. It was more like, he put us to work, and we figured it out along the way."

The serene intermingling of sweet aromas and nostalgia hovered about Timothy, summoning aspirations of a fresh start in life. He put his hand up against the display case. "Do you think I could learn how to make these?"

Before Jude could answer, the door to the back room swung open abruptly. "No, no, no, you can't be up here! Get your hands off the case." A muscular young man with a square jaw and shaven head barked. "This is for customers only! You enter around back."

"I think there has been a misunderstanding." Jude began. "You see, my name is Jude and-"

"I know who you are. Your friend Marcus called me a dozen times!" The man's eyes kept darting out the window as if he were expecting someone. "I'll tell you what I told him; just because my pop let this place be a haven for degenerates doesn't mean I will. If you want some three-day-olds, come around back and I'll give you a decent price." The man pointed at the door. "You need to leave; I can't have customers seeing people like you in here."

Jude stood dumbfounded. "People like us?"

The man nodded haughtily. "Yeah, people exactly like you, who take advantage of foolish old men."

"Your father is far from foolish."

The man looked at Jude with disgust. "This is no longer a charity. You want something, you pay for it."

"I don't want a handout." Timothy interjected. "I'm willing to work hard for honest pay."

The man turned his attention to Timothy. "What makes you think I have any openings? The man scoffed. "And if I did, why would I hire an ex-con who is probably going to rip me off?"

Jude's face was flushed as he tried to reason with the man. "Everyone needs a second chance at some point. Do you have any idea how many men your father's kindness and compassion has helped?"

"All I know," The man leaned closer towards Jude's face, "Is that after cutting all the dead weight my father put up with, I'm projecting the most profitable year in the history of this bakery."

"What does your father have to say about this new direction?"

"I'm the boss now. He doesn't need to be troubled with the day-to-day details." The man held open the door and shooed the duo out like flies. "We can't afford to hire substandard labor anymore. We've got a real business to run here."

Jude was incensed. "You are a disgrace to the legacy of your father's service to the Lord."

"Well, the Lord doesn't know much about turning a decent profit, now does he?" The man sneered. "This manager plans to retire far better off than the old fool rotting in West County."

"That so called fool, won't be laughing when I tell him exactly what is going on here." Jude scolded.

"Suit yourself. Just make sure he doesn't drool on those fancy shoes." The man sneered then went inside.

Jude looked down at the modest, tattered shoes on his feet. "What does that mean?" His face reddened.

"So, what now?" Timothy asked.

Jude pursed his lips and thought for a moment. "I have to see old man Sutton. He has to know about this. How much change you got left?"

Timothy dumped the remaining coins into Jude's cupped hands. Jude fingered through the pile of change. "I think I should visit Mr. Sutton alone. You go back to St. Anthony and I'll be there later." Just then the hiss of hydraulic brakes echoed from around the corner. Jude held his hand to his heart and looked skyward at the dark clouds above. "Good timing, that's mine." Jude took off, hobbling full speed.

As Jude disappeared around the corner, it dawned on Timothy that he hadn't left him any bus fare. Timothy dashed after Jude calling out his name, but just as he reached the corner the bus rolled by, leaving Timothy standing alone in a gust of exhaust. "For crying out loud!" Timothy yelled out.

Looking around the intersection, Timothy tried to get his bearings. He looked up to see where the sun was for reference, but the sky was dense with storm clouds that hid any spec of blue. He cinched his jacket tighter to fend off the creeping cold and then wandered off in the direction he thought they had come from. He knew he'd have to hustle if he was going to get back before the rain.

For six blocks he walked head down against the wind, through gritty streets, crossing broken sidewalks and trying to steer clear of the obstacles in his path. Some were material hazards, but most were meandering youths dealing out cons or worse troublesome diversions. Timothy didn't take interest in any of it. The dank air's aquatic aftertaste burgeoned in Timothy's nostrils, signaling the bridge was near. A reserved sense of pride came over him as he recognized his innate survival skills. Maybe he did have the aptitude to start over after all.

A thunderous rolling crackle echoed across the sky, and heavy droplets began pelting Timothy. There was no subtlety to the brute storm. It barged in and raged untamed, whipping water droplets horizontally with its freezing wind. Timothy tried to travel under the scare awnings, but there was no place to hide. In a few short minutes, Timothy's cotton jacket, clothes and shoes were completely saturated with water. With vapor billowing from his lips, he sloshed ahead fighting to lift his head up long enough to see what was ahead. He held his arm up to his forehead and squinted. There it was, it couldn't have been more than two blocks ahead of him – the bridge.

The rain hammered down more and more with each step. Timothy jogged steadily toward the waterfront hoping the storm would ease up. Between the loud booms of thunder, streaks of lightning erupted behind the dark gray clouds, momentarily illuminating his path to the bridge. By his own estimations he couldn't be more than two miles from St. Anthony. He imagined Jude was faring well on his own, basking in the comfort of public transportation.

Before long, the bridge entrance was before him. Timothy darted between the few vehicles on the road toward the far shoulder. The distance between thunder claps continued to narrow, while the intensity of electric discharge in the clouds amplified. Timothy entered the chain-link shoulder enclosure, and despite its appearance as shelter, the waterfront wind cut through his clothing, mercilessly stinging his skin. "Just need to keep moving." He told himself as he pressed onward against the elements.

It was slow going. With no more structures to dampen the wind's fury, just managing to stay upright on the wet asphalt was a challenge. Timothy clawed along the chain-link enclosure, struggling with each step. He looked forward at the cityscape beyond the far end of the bridge. The pale glow of downtown street lamps and fluorescent signs were faintly visible through the heavy rain and mist. The constant flow of midday traffic rushed past Timothy, each sloshing vehicle drowning out the storm for just a spit second.

After a few minutes, Timothy established a steady rhythm of steps and fence grabs while focusing on each visible exhale. He knew he'd reach his destination if he just continued forward and didn't stop, no matter how hard the storm pounded him. As was often the case when performing repetitive tasks, his mind drifted to thoughts of his mother. He was transported to the day he and Stephen were in the pool, and she called out for him from her second story window. It bothered him that this was always the origin of his mind's recollection of her; the uneasy calling out of his name. Her frail voice poorly masking her distress, echoing in his head as clear as the day she died. Over the years the features of her face, the feel of her touch, the sound of her laughter, had faded and grown fuzzy, but not her calling out to him. With no photographs, no home movies, not even reminiscing conversation with those who also loved her, his memory of her was more of a feeling than anything. Feelings of love and regret interposed with her haunting voice calling down from the second story window.

The sharp blast of a semi-truck horn warding off a compact car drifting into its lane jolted Timothy and brought his eyes upward again. With his heart pounding, he could faintly make out an odd rectangular obstruction directly in his path about twenty paces ahead. It was maybe four feet high and six feet wide, surely not more than three feet deep. A constant stream of torrential rain water splashed off the top of the object and down onto the pathway. Timothy figured it might be a service tunnel entrance. A bridge so large was sure to need maintenance, but he didn't remember seeing any others. As he came closer, he noticed the object's impromptu construction; a hazardous monument of discarded aluminum siding bound together with duct tape and rusted, repurposed wire hangers. It was clearly not a civic implement.

There was no way to simply step around the structure without risking injury. Metal shards poked out from every seam and corner joint. Timothy envisioned laying his soaked jacket down along the top edge and scaling over, but he wasn't sure the structure could support his weight. The last thing he wanted was to sink down into that sharp mess. The small space separating the road from the monument was his best bet, although it was choked with overgrown brush. He pulled his soaked jacket collar up tight against his neck and proceed to fight through the short stretch of untamed landscaping. The storm gave no indications of easing up, thunder roaring again as he began to push through the green jumble of leaves and branches. A foul waft of pungent filth cut through the clean storm air and assailed Timothy's nose as his first sodden steps sunk into the soft muddy ground. Timothy took one last long look at the ragged structure before proceeding. He wanted to make absolutely sure there was no better alternative before drudging further, but he knew there wasn't.

Two steps later, Timothy heard the distinct clop of a cowbell above the storm and froze in his tracks. He waited for it to repeat, but it didn't sound again. He chocked it up to his imagination and continued on. Right away he heard the bell again and realized his ankle was snagged in what looked like fishing line. He cursed whatever bridge fisherman had carelessly discarded the tangled mess, thinking that ingesting any meat pulled from the polluted waterway below was punishment enough.

"I see you!" A gravelly male voice cried out above the rain. Timothy's view was obstructed by the greenery and he could not see who was there. "I see you good!" The voice repeated angrily.

The disorienting greenery prevented Timothy from seeing who was taunting him. The branches around him rustled and sloshed, filling Timothy with anxiety. "Look, I don't want any–" The hard sting of a metal rod landing squarely between his shoulder blades sent Timothy face down into the cushioned arms of soaked foliage. He cried out in pain and arched his back tight, then frantically thrust his arms downward through the greenery into the mud trying to prop himself up. His palms gave way in the slippery mud he dropped down again, his forehead scraping against some rough branches along the way. He desperately scurried about in the low brush, trying to avoid another blow from the rod. He seemed unable to get any traction, and then remembered his ankle tangled in the line. The metal rod whizzed past his head and struck the bush directly above him sending leaves and debris down onto his face. "What's wrong with you!" Timothy cried out.

"You come to rip me off!" The voice shouted indignantly.

"You're insane!" Timothy shouted back, trying to formulate a plan to save his head from being split open. He planted his tangled foot in the mud and pushed off an awkward kick with his free leg, while leaning back on his elbows. He felt lame and powerless, but his jutting foot made contact with something fleshy and the taunting voice cried out in pain. Timothy scrambled to get to his feet. If he couldn't travel far entwined in the fishing line, at least he'd have a chance going head-to-head with his attacker. He got to his feet just in time to see the metal rod swinging down toward his head with great velocity. Timothy instinctively shot up his hands above his head to block the blow. The metal rod slammed hard between the middle and index finger on his left hand, causing an internal snap that sent a reverberating wave of pain down his arm. His right hand clasped tightly onto the cold slippery rod while he howled from the pain. Timothy looked forward through the rain at his shadowy attacker and was astonished. "You?"

There, not three feet away, stood the homeless vagrant who had decimated Gemp's windshield. He didn't seem to recognize Timothy at all; just stood there scowling and tugging on the rod. "Mine!" He growled at the resistance.

Timothy's right hand slid down the remaining length of rod and met a thick metal clump. "A golf club? You're coming at me with a golf club?" The severity of the vagrant's choice of weapon infuriated Timothy. "You could have killed me!" He shouted over the storm as the wind blew wildly through the overgrown brush surrounding him.

"Let Go!" The man gruffly commanded, yanking again unsuccessfully.

The pulsating pain in Timothy's left hand only fueled his rage. He tersely wrenched the club from the man's weathered hands with a hard twist and held it up aggressively to the man's stone face. "You know what's wrong with Old Town? Scum like you!" The man recoiled only to find his back up against rusty aluminum siding. "Not so tough now, huh?" Timothy banged the club against the metal structure.

"I ain't 'fraida you!" The man said nonchalantly, looking Timothy up and down with a defiant curled upper lip. He then murmured, "You're scum too." barely audible over the wind and rain.

"What did you say?"

The man gave Timothy a rotten smile. "I know scum when I see it, man."

His old nemesis, rage, stirred within Timothy's core. Only, instead of trying to suppress the beast, he embraced it absolutely. The stifled reservoir of hatred and frustration could no longer be contained. "You dirty, disgusting pig." Timothy snarled sloppily. "Everyone knows this town was once great, but parasites like you ruined everything!" Timothy pointed to the hazy lights of Old Town a quarter mile past the end of the bridge. "Nobody wants you around!"

Obviously a seasoned veteran of abuse, the homeless man was unmoved by the insults. "You don't like my town, then get out."

"Y-Your town?" Timothy stammered disbelievingly. The man nodded confidently. "This town was poisoned by losers like you begging for handouts. You've got nothing to offer."

"I got a job. Folks love me to wash windows."

The storm flailed wildly, mirroring Timothy's outbursts. "You are a worthless, good-for-nothing, loser that nobody wants around!" Timothy screamed into the rain. "Don't you get it, you are nothing!"

"You know an awful lot about me." The man shouted back unafraid, then slowly looked Timothy over. "You gonna beat me now or later?"

"Shut up!"

The man burst out laughing, turning his head upwards into the pouring rain for a moment then back down. "Welcome to Old Town!" He cried out hysterically.

"I said shut up!" Timothy shouted.

Timothy's anger only made the man laugh harder. "Oh, we've met before."

Timothy let out a guttural scream so loud, and so uncontrolled, that it left his throat instantly stinging and tender. "You don't know me!" He yelled hoarsely. "I hate you and I hate this dump!"

"A dump?" The man shouted quizzically. "I suppose you're right." He rubbed the rainwater into his face to cleanse himself for a moment then pointed his dirt-crusted finger directly at Timothy. "There is where all things thrown away come to rest."

It was all Timothy could take. He raised the golf club overhead with both hands and prepared to strike. Not even the searing pain from his fractured finger bones could slow him. He had fully submitted to his rage and there was no turning back. He tightened up his body and swung down with all of his might, and that's when it happened. . . .

Chapter 28

The rushing sensation of sinking down deeper and deeper into the cold water peeled away Timothy's rage like a flimsy glove. His eyes watched the blurry rippling water above him grow darker as he descended further away from the surface. Something was very wrong.

Timothy began kicking and treading against the downward current, fighting to get back up, but his efforts seemed to only drag him down further. He flailed around in the water for an extended amount of time before calm washed over him. He stopped struggling and fell still, gazing up at the pinhole of surface light above him and accepting somberly that it was too far, and he was much too deep. He couldn't believe this was how it was all going to end. Slowly, ever so slowly, he anticipated his demise with a heavy heart. He thought to himself how little he had accomplished. He despised himself for ever embracing the notion that he could get a fresh start in life. Here, at the bottom of this dark mass of water, is where he deserved to be.

As he stared up at the sliver of surface light, he noticed it changing shade and intensity. Absorbed in his self-loathing, he failed to notice the buoyant upward journey his body had begun to take. Hesitating for just a small instance, he again began to paddle and kick with all of his strength. Each thrust, each stroke, filled him with optimism and propelled him toward the surface. His rate of ascension doubled with each stride until he broke through the surface, torpedoing high out of the water with a loud gasp.

Timothy sucked in a full breath of air as he arced into the air. The oxygen flowed perfectly into his lungs, giving him an incredible sensation of strength. He was fully recuperated from his ordeal before splashing back down in the water. It was remarkable how full of energy and alert he was. Timothy speculated his body had gone into shock and was preserving itself. He didn't really care; it was the best he had felt in years.

Splashing around, he noticed a light, cloudy mist dancing on the surface of the water that dispersed with each splash. Timothy looked up and noticed that the rain had stopped and the sky was clear. Surprisingly, the air felt and tasted almost tropical. Then, in an instant, it rushed back to him; the bridge, the transient and the golf club. A frightful streak shot up his chest, and he began looking around anxiously for the remnants of whatever horrible accident he had been involved in.

"Hello!" he called out nervously while flapping his hands, but there was no answer. As he waved, he caught sight of a grotesque, yet somewhat beautiful injury. Inflamed pink and white bursts of scar tissue ran from his palms to midway up both forearms. The raised, deformed welts sprouted like fern leaves, branching and splintering up along the way. Holding his hands an inch from his face, Timothy studied the curious scars. "What the-"

"I actually think it's kind of pretty." A familiar feminine voice called from behind.

Timothy's heart seized, and he whipped around to see firsthand. "It can't be!" His eyes shot upwards. "You're not real, none of this is real!"

Thirty feet away, the back end of a pristine two-story urban track home towered above him. It was no random building; it was his childhood home, as immaculate as the day it was built. Smiling down from the second story window stood his mother, more beautiful and youthful than he had ever seen. The sight of her smiling down on him dissolved his etched memories of her uncomfortable, sickly expression that had haunted his memories of late. "It's nice here, don't you think?" His mother asked casually.

Timothy made a mental note that what he sensed while surfacing could not possibly have been shock, because it was nothing like what he was currently experiencing. He gazed up at her, soaking in all of her beauty and maternal charm. A luminescent fog surrounded her; bright, yet not at all abrasive to his eyes. He couldn't get over how vibrant and youthful she appeared, smiling down at him lovingly.

Timothy ached to speak with her, but when he opened his mouth nothing came out. He wanted cry out to her, to beg her for forgiveness. It wasn't possible underneath the avalanche of past deeds and poor decisions that weighed him down.

The unexpected, gentle collision with an inflatable lounge chair against the back of his head drew Timothy's gaze away from his mother. Its chlorine infused plastic scent and glossy texture jarred his senses. He was back in his family's pool. As the floating recliner gently spun around in the water, it revealed his slick grinned younger brother Stephen enjoying the relaxing drift. "My chair, I called it!" He announced in a chipper voice.

Timothy flinched, causing his feet to clumsily scrape the bottom of the pool which had previously not been there. He stared into the eyes of his fresh-faced brother radiated with the same soft light as his mother. Stephen was happy and content frolicking in the pool and didn't appear to be aware of the cataloging of regrets going on in Timothy's mind. Intuitively, Timothy's hand extended out toward Stephen but stopped; his whole body was immobilized. Before him, Stephen's carefree expression conceded to a sobering, contemplative gaze that both saddened and frightened Timothy. As their eyes locked, Timothy's paralyzed body raised slowly up out of the water, hovering momentarily until Stephen smiled and splashed water in his face. Timothy's paralysis vanished and he plunged back down into the pool, submerging briefly then bobbing up. He quickly wiped the water from his face, not wanting to lose sight of Stephen. "What is this place?" He blurted out as Stephen pushed off playfully into the surrounding mist.

"I told you, it's my chair. I called it first!" Stephen giggled as he floated out of sight, not seeming to hear the question.

Timothy felt no urge to rush into the mist after him. It was clear that Stephen just wanted to enjoy playing in their family pool like old times. It wasn't fair to burden him for the selfish reason of cleaning his own conscience. Timothy turned back around and discovered both his childhood home and mother had dissipated into the mist. Strangely, he felt more comfortable that way. Isolation was what he knew. The soft glow above began to wane as all periphery details softened and blurred slightly. The pool tiles beneath his feet gave way to a dark aquatic abyss, forcing him to tread once again. He sucked in a deep breath of air and shouted out, "I'm sorry!" His voice flubbed like a flat note wrapped in wool; not seeming to travel any further than his own ears. No ringing in the distance, no echo, just immediate silence. "I'm sorry!" He repeated more urgently, but it was no more effective.

As silence encircled tighter, his heart beat increased. The vacancy was filled with the sound of his pulse throbbing in his ears; its intensity increasing proportional to his climbing heart rate. From behind, a large splash of water washed over his head. As he wiped droplets from his face, he heard Stephen playfully exclaim, "You're not supposed to be here, cotton head!"

Timothy hesitated, and kept his back to Stephen. He tried to understand what it meant. Stephen used to call him lots of names, but 'Cotton head' wasn't familiar. Timothy massaged his weary eyes while kicking to stay afloat. He no longer felt strong and vibrant. A dull pain wormed in his head seeming to cause him to labor harder for each new breath.

"It's going to be all right, he's never stopped loving you." His mother's soothing voice assured him. "He's never stopped loving you." She repeated. He removed his hands from his eyes to find her directly in front of him, looking even more spectacular than she did up in the window. Timothy broke away to look behind him but Stephen was nowhere to be seen. "Timothy." His mother called his attention back to her. "There is something you need to know."

"No mom." Timothy interrupted. "I have to tell you something. I really messed up." Tears flowed from his eyes.

"Shhh. . ." she consoled him, her face glowing brighter.

"I'm sorry. I'm so sorry."

She put her index finger up to his lips. "Listen to me. I need to tell you something son."

"What?" Timothy asked, not knowing what could possibly be more important than his apology.

She looked deep into his eyes. "It's going to hurt." His face radiated confusion upon hearing the words. "A lot." She added.

Chapter 29

 "Clear!" The scrawny EMT shouted for the third time before discharging the paddles. Timothy's chest contracted sharply then went limp. The EMT watched the defibrillator gauges intently but saw no change in the readings. In frustration, he ripped the leads from Timothy's chest and proclaimed, "Abandoning resuscitation." The driver cut the siren.

The second EMT working in the confined space of the fast moving ambulance shot across a disapproving glare, and then began compressions on Timothy's motionless body with his dark, husky hands. "You forget protocol?"

The first EMT looked on cynically. "What's the point? He's gone." Taking Timothy's badly maimed hand in his own and looking at the branching burn pattern he added, "He's cooked. That strike fried his ticker." The EMT dropped Timothy's hand. "You're wasting your time."

"That's not our call."

"I've been doing this a long time. I know when a customer has checked out for good." The EMT shoved his partners clasped hands off Timothy's chest. "Put your giant paws away, it's over."

Reluctantly, the second EMT succumbed to his partner's insistence, and turned his attention to a warped stack of forms, still damp with rainwater. The mundane morning had given way to a hectic afternoon, courtesy of wet asphalt. The grimy streets of Old Town were known to glisten with oily sludge whenever subjected to rain; today was no different. "What is that, seven?"

"I never keep track. Every day is a fresh start for me. If you start keeping score you'll be remembering their names and attending their funerals before you know it."

"That's not so bad." The second EMT replied. "Two out of three go unclaimed. I've been thinking about attending the group service in December."

"You're crazy." The first EMT said, shaking his head. "You're going to get your John Does all mixed up. You'll need to come up with pet names for them all. Who's got time for that?"

The second EMT frowned. "Someone needs to care."

"Like this guy, you can call him, 'Fry Young'. Get it? He's pitching for the Red Sox." he pointed to the bright pink patch of raw skin peeking through a burnt hole on the sole of Timothy's shoe.

"You're heartless."

"No, if I called him, 'Lobster Claws' that would be heartless."

Without warning, Timothy's abdominal muscles clenched and he shot upright with a loud gasp yelling, "Mom!"

"Holy Christ!" the first EMT shuddered.

"I'm sorry!" Timothy cried out then looked around with confusion at his surroundings. "Wha-"

"Lie down; you've been in an accident." The second EMT placed his oversized hand on Timothy's chest and gently guided him back down. Timothy resisted at first, then collapsed onto the gurney and lost consciousness. "Stay with me." The EMT grabbed Timothy's hand and applied sharp pressure to his red finger nails, but Timothy was unresponsive. His chest undulated feebly. "Oxygen." The EMT called out.

The first EMT placed a mask over Timothy's face. "At least we know he's got family."

The second EMT ignored the disingenuous remark and began fitting Timothy's hand with an IV. "Get the monitor back on him."

"Never had that happen before. It's a good thing I shocked him that third time."

"Yeah, you're a real life saver." The second EMT said dismissively. "Try to keep him stable until we get to the hospital, if it's not too much trouble." He then banged on the back of the driver's seat. "Make it hot!" The siren chattered, and then blasted a patterned loop, saving the first EMT from having to rationalize his behavior.

For the next three weeks, Timothy lay unresponsive in an Old Town Community Hospital bed. A deep coma preserved his body, forcing it to heal. Damaged red and white flesh on his palms, where the golf club had conducted the lighting strike, was hardening and taking its permanent lumpy form. The aberrant beauty of branching Lichtenberg scars, diverging up his forearms, offset the appearance of his gruesome palms.

Nearly all of his bodily hair had fallen out days after the accident. Now, a soft patch of silver stubble filled in the surface of his scalp; an unsettling contrast to his previously dark brown locks. His eyebrows and eye lashes however, had yet to return.

Nursing staff came and went at all hours of the day, performed their rudimentary duties with lackluster apathy. Not that it mattered; Timothy would be equally unaffected by tender loving care while in his deep sleep. His slumbering consciousness was completely disconnected from the still, impaired form lying in the long-term bed. He was unaware of the catheter, feeding tube or decubitus ulcer forming on his left shoulder blade. He had no idea that all of his physical, bodily needs were being met by total strangers; the grade of which he'd never stoop to mingle with in the wild. The coma protected him, shelving his superfluous dignity, a healing body's greatest distraction.

Chapter 30

An indifferent blanket of fog awaited the dawn. The rising sun cast impartial shadows of industrious architecture across the dog-eared streets of Old Town. A staccato symphony of rattling diesel engines reverberated while long, shady, west pointing fingers stretched out across the city.

The bitter aroma of dew-slick asphalt clung desperately to the clammy morning air; as if aware its short existence would burn off in a few hours. Pressurized hoses sprayed down storefronts and back alleys in preparation for another grueling round with the haggard, once-great metropolis. Above the urban din, birds chirped, the wind gusted, and the lost residents of Old Town persevered. It was Jude's favorite time of day, what he referred to as, "Wind corralling time." He looked out over the city from his third story bell tower window and prayed it would be the last time he would enjoy the view for a while.

Fourteen hours earlier Jude petitioned for Timothy to be discharged into his care for rehabilitation. It was a big responsibility to take on, and normally he wouldn't have entertained the idea, but there was no one else, including Gemp, who would agree to it. Releasing Timothy into Old Town's subhuman adult care was not an option for Jude. The accident weighed on his conscience, strengthening his resolve to guide Timothy to that elusive second chance.

Three weeks had passed since Timothy had awoken from the coma, and he was now ready for outside treatment. It was never expected that he would wake up, or even survive for that matter, so rehabilitation was sure to be tough. Jude had only visited Timothy once since waking, but he was asleep at the time, making it hard to gauge how bad the damage was. Committing to Timothy's care was only half the challenge. Successfully convincing Timothy that his best option for recovery was taking up residence at St. Anthony was a long shot, but Jude was unswerving.

"Care for a cup of tea before you head out?" Mariam Kidd, the elderly, short statured cook at St. Anthony asked with a curt austerity, common in women from her generation. She already knew Jude's answer and had his favorite cup in hand, complete with an unmeasured splash of lemon juice and honey. In Mariam's eight years of service she had never known him to decline, and she had also never served him tea prepared the same way twice. Jude half nodded, his mind preoccupied with concocting the ultimate persuasive pitch. "I reckon that boy won't be agreeable to your proposition. They're stupid at that age." Mariam offered tactlessly.

"True." Jude's ponderous gaze broke into a warm smile and then he downed the entire cup of tea in one shot, his eyes watering from the unexpected surplus of lemon. With lips pursed, he privately thanked the Lord for her inconsistent service and unsolicited candor which always managed to keep him alert.

"You are wasting your time Brother Jude. Why would you nurse a boy like that back to health, so he can go out and beat up more bums? He's no good."

Jude backed away from the window. "I hope you are wrong."

"If it was horse racing you'd be losing money. That's a fact." It was true. Two out of three parolees were holding round trip tickets. "Some folks are too far gone. You know that. Lord knows you know that."

The bleak assessment obscured Mariam's unrefined charm. Its implications annoyed Jude, but he hid the fact best he could. Gripping the handle of his cane tightly, he hoisted himself out of the chair, put on his long coat and gloves and then checked his watch. "What time did Sarah say she would be here?"

"Soon enough." Miriam answered while clearing away Jude's cup and saucer. "She'll be over after dropping off-" Miriam stopped then held silent for a moment, listening. "I think I hear her now."

Outside, Sarah McGreggor, a painfully plain young woman whose regrettable features made one assume she was ten years older, pulled up in a boxy, well-worn van and honked. Jude made his way outside and told Miriam, "See to it that the bell tower loft is prepared and stocked for the boy."

"Don't get your hopes up. I told you, they are stupid at this age." Miriam called after Jude but he didn't look back before walking out the front door. She followed and stood in the doorway, waving mechanically to Sarah with a stern face. "You and your strays." She muttered to herself.

The ride to Old Town Community Hospital was quiet, peppered only with Sarah's stroppy one word replies to Jude's probing small talk. Jude wasn't sure if it was a result of a superficial world passing her over or if she was just naturally clunky. Regardless, he felt pity for the frumpy woman. The stench of stale smoke eventually prompted Jude to roll his window down. "Is the gum effective at all?" He asked, referring to the ample supply of nicotine gum he had given her two weeks prior.

"Martin chews." She mumbled.

"Sorry?"

Outwardly aggravated at having to explain her confusing mumblings, she sighed and clarified, "Martin, the bartender at Cleo's. . ." She hesitated with raised eyebrows, waiting for Jude to recall the man, but he didn't. "That gum was kind of gross so I gave it to Martin and he likes it a lot."

"I see." Jude said quizzically. "Has it helped him quit smoking?"

Sarah guffawed, "That's the thing, and he doesn't even smoke! He says he likes the way it makes his scalp tingle."

In his mind, Jude recalled paying the checker at the pharmacy sixty-two dollars and change, and his heart sank. He made a mental note to never let Mariam get wind of this. "I don't think that is the intended use."

"He's weird, but I get a free beer now and then, so it's all good."

"Do you think that is the best place for you to be spending your free time?" Jude asked. Their conversations had a tendency to digress into fatherly advice; a pattern which inevitably fostered her avoidance.

Half of Sarah's blotchy face dimpled in frustration. "It's just a beer and some good times a couple days a week for Christ's sake! Is it against the law for me to unwind?"

Jude sat silent for a moment, waiting for the most effective words to come to him. He knew, 'a couple times a week' probably meant nearly every day. "No, it's not against the law, but maybe you can find a less precarious way to unwind."

"My phone is not exactly ringing off the hook. When I walk into Cleo's, no one cares where I came from or what I've done. No one judges me."

"What about Lucas?" Jude asked, not missing a beat.

"He's sixteen years old!" Sarah's voice grew louder. "What teenager wants to unwind with his mother?"

"What I meant was, does he approve."

This struck a nerve. "What do you want from me Brother Jude?" Sarah's lower lip protruded as she spoke. "You think it's easy not shooting up when every molecule in my body is begging for a fix? If you had any idea at all what that's like, you wouldn't be harassing me over some smokes and a couple of beers."

An out of place, slow gliding hawk caught Jude's attention as it sailed across the horizon, high above the outskirts of town. "Be sober and vigilant. Your opponent, the devil, prowls around like a roaring lion looking for someone to devour. Resist him."

"You don't get it. It's harder than you think." Sarah muttered.

"Then make it easier."

"What does that mean?"

Jude looked back at Sarah. "It means unwind with your son while wearing a nicotine patch."

A sarcastic sigh blew past Sarah's lips. "Not all of us are as holy as you Brother Jude."

Being right never yielded any sense of victory for Jude; only paranoia that his modesty had eroded. Still, he was willing to ransom popularity for Sarah's sake. "That's a cop out."

"If you say so."

"I do." He refused to succumb to the tendrils of her denial. "We're not all that different. Everyone struggles – Everyone. But, you can't begin to fight if you don't acknowledge the foe. Sometimes you are your own worst enemy."

Sarah was not ready to yield to wisdom. "Have you ever been possessed by addiction?" Jude looked away from her incredulous glare. "That's what I thought. So don't lecture me on what I should or shouldn't do, because I guarantee you, none of it is even remotely as awful as the things I used to do before we met." Jude decided it was pointless to agitate Sarah further, and the remaining ten minutes of the ride went back to being just as drippy as the first.

"Pull up there." Jude pointed to a patient loading zone. Sarah coasted up to the blue striped curb and parked. "Wait here. I'll be back shortly."

"How long?" Sarah was incapable of waiting patiently.

Ignoring the question, Jude placed his hand on Sarah's shoulder to emphasize his sincerity. "I appreciate you helping out today, but I have one more favor. Pray that I don't come back down here alone." Then he gently stroked the side of her expressionless face before gathering up his cane and disappearing into the aged building.

Old Town Community Hospital, referred to as 'the sick tank' by locals, was one of the city's greatest examples of regulation neglect. The administration exerted minimum effort to maintain their façade as a viable healthcare institution. The deficiency was tolerated mainly because the diversion of funds inflated the mayor's job creation figures. The money chased its own tail, exchanging hands amongst lobbyist, politicians, union heads and minimum wage earners. None of it aiding patient care.

"Good morning Brother Jude!" An older gentleman behind the front desk stood and smiled.

"Good morning Nick. You look well."

Nick extended his arm with an adhesive visitor's pass dangling from his index finger. "I've already filled it out for you."

"Thank you." Jude placed the badge on his breast pocket.

"Room five-twenty-five. I saw him earlier in PT. He looks good after all he's been through."

"Thank God for that." A stitch of regret tightened Jude's chest. "Unfortunately, I haven't been tracking his progress as close as I should."

"There's a good chance you're about to become very acquainted with his progress."

Jude thanked Nick again and then anxiously took the elevator up to the fifth floor. After exiting the metal car, he passed the nurses' station and mingled briefly with familiar faces he had come to know over the years. Eventually, Jude continued down the corridor until a distressed dark-skinned doctor discreetly beckoned him into an adjacent room. "Is everything okay Dr. Martin?" Jude asked cautiously.

The tall doctor removed his glasses and rubbed his eyes. "You know me, right?"

Jude nodded, confused by the peculiar question. "For many years, yes."

The doctor put his glasses back on then looked intently at Jude. His near persecuting gaze oscillated between each of Jude's eyes, probing for any hint of deceit. "You know how I feel, right?" Jude stared back silently. "You know, from our late night discussions at the coffee shop."

"Yes of course." The two men had shared several spirited theological discussions over the years, Dr. Martin holding firm to a position of non-belief.

"I've pretty much witnessed everything come through this hospital that a person like you might call a miracle. I have never been unable to site reasonable scientific explanations." Dr. Martin lowered his voice. "That boy of yours flat lined for eight minutes on the way here, and was then resuscitated. It's not that uncommon, it happens. Significant debilitative brain trauma from lack of oxygen afterwards, I've also seen that in other young people."

"How bad is he? I thought he was healing?" Jude silently cursed himself for ever getting on that bus. "Are you suggesting his injuries too extensive for us to provide adequate care?"

Dr. Martin shook his head. "That's the thing. When he got here he was an unresponsive lump of flesh. His physical wounds healed some during his stay. We checked his mental status, but there was no improvement at all. Then three weeks ago he just opens his eyes and is back. We get him un-tubed and discover he's fully functional. No sensory, speech or motor skill impairment. No loss of short or long-term memory. We ran every test, and aside from losing partial hearing in his left ear, his nervous system appears completely restored. Rapid recovery of conscious awareness after a trauma like that, with no significant loss of brain function; that's something I've never seen before."

The news sent a sense of relief over Jude. "That's wonderful, praise God!" He said joyfully.

Dr. Marcus pointed to his own face. "This, I saw with my own eyes. It doesn't make any sense."

"There are some things which man was not intended to make sense of."

The doctor frowned. "It bothers me."

Jude smiled, "I find that giving thanks is an excellent remedy for bother."

Dr. Martin thought about it. "I suppose I'm thankful I was lucky enough to study this physiological anomaly first hand."

"And I'm thankful you were blessed to witness such a wonderful miracle." Jude beamed.

"When he opened his eyes I immediately sensed mental clarity. After all these years, I can see it before we conduct the first test." Dr. Martin held his finger up, pointing to Jude's face. "What surprised me, is that your face was the first thing that popped into my mind as I watched him grope around after waking up."

"I may have a bad leg, but don't underestimate my skill manipulating this cane."

"That's not what I meant. It was that perpetual look of content you always seem to be wearing that came to mind." Dr. Martin led Jude back into the hallway. "I don't know that we'll ever agree on miracles, but I do know one thing for certain, I envy your faith Brother Jude."

A nurse stepped in-between the two and said, "Oh, there you are Doctor. Five-two-five is ready for discharge."

"Let's go see that boy of yours."

The look on Jude's face as he entered the room instantly made Timothy insecure. He clasped his hands together to hide his mangled palms while Jude's intrusive eyes inspected him. Only when the eyes hesitated upon his head did he remember his most noticeable injury. "What's the matter? You act like you've never seen a toe head before." Timothy pointed to his near-white crew cut. "They say I might be like this forever."

"It's- it's nice." Timothy's nervous system may have been intact, but Jude thought he looked ghastly. Pale mottled skin, snowy hair, and dreadful scars from the elbow down made it difficult to hide his shock. If his outward injuries had healed as Dr. Martin had indicated, Jude was having a hard time telling. "I-I hear you have made an incredible recovery."

"I'm alive if that's what you mean." Not wishing to be at the mercy of his insecurities any longer, Timothy unclasped his hands and held them up. "I got a new set of mitts too." Jude stared at the deep clefts of pink and white skin adorning his palms then looked away. "They look bad, but they don't hurt at all." Timothy took a finger and traced one of the raised fern-like lightning scars up his forearm. "At least these aren't as ugly."

"I'm sorry this happened to you Timothy." It was at times like this that Jude's faith was most tested. He believed in his heart that God had a plan and that everything happened for a reason. But this, the mauling of a boy on the verge of a second chance, tested him. "They say you are well enough to continue your treatment elsewhere now."

Timothy alternated lifting each knee. "My muscles kind of shrunk while I was gone, that's the main thing I have to fix." He tapped his left ear. "This ear doesn't work right anymore, and the doc says it's busted for good. At least it's the one with the bad lobe. No biggie, I got another one."

"That's a good way to look at it." Jude watched Timothy snap his fingers next to his ear and suddenly felt pressed for time. He berated himself for failing to formulate the ultimate persuasive pitch earlier that morning. He only had one shot to persuade Timothy to spend his recovery at St. Anthony. "I don't know if you've given any thought to your next move, but I would be glad to put you up until-"

"At the church?" Timothy interrupted. It was already going wrong. "Thanks, but I already told you I don't believe all that stuff anymore."

Sucking in a breath out of rhythm, Jude tried to salvage the offer. "Since being rebuilt after the riots, St. Anthony only operates as a shelter. It's pretty quiet most of the time."

"Where did everyone go?"

"The congregation combined with St. Mary about two blocks north." Jude hoped Tim would reconsider.

"I don't know. I feel weird about getting help from people who, um. . ."

"It's no bother. You can stay with us while you heal and sort things out, and get your head straight – I mean, get focused on what you want to do once you are all, ya know, smoothed out and stuff. Not that you look horribly disfigured or anything. I'm just sayin' there is a room and supplies for you. Oh, and a bed of course." As each word exited Jude's mouth it cascaded downward into the freight train pileup that was his ultimate persuasive pitch.

Now Timothy was looking at Jude as if *HE* were a disfigured mess. "What's this about? Are you trying to, like, convert me or something? It's pointless."

"No! I mean, maybe, but no, not yet, n-no."

"What is wrong with you people?" Timothy's lips curled with disgust. "I told you already I don't need your Jesus, but here you are again bugging me about it. You Christians don't respect anyone."

Dr. Martin squirmed away, "I've gotta go check on something else."

Not having anything to lose, Jude asked, "At some point you believed in Jesus, what happened?"

"What happened?" Timothy's mouth gaped in disbelief. "I'll tell you what happened. He never did anything for me when I believed in him except let my mom die."

"I'm sure that was hard for you."

"She was my faith – all of it. God died when my mom died." Timothy covered his eyes with his scarred hands. "Are you happy now? You see what joy your precious savior brings?" Tears fell from behind his hands. "Will you just leave me alone already?"

It would be hard to make a bigger mess, but Jude pressed on, "God so loved the world that-"

"Get out!" Timothy shouted, prompting the sound of Dr. Martin's returning footsteps.

"I'll go then." Dust had finally come to rest on Jude's feet. He took three steps then turned and spoke one last time. "Even though you have abandoned him, he's never stopped loving you." Having said it, Jude exited the room.

A dizzying tirade filled Timothy's mind as he replayed the conversation in his head. "God so loved the world that he sent you to annoy me! No respect for other people at all!" His rant continued even after Dr. Martin reentered the room. "Can you believe that guy?"

Dr. Martin played it down. "I think he meant well. Now I have some paperwork to go over with you."

"And then he has the gall to speak on God's behalf. Apparently, our good Lord asked Brother Jude to inform me that he's never stopped-" Timothy froze.

"Everything okay?" Dr. Martin asked.

It didn't seem possible, but Timothy grew even paler. "No, I need you to catch up to him."

"I don't understand."

"Brother Jude." Timothy sat up and pleaded. "Please hurry; tell him I accept his invitation."

Chapter 31

" Maybe he's got a brain tumor." Miriam whispered to Jude as they followed Sarah and Timothy up the stairs to the bell tower loft. Seeing Jude return with Timothy irritated her. Admission of her miscalculation would only come after exhausting a number of implausible explanations, a brain tumor being first. "Hair that shade of cotton isn't natural." She huffed. "He most certainly has a brain tumor."

Jude prayed Miriam's obnoxious speculations would not reach Timothy's good ear, and that she'd run out of breath before having the chance to declare that he was doomed to return to prison. To distract Miriam, Jude pointed to Sarah and Timothy several steps ahead and whispered, "Those two seem to have hit it off well."

Miriam scowled. "Strays run together."

Jude wished he'd left well enough alone and purposefully labored slower with his cane for the last flight of stairs to widen Sarah and Timothy's lead.

"Here it is." Jude announced when they reached the modest top floor loft. A bittersweet panoramic view of Old Town and the water front surrounded the plainly furnished space. A simple wooden writing desk and chair sat in the corner, with a low bed, storage chest and second chair resting opposite. The tall parameter windows camouflaged the small quarter's true size.

"Staying up here will definitely strengthen my legs." The climb left Timothy drenched in sweat.

Sarah laughed at the remark long enough to make her crush obvious. It wasn't hard to gain her affections. "And it's small since you don't have any stuff." She added, not realizing her poor choice of words dished out a unique offense to each one of them present.

"There are fresh linens and clothes in the chest. Please be mindful of your wounds, we don't want any stains." Miriam continued in her best school teacher voice. "Meals are served three times a day and there is no snacking, so be prompt." Westminster Chimes unexpectedly erupted from above and filled the loft with sound. Miriam sang along, raising her voice sharply to declare, "No foot shall slide!" A dozen E whole notes followed leaving the group reverberating.

"What was that?" Timothy asked with wide eyes.

"The lunch bell." Miriam answered. "I'm sure you have some freshening up to do so it won't be possible for you to make it in time. Listen for six chimes later and come down promptly for supper."

To Miriam's displeasure, Sarah spoke up. "Don't be silly, I'll grab him a plate."

"Meals are to be eaten in the dining hall only!" Miriam said sternly. "That is the way we do things here."

Jude waved his hands above his head. "Everyone settle down, I think we can make an exception today." Jude placed his hand on Miriam's shoulder. "You did a very nice job preparing this room for Tim, thank you."

"Yes, thanks." Timothy said quietly, feeling very unwelcome. "It's no problem, I'll eat at six."

Eager to please, Sarah said, "Don't let her get you down; I'll be back with some food."

"No, really, I'm not very hungry, and I could use a few minutes to get settled in." Sarah began to protest, but Timothy insisted. "I just need a few minutes to myself."

Miriam smiled, "Good, then I'll see you at six o'clock Timothy."

"It's Tim."

"What?"

"My name, it's just Tim."

Miriam probed. "I highly doubt that is the name your mother and father gave you."

Timothy felt a drop of anger begin to boil deep inside his soul. "Just Tim."

"Miriam, you and Sarah go down, I need to wrap up a few things with Tim." Jude pointed to the stairs so there would be no misunderstanding of his expectation.

"Very well." With Sarah in tow, Miriam slinked down the stars and out of sight.

Jude leaned on his cane and dragged his index finger in a horizontal arc. "You get an incredible view of the city from up here."

Timothy stepped up to the window and looked around. As far as his eyes could see there were rundown buildings and filthy streets in disrepair. "This town is a mess." He watched a woman scamper across a nearby street to avoid one of the many unwanted solicitations that plagued practically every pedestrian route. "These people don't know how to behave. It's disgusting."

"It's an opportunity." Jude said calmly.

"For what?"

"To help them, of course."

Timothy laughed cynically. "I've been around these people. They aren't helpable. Some people are just too far gone."

The irony was a reminder not to give up. "I'm curious, why the change of heart at the hospital?"

It was a question Timothy hoped to avoid. "I um, guess I just didn't have anywhere else to go."

It would be easy to point out Timothy was wrong, but Jude let it slide. "Why don't you come over here so we can talk." Timothy sat in the chair at the desk across from Jude. It was difficult for Jude to keep his eyes off Timothy's white scalp while talking. "I'm sorry this happened to you. We don't always know why things happen, but I believe they happen for a reason – that God has a plan." Timothy showed no reaction. "That sounds silly to you, I know. Since I have the means to help you - that is what I feel I have been called to do."

Timothy pointed at the window. "Like those losers out there?"

"We all face challenges in this life – every one of us. Sometimes we need help and sometimes we provide help."

"Right." Timothy snickered and looked down at his feet.

Jude observed the familiar skeptical body language, and then remembered Gemp's warning not to be shy. "You see all this?" Jude extended his arms out. "This is all temporary. None of it will matter to you a hundred years from now. We're just passing through town, and you can't leave with any of it."

"That's what you say to losers so they don't feel so bad about not having anything. I'm a realist. I don't believe that stuff."

"That stuff is the truth."

"If it makes you feel better to help me I'll take it, but don't expect anything from me in return." Timothy motioned to the window. "Like everyone else, I got nothing to give."

Jude continued. "All I'm asking for is-"

"Ah, the catch! There's always a catch. No one does anything for nothing."

Jude tried again. "All I'm asking is that you keep an open mind, and consider what I'm saying."

Timothy jutted out his chin and proclaimed, "Jesus saves!" In his most obnoxious, mocking southern accent. "Save your breath, I've heard it all before. The sad truth is, you die and that's that. You've got to get what you can in this life while you're still breathing." Timothy channeled his father. "You sure you still want to nurse me back to health?"

He had heard this denunciation countless times, but it never left Jude deterred. "Yes, I am prepared to do so."

Unwavering commitment was foreign to Timothy. "I can't figure what you Christians get out of helping someone like me. Maybe it's just good old-fashioned curiosity. You can't resist the urge to look down from your perfect little holy perches and see how the rest of us live."

"We're not perfect."

"Just forgiven right?" Timothy laughed. "I've seen that stupid, stuck-up bumper sticker before. You guys really have some nerve."

The jab rolled off Jude as if never spoken. "We're not so different you and I. We're both afflicted with sin, only I recognize it and repent."

Earning credibility with Timothy was near impossible. "Talk is cheap, especially coming from a priest who has never had to wade through the wreckage of real mistakes."

"That's not an accurate statement."

"Oh, I'm sorry. You're not Father Jude; you're Brother Jude – whatever that means. Who can keep up with these ridiculous boy scout ranks?" Timothy had no respect for religious hierarchy. "Did you bring me here to help you get your priest badge?"

"No. I hoped to be a friend to you. Someone who can relate to you and help you through this stage of life."

Timothy pointed to Jude's cane. "My legs are going to heal, and when they do, I don't expect we'll have much left in common."

"There's more than just your physical health at stake." Jude sensed Timothy's glass was pretty full now. "I hope we have more in common when you ride up on the city limits."

The two sat silent for a few moments until Timothy piped up and asked, "Did you ever talk to that guy's dad? The bakery guy?"

The question brought back memories of parting ways with Timothy before the storm. "I did. Unfortunately, the bakery is under new, less tolerant ownership. I don't expect that to change anytime soon."

"I shouldn't have gotten my hopes up." Timothy grumbled.

"That was just one opportunity. There are others."

"Like what?"

Jude stood up, suddenly exhausted from the day's trials. "We can talk about it when you have healed more. For now, just get your bearings. Let me know if there is anything I can do to make your stay more pleasant."

The hospitality made Timothy feel like a heel. He wondered why Jude's kindness brought out hostility and suspicion in himself. "Brother Jude."

"Yes."

"Thank you." It felt good to have an ally, but Timothy couldn't shake the expectation of imminent disaster.

Chapter 32

*O*ver the next week and a half, Timothy acclimated to the St. Anthony routine, taking on small chores and being careful to use minimal resources. The goal was to stay out of trouble long enough to heal, and then split. He quickly recognized what a sweet deal Brother Jude had provided him. Staying at the church, even with quarterly bells, was marvelously serene; within days Timothy found himself comforted by their routine rather than annoyed. There was, of course, the daily invitation to God's love wrapped in casual conversation that he had to endure, but even that felt okay after a while. Timothy came to appreciate Jude's genuine interest in helping him. It was something he had not experienced in his entire adult life.

Each morning, Miriam played nearly unrecognizable gospel hymns on a weathered upright piano at the center of the first floor. It warbled flatly throughout the church as if crying out in desperation for a good tuning. Miriam called it her 'little janky piano'. Timothy was certain it must be missing no less than five strings. Even so, Miriam always managed to draw a small impromptu chorale that didn't seem to mind the pitch. None of them could carry a tune, especially Sarah whose squeaky voice dominated center stage. After a while, Timothy began to recognize some of the songs, and they didn't seem so terrible after all.

Most of the strength in his legs had returned with an added windfall of stamina. He could scale all three flights in under a minute, energetically skipping every other step. His hands felt more his own as the swelling reduced and he got used to their new toughness and limited grasp.

Something else happened to Timothy over the course of his stay; he developed a hunger for being productive. No one had ever expected much from him so he hadn't exerted himself. It felt refreshing that he was more than just a liability. Timothy enjoyed helping out around St. Anthony but decided he was ready to find outside work.

Most mornings Sarah would come by early after dropping Lucas off at school and work alongside Timothy in the kitchen. She was not at all the kind of girl he would have chased in his pre-incarceration days, but he enjoyed the female attention. He especially liked that she didn't talk about the Lord all the time, and he never had to correct her for calling him anything other than, 'Tim'.

This morning he was up early, cleaning and slicing a large mound of potatoes for breakfast. He had never spent much time in the kitchen when he was younger but seemed to have a natural ability, for slicing potatoes at least. He waited for Miriam to leave with a basket of soiled hand towels then scooted over to Sarah to announce, "I'm going to get a job."

"Really!" Sarah bubbled with enthusiasm. Unwarranted, over the top enthusiasm that Timothy worried would catch Miriam's attention even though she was two rooms away.

"Yeah, I need to make some cash and get out on my own."

"You could crash at my place for a while if you want." Sarah blurted out desperately. "It's small but-"

"No." All the fawning in the world wouldn't make it a viable proposition. "I need to go out on my own. Get a job and then get my own place. Do it right."

Timothy's determination only made Sarah more enamored with him. The tattoos, scars and prison time didn't hurt ether. "Did I ever tell you that you remind me of a guy I used to date?"

"Are you listening to what I'm saying? I'll never get ahead hanging around a church. I have got to get a real job!"

"That's great news!" Jude surprised the two as he entered the kitchen. "I'm glad you are feeling better. Praise God!"

Timothy and Sarah exchanged an unsure glance then Timothy said, "Really?"

"I hear you skipping steps up to the loft, it's exciting!" Jude patted Timothy's back. "We should talk about your options when you have some time."

Timothy's eyes lit up. "I've got time right now!"

Jude pointed to the remaining stack of potatoes. "Who's going to finish breakfast?"

"I've got this, go ahead." Sarah insisted.

Miriam entered the kitchen with a freshly cut bouquet of daisies. "Those potatoes aren't going to peel themselves." She announced sourly then threaded one of the flowers through Jude's lapel button hole. The stem hung crookedly, and despite repeated attempts to straighten it out, the flower always came to rest with half of its pedals folded. "I suppose that will do."

"It's beautiful." Jude smiled, but Miriam remained stoic, only grunting in return. Jude turned to Timothy. "Let's head upstairs and see what we can do for you."

"Awesome!" Timothy exclaimed.

Jude led the way upstairs, cane in one hand, Bible in the other. Even though Jude was very proficient with the stick, Timothy was always one step behind, ready to catch him if he stumbled. Once up top, the two settled into their usual conversation spots. "So tell me Tim, what kind of work do you think you would be happy doing?"

The question surprised Timothy. "I don't know, just whatever." He hadn't counted on having much say in the matter. "There are only certain people who are going to hire me. So, I'll take what I can get."

"You've been very helpful around here. Any business would be lucky to acquire your services."

"My services?" Timothy shot Jude a dubious look. "Doing chores is doing chores. Don't make it sound so fancy."

Jude laughed. "Nothing fancy about promoting what you do well. You need to take an inventory of your skills and sell yourself to employers."

"Right." Timothy held up his hands like lobster pincers. "Are there any seafood restaurants in need of a mascot?" Jude laughed at Timothy's self-deprecation. "Or maybe. . ." Timothy rubbed his head. "There is a giant in town needing help with an earwax problem."

"Stop it." Jude laughed out loud, a rarity.

Timothy was not impressed with his comedic success though. He gazed coolly out the window while Jude's laughter dissipated, telling himself not to get his hopes up. "You need to be realistic. It's going to be hard to find someone willing to hire me."

Jude began to sing, "All things are possible. . ."

The incessant optimism grated on Timothy's nerves. "Life isn't all prayers and singing for the rest of us. We don't have it so easy."

"Trying to navigate the waters of life alone will always be harder. I keep trying to tell you there's a better way." Pessimism didn't stand a chance against Jude.

Timothy tilted his neck back, cast his eyes up to the ceiling and let out a heavy sigh. "Yes, you might have mentioned it a few million times before." He closed his eyes.

"We're all faced with the same lifelong struggle. We are born with this affliction called sin. Every one of us." Jude paused, and waited until Timothy opened his eyes again before going on. "But there's good news Tim. God loves us so much that he sent his only son Jesus to demonstrate what he wants for us. Jesus was perfectly obedient to God's will, even to the point of paying the price for our sins. If you accept Jesus as Lord with a sincere heart, and repent for your sins-"

"I'll be born again! Yeah, yeah I know." Timothy interrupted sarcastically.

Undeterred by the outburst, Jude continued. "Not only will salvation be yours, but death will have no power over you in the kingdom of heaven."

Timothy smirked arrogantly. "There's just one problem Brother Jude; I can't really accept Jesus when I don't even believe in God."

"No God? How do you explain all this?" Jude waved his hand in the air.

"We're just a freakish accident that occurred randomly. It could have never happened or happened a million times. We don't know." Timothy's adrenaline began to flow as it always did when he recited the dogma of his father.

"Random?"

"Completely! We're not cowering in caves anymore, inventing gods to explain the magic of nature. Science provides real answers." Timothy nearly shouted the declaration.

"Scientific exploration has surely been fruitful for man." Jude thought for a moment. "What would you say is mankind's greatest scientific achievement?"

The corner of Timothy's mouth cinched up as he thought about the question. "I guess computers. They have propelled society forward at an unprecedented rate. An eon's worth of progress has been accomplished in a few short decades. Every aspect of society has benefited from our colossal strides in technology." Timothy's eyes lit up more as he spoke. "Think about all the advances in computing that took place just during my time in prison! Computing advances computing!"

"Do you weigh this computing achievement evenly with mankind's latest achievements in areas like civics, cosmology, or artistic expression?"

Timothy shot back without hesitation, "Those things are important, but not everyone agrees with, or understands each other's ideas. Put the latest gadget into the hands of any person on the planet, and they instantly feel how advanced we've become."

"So, is it safe to say, you feel computing is the pinnacle of all mankind's achievements so far?"

"We have artificial intelligence that can beat world chess champions! We create machines that outthink and out reason the sharpest minds." Timothy's face flushed as he spoke. "We don't need the crutch of God anymore to explain the unexplained. All that is needed is time. With enough time we can figure out just about anything."

"The computers. . ." Jude's fingers tickled an invisible keyboard in front of him. "What are they made of?"

"I don't know, circuits and chips and stuff."

"I mean, what basic materials are they manufactured from?"

Timothy thought back to the time he helped his uncle install additional memory in his personal computer. "Mostly metals and plastics I think." A further look of wonder appeared on his face. "Think about how great plastic is! Can you imagine a world without plastic? Another milestone for man!"

Jude nodded in agreement. "Yes, plastic is good."

Coming back down, Timothy asked, "Why are you asking me this?"

"Because I find it fascinating."

"The plastic and metal isn't the fascinating part, it's that we can create intelligent electronics!" Timothy explained.

Slumping back slightly in his chair, Jude continued, "What fascinates me is that when I think of all of the natural wonders in the world: the oceans, the deserts, the heavens, the mountains, living creatures, none of them are made entirely of metal and plastic. And I suspect you'd agree that these natural wonders are far more. . . wondrous, than anything created by man, right?"

It wasn't what Timothy was expecting. "You're comparing apples to oranges."

"I'm comparing man-made wonders to natural wonders."

"Okay, then obviously nature blows away any computer." Timothy still didn't understand Jude's point.

"If computers demonstrate man's most intelligent engineering, doesn't it seem at least plausible that the vastly superior, awe-striking natural wonders of this Earth, made of far more intricate organic particles, and formed to survive and thrive throughout the ages, were also the product of some form of intelligence?" Jude took the daisy from his lapel and spun the stem gently between his fingers. "It's remarkable how often the very people blessed with the acumen to engineer the testaments of man's vast intelligence, vindictively reject even the possibility that our universe was architected with purpose." He held out the flower. "They have a front row seat to the marvels of this universe and still snub their noses at the possibility of a divine origin."

The observation flustered Timothy, sending him back to his old adage. "Because they understand that natural wonders are simply the by-products of random elemental collisions. Gases, liquids and solids inevitably took form."

"But what caused it to happen? What caused the gases, liquids and solids to form?" Jude asked.

"Someone didn't pay attention in science class." Timothy said condescendingly. "The basic laws of nature determine the behavior of matter. These laws are consistent and verifiable, so we can trust them."

Jude tried again. "What I'm asking is: where did the natural laws themselves come from?"

"From years of observation by the greatest scientific minds in history."

"I'm going about this the wrong way." Jude took a moment to formulate his question more successfully.

Timothy exploited the pause with further lecture. "We observe, form a hypothesis, test and retest until we have proof positive laws."

Before Jude could present his restructured question, the door opened. Sarah entered carrying two tall glasses of orange juice. "Freshly squeezed." She announced, but mostly to Timothy. Each of them took a glass and thanked her to which she smiled, again, mostly to Timothy. They remained pleasantly silent waiting for her to leave, but she did not take the cue. "Have you figured out where Tim can work yet?"

"We're still hammering it out." Jude answered.

Sarah turned to Timothy and commandeered the task. "I can talk to Martin at Cleo's and probably get you a job. He owes me a favor anyhow."

Before Jude could regain control of the situation, Timothy's eyes lit up with interest. "Really, you think so?"

"Now-" Jude tried to apply the hand brake.

"Sure! You'll probably get some of the tip money too."

"Cool!" Timothy said enthusiastically.

Jude stood up from his chair and led Sarah gently by her elbow back over to the door. "We're going to explore all of Tim's options so he can find the best opportunity." Jude said as he led her outside and then shut the door. He turned back momentarily and shouted, "Thank you for the juice!"

Timothy was irritated. "Why'd you do that? That sounded like a good job."

Jude sat back down and pointed at Timothy. "Because I think you are better than that." Timothy's nose crinkled up in dismay. "Yes, better. I don't think you should spend your second chance working in some bar."

"Money is money, I don't care. Tips would be sweet."

"There is more to consider than just income." Jude said assuredly. "Be less fixated on making a flashy living and more concerned with making a good life. This is your second chance Timothy, remember?" Jude pointed at the door. "Stay clear of things that compromise your chances for success."

"I understand." An old feeling stirred in Timothy's chest, one of being cared for. He hadn't expected it, and it made him somber. "I appreciate the advice. I'll be careful."

"I pray to God that you will." A passionate sincerity coated Jude's words. "Things can switch directions in a flash. It's up to you to keep your head in the game and make good decisions."

"Okay, no bar. What now?"

Jude's face relaxed. "A good friend of mine owns an extended warranty company across town called, 'J-7 Comprehensive Care'. I told him about you when you were first released from the hospital. He agreed to give you a shot when you were well enough."

Timothy was substantially less enthusiastic with the prospect. "Warranty company?"

"The guy's a brilliant business man, just like his father. You would learn a lot." Jude laughed to himself, seeming to remember childhood antics from long ago. "Jesus. That's his name, Jesus."

"Figures."

"He's from a long line of Jesus'." Again, Jude laughed. "Both his brothers, his father, his uncle, his grandfather, his great-grandfather – all named Jesus."

Timothy listened, but didn't think it was as funny. "That's kind of stupid. How could they tell them apart?"

"Come here and see." Jude got up and went to the window. "See that check cashing place three lots from the corner?"

Squinting, Timothy counted the shops backwards from the corner. "You mean J-6 Check Cashing?" As soon as he said the name, Jude burst out laughing. Timothy wasn't amused. "That is so lame."

Jude pointed across town, in the opposite direction. "J-5 vacuum and sewing machine repair on Washington was a fixture in this town when I was a kid. Gramps J. could fix anything mechanical."

Timothy rolled his eyes. "How hard could it be to name a baby?"

"It was what they wanted." Jude wandered back to his chair as he spoke. "Me and the other guys always teased him, but he didn't flinch. His family was very proud that every generation had a father and son Jesus. It was their way of honoring their faith."

Timothy followed Jude back to his seat. "Sounds more like child abuse."

"J-7 thought so." Jude smiled.

"I never totally understood if Jesus was the son of God or God himself?"

Jude nodded and listened. For the first time, Timothy brought more to the table than sweeping denunciations and perversions of scripture. It was exciting. It was progress. "We believe in the Holy Trinity. We accept that the Father, Son and the Holy Spirit are separate beings, but of the same substance, none lesser than the other. God gave us the word. Jesus, his only son, was the word made flesh. He was sacrificed so that our sins would be forgiven and we'd receive the gift of eternal life. He conquered death, and reigns alongside the Father in heaven."

"Alongside, but they are really the same person?" Timothy's forehead crinkled. "That makes no sense."

To Timothy's astonishment, Jude nodded in agreement. "The mystery of faith is beyond the confines of human logic. As believers we accept it on faith. We humbly offer submission to its mystery and wonder, aware that full comprehension is incongruent with our humanity."

"So you believe in something you don't completely understand, and are sure no one will ever be able to completely figure out?" Timothy asked, frustrated by the idea. "I don't know how you can do that. I would have a hard time not obsessing over how three guys are actually the same God."

Jude's finger bobbed at Timothy. "When you accept the gifts of His grace and love, those kinds of obsessions become meaningless."

Timothy contemplated the idea for a moment before asking, "What is the Holy Spirit, or Holy Ghost, or whatever it's called?"

"They are the same thing."

"Wait a minute. The two are one, who is also one of three, but ultimately just one?" Timothy shook his head. "You're killing me!"

Jude explained further. "There is only one Holy Spirit in the Holy Trinity. The different names are due to different translations of the Bible, but they represent the same being."

"How many translations are there?"

"The Bible is the inspired word of God. Although its content spans several millennia, its message has remained the same. In order to share it with people of different languages and cultures, new translations are necessary."

The answer seemed reasonable to Timothy. "Okay, so you just use the English one."

"Well. . ." Jude braced for more confusion. "Actually, there are more than fifty unique English translations of the Bible. All contain twenty-seven New Testament books, but there are two distinct variants of Old Testament canon: Forty-six Roman Catholic books compared with thirty-nine Protestant books."

"Fifty versions?" Timothy gawked.

"The English language is constantly maturing. Our vocabulary, the way we construct sentences, how we spell words, adoption of slang words and phrases, all impact the readability of scripture. It becomes necessary to revisit and update translations of the Bible so that readers living today can relate."

"So you're saying, no one wants to read a bunch of Thy's and Hither's anymore."

Jude nodded. "You have to be careful. Every generation has the challenge of keeping the language contemporary without distorting the message. The word needs to be both accessible and faithful to the original message."

"I bet it's been screwed up plenty of times."

"Most translations are fine and succeed in conveying scripture's meaning. On a rare occasion, an attempt to contemporize scripture borders on rendering the word profane. That can be upsetting to more traditional readers and create friction."

Timothy smirked. "So much for brotherly love."

"You will cross paths with people who are fiercely loyal to a particular translation which they grew up with, or can relate to on a personal level; there is nothing wrong with that. I rejoice in the fact they are reading the scriptures." Jude leaned forward. "That's the important thing - actually reading the scriptures. Leave distracting academic debates over translations to those who can afford the luxury. The message is clear and universal if you are willing to listen."

"What if you don't get it?" Timothy asked.

"Sometimes you need to re-read scripture or come back to it later before its application to your life is revealed." Jude closed his eyes and spoke quietly. "Before I read scripture, I close my eyes and pray that the Holy Spirit will bestow the full blessing of their teaching and wisdom upon me."

The serene moment was broken by Timothy declaring, "That's asking too much from people. The Bible is a huge book, and now you have to do some special prayer each time you want to read it?" What was a blessing to Jude was a chore to Timothy. "You know what I think? If you want more people to read the Bible you should cut it down to just the useful parts, like the Ten Commandments and some of the better Aesop's fables. Keep the entertaining ones like the story where the kid kills the giant. Oh, and that part where all the creepy frogs and locusts show up is good too. People like blood and horror. Then in Act III Jesus shows up, and we all know how that ends. You have to do more than re-translate; you need to make it entertaining."

The gross misunderstanding should have troubled Jude, but instead he delighted in Timothy's childlike assessment. It was an opportunity to teach. "The Bible contains inspired works of history, poetry, literature, law and prophecy; none of which should be discarded for length's sake. Its content and message are perfect inasmuch as the reader seeks its message with a sincere heart."

"Perfect? More like perfectly confusing." Timothy scoffed. "I don't understand why you guys make this so complicated. You could get so many more people saved, or whatever, if you just made some simple changes. Get everyone to agree on one translation. If you don't want to cut it down then at least put all the stuff into categories so we can skip the boring parts. Oh, and remove the duplicates. Isn't the story of Jesus in there like three times?"

Although crude, Jude was pleased that Timothy had some knowledge of the Bible. "There are four Gospels, or accounts, of Christ's life."

"How many times do you need to tell the same story?"

"We believers are thankful to have multiple accounts of Christ's life from those who lived in his time."

In Timothy's mind it was all the same, wasted space. "Sounds like I'm not the first to think of this. You said the Protestants dropped. . ." Timothy tried to compute in his head. "How many books was it?"

"It's wasn't quite like that." Jude emphasized.

"How can the Bible possibly be perfect when there are so many disagreements about it? You Christians have issues."

"It is important to remember that from the day Jesus declared St. Peter's vocation, propagation of his message of salvation was in the hands of men. As well intentioned as most ecclesiastics were, they were still men."

Timothy recalled his discussion with Angelo in the jail infirmary. "And man cannot escape his sinful nature."

Jude was impressed with the admission, not knowing its true origin. "The man who accepts Christ as his savior doesn't outrun sin. He repents, is forgiven, and strives to resist sinning again."

"But if he folds too many times, he's out for good, right?"

"No, when he folds, he repents." Jude looked away. "Jesus was the only man who has ever lived without sin. The rest of us have to resist it daily, including those tasked with leading the church over the centuries. Amidst the unquenched ambitions and egos of men, struggles for political domination, breaches by false prophets and tyrants, splintering of the Universal Church, the Christian community and the word of God have survived largely unscathed. To this day, the message of God's grace and Jesus's gift of salvation transcend our sinful nature, and reach the hearts of new believers."

"So you admit there are a lot of phony Christians."

"I'm saying every person, Christian or not, is born with sin." Jude wiped sweat from his forehead. "Some resist and some fold."

"Between the crooked TV preachers, abusive priests, and gossipy church ladies, you guys don't have much credibility. I'm sorry." Timothy added blushingly.

"Inevitably, there are bad apples, and varying degrees of commitment among any large congregation. Influential assemblies are an enticing target for exploitation. I assure you, those who prey on the innocent while invoking God's name will have their day of judgment." Jude shook his fist. "Gossiping, although bad, it is a less sinister offense. Even the best Christians succumb to bad behavior sometimes. Resisting sin is a daily ordeal."

"I don't think I have to resist it daily. I'm a pretty good person now, even though I messed up before." Timothy declared confidently. "It's not like I go around causing mayhem and stealing stuff."

"God hates all sins, not just the ones that make the news." Jude held up his palm. "Don't answer these questions, just think about them. Have you had hateful or vengeful thoughts against others? Have you been disrespectful to your elders?"

Timothy interrupted, "That's not fair! Miriam never has anything nice to say to me, and she watches my every move with suspicion. Of course I have bad thoughts about her! Who wouldn't?"

Jude held up his hand again. "Slow down, just listen." Once Timothy sat back, Jude continued. "Have you been jealous of what others have? Have you been ungrateful for what you *DO* have? Have you had impure thoughts?"

"Oh c'mon, that's just human nature!"

"Precisely."

"You can't expect people to go around feeling guilty all the time about things they think about privately but don't act on." Timothy argued. "It's absurd!"

Jude countered, "What about the things you don't think about and don't act on?" Timothy looked confused. "Have you been kind to others at every opportunity? Have you been charitable?"

"I've got no money!" Timothy protested.

"What is the going rate on a friendly smile, or providing assistance without expecting compensation?" Timothy reluctantly nodded, conceding that inaction was as much a problem. "The unwillingness to put one's pride aside and recognize this human infirmity of sin is a barrier to embracing faith. Until you confess this reality of our nature you cannot repent, and you cannot remain vigilant against weakness and temptation."

"You're not going to break me down and make me dependent on Jesus to escape condemnation from this supposed inherent sin. I think I can successfully pull off being a better person on my own without Jesus." Timothy regretted his arrogant tone as soon as he spoke. "It's nothing personal; I just don't need that."

The conversation's defensive turn didn't bother Jude. "God wants a relationship with you. The only thing separating you from God is sin. Jesus paid the price for your sins and invites you to have an eternal relationship with him and the Father. Being a better person isn't something you pull off; it's the by-product of accepting the Lord's gift of salvation."

"Sorry brother Jude, I need more to go on than that. Where is the proof?"

Jude flipped through the heavily marked up Bible in his lap. "For some, the totality of God's love and grace recorded in these pages serves as proof enough. Others consider the innumerable testimonies of faithful believers throughout history who have been blessed, and found peace through fearing God as proof enough." Jude closed the Bible. "There are temporal enthusiasts who, from the sidelines, spend their efforts dissecting and scrutinizing the word of God in search of the proof you speak of. These efforts are in vain."

Timothy's eyes widened. "You agree there is no proof?"

"Faith is just that - faith. It means believing what cannot be proved or disproved."

"I can't believe you are saying this!"

"Remember, God is unrestrained by the physical laws and human reasoning of this universe. Something far more compelling than any legalistic body of evidence assembled by man awaits those who genuinely seek the truth." Timothy was hanging on Jude's every word. "Since the day the Lord created you, he has loved you. He longs for you to repent and accept the gifts of the Holy Spirit and eternal life." Jude raised his hands. "Amidst your grievous offenses and denials, he has never given up on you. He beckons you to shed this worldly existence and accept his invitation. Your personal experience from doing so will provide all the proof you seek."

"I have to believe to believe?" Timothy asked hesitantly.

Jude placed his hand on Timothy's shoulder. "The moment you accept his invitation, you'll understand. You'll never be the same again." Jude's grip on Timothy's shoulder tightened. "Our unique personal relationships with Jesus can't be published in a scientific journal as evidence, but they are the most compelling substantiation of God's love for us."

"I'm supposed to engage in a relationship with an entity I don't even think is there in order to see that he really is there. Am I getting this right?"

Jude smiled. "What are you afraid of? You've got nothing to lose."

"Honestly, I'd feel pretty silly talking to an imaginary friend."

"Start small. You can say something like, 'Lord, I haven't known you, but I want to. If you are real, as Brother Jude claims, I invite you to make yourself known to me.' See, it's painless." Jude motioned for Timothy to speak. "Now you try."

All at once, every pore on Timothy's body seemed to excrete perspiration. His whole body felt clammy and cold and his vision blurred. His mother's face appeared in his mind and the metallic St. Anthony necklace suddenly felt like it was searing his sweaty skin beneath his shirt. "Um, God. . ." He rubbed his eyes as his breathing shortened. "This is Tim." He stopped and panted for a moment, then abruptly stood up and staggered. "I can't do this."

"Relax, you were doing great!" Jude encouraged.

"It's not. . ." Timothy felt dizzy but wouldn't sit back down. "I can't say this stuff. I'm not being sincere."

The visceral reaction surprised Jude. "This is simply an extension of you sincerely wanting proof."

The episode was too much, Timothy sat back down. "No, I don't want to do this right now."

"No problem Timothy, we don't have to do this now." Although disappointed, Jude knew when to back off. He smiled warmly hoping to ease Timothy's anxiety. "It's not like Jesus is going anywhere. He'll be there when you are ready. He's never stopped loving you."

There it was again, those haunting words. "Why do you keep saying that?" Timothy barked accusingly.

The sharp tone of the question made Jude recoil. "I just meant that-"

"You said that to me at the hospital too. Don't you remember?"

"I guess I might have said that." Jude said lots of things, but he wasn't sure exactly what and when. "I can't remember specifically. If the Holy Spirit inspires me to say it, I do."

Timothy's eyes moistened involuntarily. "Did you ever wonder why I had them call you back to my room that day?"

"I figured you realized coming here was better than rotting in county rehab." Timothy's mood swings worried Jude. "Am I missing something?"

Tears trickled down Timothy's cheeks. "The day of my accident, something weird happened to me while I was unconscious that I've never told anyone about." Timothy wiped his eyes shamefully. "I guess my brain went into shock and concocted an apparition of my mom and brother. It really freaked me out." Timothy looked Jude square in the eye. "It seemed so incredibly real."

Jude wondered if Timothy knew he wasn't just unconscious, but clinically dead. "I can see it was upsetting to you."

"Right before I came out of it, my mom said, 'He's always loved you.'" More tears streamed down Timothy's cheeks. "And then you also said it at the hospital. I can't make sense of it."

Again, the door opened and Sarah entered with a single breakfast plate, presumably for Timothy. "You guys have been up here for a while so I brought you some breakfast."

Timothy turned away sharply to hide his tears. Jude engaged Sarah to provide more privacy. "Over easy eggs, there's no better way to start my day."

Sarah froze, realizing she hadn't prepared anything for Jude. "Oh, yeah. . ." She put down Timothy's plate of scrambled eggs and potatoes then hustled out the door saying, "Coming right up Brother Jude."

Jude stood up and patted Timothy on the back. "I'll call J-7 and let him know you'll stop by his office tomorrow." He pointed at the plate of food. "Eat up and take it easy today. I have a feeling tomorrow will be a great day for you."

"I hope you're right." Timothy said with a sniffle.

Chapter 33

*T*he following morning, Timothy was up before dawn. He watched the sun come up over the city and wished he was somewhere else. "This town is a pit." He said to his reflection in the window.

He had on the suit Jude had laid out for him the night before. A little big, but it still felt better than anything his skin had touched in years. He was wearing two pairs of socks to keep his feet from swimming around in Jude's large dress shoes. His pocket bulged with the directions and bus fare Jude had given him. He looked at his reflection in the window and didn't recognize himself.

Timothy quietly made his way down the stairs and outside where it was still dark. It would take him nearly two hours to reach J-7's office so he needed to head out early. As he walked to the edge of the church property, Sarah pulled up in her van. "Hey Tim, going to your big interview?"

Timothy nodded. "You know that. I told you about it yesterday."

"Why don't you let me drive you? We can stop for coffee on the way."

"Nah, I can't." An odd enticement came over Timothy as he studied her plain features and frumpy posture. He supposed not being with a woman for so long had ruined him. "I appreciate you offering, but I could use the alone time to prepare."

"Aw, c'mon, it'll be fun!" Sarah whined.

A dirty black plume of smoke over the skyline caught Timothy's attention and reminded him the city was waking up. "Another time, I really need to go now." He jogged across the street without saying goodbye, and headed toward the bus stop, never looking back at her.

A torn up sofa in the gutter obscured the bus stop. Sprawled out along its length laid a disheveled man, reeking of liquor. As Timothy drew near, the man sprung up unsteadily, revealing a 'free couch' sign beneath him and proclaimed, "This is my couch!"

"Great." Timothy loathed the company. Before any further conversation could take place, the man flopped back down and was out.

Directly across the street, a craggy Asian woman was dumping what looked like fish guts into the gutter. Timothy looked on with disgust until she noticed and angrily shouted something foreign at him. He wasn't sure what she said, but her tone was vulgar.

Soon after, the sound of squeaky air brakes cut the morning stillness and Timothy boarded the bus. At that early hour he had his pick of graffiti laden seats. He shimmied halfway back and settled in. As the bus pulled away, he realized he had taken the same seat as the day he and Jude went to the bakery. He got up and took another seat across the aisle. Looking out the starboard window, Timothy spied the neon J6 Check Cashing sign at the end of the street. The bus slowed for the light giving Timothy a chance to peer inside the storefront. He saw a man in his pajamas banging on the glass partition. The stoplight changed and the bus lurched forward before Timothy could see if anyone emerged from the back to help the man.

The sun rose slowly revealing a coat of graffiti on everything in the city, including bushes and trees. "These people are animals." Timothy said to himself as he passed two youths spray painting a parked ambulance.

At the halfway point, Timothy got off the bus and checked the directions Jude had given him. The sound of an approaching grocery cart with squeaky wheels made him nervous so he read fast. He needed to catch his next bus two blocks away. Looking up from the paper he saw a make-shift memorial next to him on the sidewalk. Propped up against a faded, blue mailbox sat spent candles, rosaries and dead flowers. He saw torn remnants of police tape mixed with trash that had blown up against an adjacent storefront. He wondered what pathetic story they told. "Got to keep moving." He told himself.

The next two blocks were mostly uneventful. The sweet smell of tamale' carts deploying to street corners was a welcome change from the stench of garbage and industry. He passed an insurance billboard urging people to compare rates. It said, 'What do you have to lose?' in bold letters. Below that read, 'You may be pleasantly surprised!' It reminded Timothy of his conversation with Jude the previous morning. It left him conflicted. Jude seemed to genuinely care about him, something he craved and knew he needed. But the price for accepting that guidance was giving up his independence at a time when he was anxious to get out and take on the world. And all the Jesus talk was becoming exhausting. Jude was so comfortable living in his faith, and would happily engage all of Timothy's intellectual sparring, without trepidation. He was without doubt. What bothered Timothy most were the times he found himself questioning if Jude could be right about any part of it. How can a guy be content living in Old Town? Walking down the street, wearing Jude's formalwear with these questions festering in the most private corners of his mind was bothersome.

In the distance, Timothy spotted a flock of dogs rustling through an overturned trash can just a few feet from his next bus stop. "Great." Timothy grumbled, and wondered if he could manage to flag down the bus a quarter-block back. Today wasn't the day to mix it up with strays. Fortunately, the problem resolved itself when an angry shopkeeper appeared on the sidewalk with a hose and shooed the mongrels away.

Timothy caught his next bus and began strategizing. He rehearsed everything in his head on the ride over. How he would shake hands firmly, make eye contact, and answer questions confidently. He'd agree to take any open position.

Just as Jude's instructions had indicated, the route stopped directly in front of the three-story professional building. "Here goes nothing." Timothy said under his breath as he stepped off.

The warranty office was on the ground floor and easy to find. Timothy smoothed his collar and lapels before rapping on the door. Before anyone answered, he quickly cupped his hands over his nose and mouth and tested his breath. Coffee. "It could be worse." He said then dropped his hands.

The door opened and a middle-aged woman greeted him. "Can I help you?"

"Um, uh, yes. . ." He tripped over his words making himself more nervous. "Uh, my name is Tim Clement and-"

"We're not interested in buying anything." The woman interrupted.

"Oh, no, I'm not selling anything." Timothy remembered Jude telling him to sell his talents and found it ironic. "I'm here about a job. Brother Jude from St. Anthony talked with, um, Jesus about it." He felt ridiculous referring to anyone by that name.

"I'm afraid the owner won't be back until tomorrow. You'll need to come back."

"Can I at least fill out an application since I'm here?" Timothy could hear desperation in his own voice. "And then I can come back tomorrow."

The woman appeared completely befuddled by this. "I don't think we have any job application forms. Jesus is more of the face-to-face type. You just need to come back. I'll let him know you stopped by." And then, with a polite smile, she shut the door on him.

"That didn't exactly go as I planned." Timothy was annoyed but not completely discouraged. As he walked away he admired his professional reflection in the window and decided he wasn't going to waste this trip downtown in Jude's suit. He walked over to the building directory out front to see if there were any other prospects. It surprised Timothy that most of the office suites were vacant. A T-shirt company on the top floor caught his eye, and he decided to see if they were hiring. The elevator was on the fritz, so he located the stairwell and went up.

When he arrived at the office he tried the handle but the door was locked. He then saw the service buzzer. He reached for the button but the door opened suddenly, revealing a screen door and attractive young woman on the other side. "Oh, Hi." Timothy said uneasily.

"I heard you try the knob." The girl looked like she was in her twenties. "No one ever follows the directions. It's a pretty big buzzer, but maybe we need a bigger one."

Timothy couldn't tell if it was an insult or if she was playing around. He chose to ignore the comment completely. "I saw your shop and wondered if you guys were hiring." Looking over her shoulder he could see all kinds of sports and skating T-shirts hanging up, in stacks and lying in piles on the ground.

"We don't have any regular jobs right now."

"Oh, okay." Timothy said, unable to disguise his disappointment.

"But we're always looking for new designers." The girl added. "Are you an artist?"

It was a good question. Timothy hadn't thought about Stevie or MarGreat since the day of his release from prison when he threw all his notebooks away. Would he be able to draw again? For a paycheck, sure. "Yes, actually I am." He heard himself say.

"Cool, have you done any packaging or logo work?"

It was a foreign language to him. "I just draw stuff." He knew it sounded dumb. His father used to chastise him for using the word 'stuff' in a sentence. "Characters. Comics." He elaborated with circular hand motions.

"Hold on." The girl ducked inside for a moment then returned with pen and paper. "Show me." She propped open the screen and passed Timothy the items, her eyes growing wide after noticing the scars on his hands. He took the paper and placed it up against the outside wall and drew MarGreat's glasses. He then drew her lumpy head and obstinate features, finishing with a bow up top. Timothy smiled. It was like seeing an old friend again. He passed the drawing and pen back to the girl who seemed stunned once she looked at it. She folded the paper in half and asked, "What school did you go to?"

"You mean like what art school?" Timothy asked.

"I mean-" The girl reached past the cracked screen door and grabbed the main door's handle. "You should ask for your tuition back." She then pulled the door shut.

"Strike two." Timothy groaned. He didn't really think he'd get any work from the girl, but he didn't expect the harsh treatment.

He decided to explore the rest of the building. After traveling the full length of the corridor, he rounded a corner and continued all the way down to the end. There was only one other operational business on the third floor, just before the west stairwell. The sign on the door read, 'Claims Processing'. Determined, Timothy yanked on the door handle but it was tightly secured. He knocked hard on the door and waited, but no one answered. Again he pounded on the door.

This time he heard a man yell from inside, "We aren't open!"

Timothy wasn't going to let this one get away. "Hey, can I just talk to you for a minute?"

"I said we're not open yet."

Timothy began to walk away then turned on his heel and pounded the door again. "I just need a minute of your time." He pleaded.

After a few muffled footsteps, the door opened. A large muscular man wearing a golf shirt and casual business slacks poked his head out looking very irritated. "You got an open claim?" He asked.

"No, I was just wondering if you guys might be looking for some extra help."

"Are you kidding me?" The man's ruddy face blazed. "You interrupted me for this?"

"I was in the-"

"This couldn't have waited until we opened?" The man looked at Timothy like a lowly bug. "You think we're going to hire someone so dumb they can't figure out when we're open? Get lost!"

The man leaned back in and began to shut the door. In desperation, Timothy planted his foot in the door jamb preventing it from closing. "I'm sorry, I-"

Like a freight train, the brute burst out the door and shoved Timothy so hard that he stumbled and fell against the opposite hallway wall. "I said get lost, idiot!"

A streak of adrenaline shot though Timothy, the kind he hadn't felt since the day of his accident. He clenched his jaw and fought off the impending rage as he staggered to his feet. "What the heck! Was that really necessary?"

"You're trespassing. Get out!" The man pointed to the stairwell. "If you're not out of here in five seconds I'm calling the cops, freak!"

Timothy began to walk away then noticed Jude's suit jacket button on the floor. "Great, look what you did." He stooped down to pick it up.

The man became unglued and came out into the hallway to scream at Timothy. "What I did? No one invited you here! You got a lot of nerve!"

Timothy kept his eyes downcast during the verbal lashing. Only when the frothing man ran out of insults and turned away did Timothy raise his head and see the slogan on the back of his shirt, 'You've got nothing to lose – You might be surprised!' "Yeah, I was surprised." Timothy muttered to himself.

"What'd you say?" The beast swooped down on Timothy, snatched him into a headlock, and dragged him into the stairwell. Amid a barrage of cursing and name-calling, he heaved Timothy past the top step, sending him tumbling down the stairs. "Waste someone else's time!"

In a ball at the bottom of the stairwell, Timothy fought to regain his breath. His body hurt in so many places that he didn't know where to feel pain first. Blood dripped down into his left eye from his stinging split brow. Strangely, his rage was nowhere to be found. Instead, he felt relieved that things had finally incinerated in a spectacular explosion of failure. He no longer had to wait anxiously for impending doom.

Timothy rolled over on to his side and coughed hard. Pulling his knees into his chest, he felt the sting of shredded fabric strands cutting into his badly skinned knees. He was sorry that Jude's suit had become collateral damage.

In the distance, a police siren spun. Timothy hoped it wasn't for him; he wasn't keen on having to explain any of this to his parole officer. Getting to his feet was painful. From his ankles to his hips, dull and sharp pains surfaced no matter how he distributed his weight. His shoulders, arms and ribs weren't any better. A surge of nausea tightened his belly while his inner ear beckoned the ground. With a groan he collapsed forward and assumed a crawling posture. Eyes squinted closed, he maneuvered downward one step at a time, the angular edge of each stair being his only guide.

The arduous descent was miserable. Only the eventual absence of sirens provided any relief. All other discomforts festered, his ribs emerging as the front-runner of pain. An empty reach of stair step signaled he had reached the ground floor. He rubbed his crusty eyes and blinked rapidly trying to make out his surroundings. He heard a man and a woman talking. The woman said, "I haven't seen anyone come through here." Timothy was sure they were talking about him and panicked. He noticed an abbreviated section of steps descending beyond the ground floor into a dark maintenance area. He crawled around to the summit and then gingerly scooted down their length taking in the pungent odor of urine along the way.

"What the hell happened to you?" A crackly voice in the shadows asked.

Timothy's heart jumped. "Who's there?" He called out.

A skinny old man slowly leaned out from behind the racked fire hose and stared at the wound on Timothy's head. "You need to leave, this is my place. You'll bring nothing but bad luck man."

"Be quiet." Timothy looked up the stairs behind him. "I don't want anyone to know I'm here."

"Then leave."

"I'm not going anywhere." Timothy said in a sharp whisper. "I just need to catch my breath for a bit."

The old man frowned and started climbing up past Timothy. "Ain't no way I'm being seen here with a mess like you. They'll think I did it." As he passed, his horrible odor caused Timothy to gag.

Coughing and wheezing, Timothy rested his head against the wall, closed his eyes and panted. He felt foolish for getting his hopes up. He rebuked himself for trying to overcome his natural penchant for failure. "I'm such a loser; even the bums can't stand me." His mumbled proclamation faded into the shadows with a quiver. Facial membranes moistened and swelled involuntarily, directing salty streams to flow down his face. He shook hard, riding out the first violent sob. He had come to both love and hate the first gush of a cry. He likened it to fighting off the inevitable effects of food poisoning, until you have no say in the matter. After the dam bursts, you realize the thing you resisted provided you the most relief.

Croaky gasps and somber whines coalesced beneath waves of grief pounding him into submission. The fortitude of Timothy's self-righteous independence lay decimated on his sodden cheeks. The divergent spec of hope stirring in his heart for the past few weeks shriveled up into a black void. A second-hand bag of witty retorts, misappropriated from a father who had repudiated him, would never fill that space.

More waves of anguish excised Timothy's suppressed hurts, demanding self-review. Stephen's smiling face hung in Timothy's field of view day in and day out, eyes open or shut. He could never shake the naïve visage. His heart ruptured with remorse for failing to keep his promise to his mother. His soppy voice cried out to her for forgiveness but only silence answered back. The silence reminded him how alone he was. Completely alone if not for Brother Jude's unsolicited kindness, which he had kept at arm's length.

He was without a family. The pain of being branded a loser and discarded by his siblings scalded terribly. Even though those jackals had never been kind to him, he hated being shunned. What he wouldn't give now for a tall helping of their cruelty.

As he wallowed in loneliness, Timothy's throat swelled nearly completely closed thinking how his father carried his disappointment to the grave. There would never be an opportunity for Timothy to reconcile no matter how well he succeeded in rebuilding his life.

But rebuilding his life was an impossible prospect from where he sat, dripping at the bottom of the steps. The world was a hard place to get by in. It was superficial and judgmental. If one could get past his freaky appearance they'd no doubt be repelled by his degenerate past.

Footsteps traveled down the stairs overhead and reached the first landing above Timothy, then went silent. He felt eyes peering down upon him then heard something fall to the ground above. Timothy twisted around and looked up to see. By the time he finished wiping his eyes dry and adjusted to the light, all he saw was the back of the young girl from the T-shirt shop hurrying away. His spirit was already so obliterated that he felt no embarrassment. There was nowhere lower to go. Timothy listened as her footsteps fled back up the staircase above him.

After the patter trailed off, Timothy heard the squeaky hallway door swing open. He knew the stairwell was no longer safe; he'd have to keep moving. Crouched down, he waited for silence but instead heard, "Tim, what happened?"

Timothy looked up and saw Jude limping down the service steps with his cane, looking horrified. Timothy flattened down the lapels of the jacket. "I'm sorry Brother Jude, your suit got messed up."

"Forget the suit, what happened to you?" Jude asked urgently.

Unable to rise, Timothy slumped back against the smooth wall, his cheek lying against it like a vertical pillow. The cool surface provided a brief moment of refreshment for his flushed face. Then he wailed even worse than before. A deep feral eruption of grief whose sound would break the hardest of hearts, echoed wretchedly up the stairwell. In concert, a cocktail of tears, blood, saliva, sweat and mucus spewed from Timothy's face while he bawled hysterically. "I can't-" He gasped to speak. "I can't do it Jude! I just can't!"

With as much tenderness as he could manifest, Jude delicately blotted Timothy's face and head with his handkerchief and tried to soothe him. "It's going to be okay Tim. This will pass."

"I'm nothing. Less than nothing!" Timothy wailed.

Jude mouthed a silent prayer then spoke softly to Timothy. "Every life is a gift, including yours. God doesn't waste life."

"This is no gift." Timothy coughed hard and gagged. After spitting on the ground he added, "This is my sentence. I accept it. It's what I deserve."

"No, you were intended for more than just suffering. God has a purpose for you; you need to find it."

Timothy emitted a sad chuckle. "All I've found is misery. If God is real, then he must really hate me for what I've done."

"No Tim, he loves you. He's always loved you."

"Shut up already!" Timothy sputtered angrily. "What do you know about being hated?" Timothy scowled at Jude. "What does some stupid priest in training know about living in the real world? The rest of us who aren't holy enough to be called to the so-called greatest vocation are just trying to get by."

Jude stared blankly at Timothy for a moment then spoke. "Sorry if I gave you the wrong impression, but I have no aspirations of becoming a priest." Jude cleared his throat. "However, I can still tell you, without any reservations, that God does love you and wants a relationship with you. He has a plan for you."

"A plan to torment me."

"This pain belongs to you. You can't blame God when it was you who refused his hand and decided to go it alone. I can't imagine anything more painful than living apart from God." Jude removed his Bible from his coat pocket and flipped to a bookmarked passage and read. "Jeremiah 29:11 – For I know well the plans I have in mind for you, says the Lord. Plans for your welfare and not for your demise, so as to give you a future of hope." Jude looked up at Timothy whose head was against the wall with eyes shut. "You hear that? A future of hope." Aside from heavy breathing, Timothy was unresponsive. Jude continued, "The greatest vocation is utilizing the gifts the Lord has given you to become an instrument of His will. There is no greater calling. There is no greater joy. His plans for you include so much more than just getting by."

For several minutes Jude and Timothy sat silent except for an occasional sniffle. After he had calmed down, Timothy grumbled, "Even if I wanted to, I'm not good enough."

"The depth of God's grace and mercy is vaster than any of your sins. Listen to this. . ." Jude flipped through his Bible again. "The Pharisees and their scribes complained to His disciples, saying, 'Why do you eat and drink with tax collectors and sinners?' Jesus said to them in reply, 'Those who are healthy do not need a doctor, but the sick do. I have not come to call the righteous to repentance, but sinners.'" Jude closed the Bible. "It is His desire that all souls repent and find salvation, especially those most in need of his grace."

Shuffling footsteps and a foul odor materialized at the top of the stairs. "You brought friends?" The old homeless man frowned. "This ain't right, not at all!" The man retreated, mumbling obscenities to himself.

Jude remained wholly focused on Timothy, never looking back at the man. "During St. Paul's third mission to Corinth he wrote that everyone who sincerely calls on the name of the Lord shall be saved."

"Oh, stop with all the Bible stuff already. I can't take it! It's not for people like me."

"Just listen, 'If one confesses with their mouth and believes in their heart that Jesus is the son of God, died for our sins, and was raised up, he will be saved.'"

"And you believe that?" Timothy asked dejectedly.

"I do."

"Even someone like me who-" An uncontrolled sob jerked past his airway. "Whose brother is dead because of him?"

"Especially someone like you." Jude replied assuredly.

"St. Paul lived a million years ago." Timothy coughed. "A lot has changed since then. I doubt any of it is still relevant."

"Our sinful nature, and Jesus' gift of salvation remain the same."

Timothy finally looked at Jude. "Brother Jude, I don't think you get it. I killed my brother. He's dead because I didn't stop gambling when I should have."

Jude nodded gently. "There was a man who hunted down Christians. He persecuted them mercilessly. Men, women and children; it didn't matter to him. He had them imprisoned, tortured, and in many cases killed. Do you think that man had any chance for salvation?"

Timothy shook his head. "Of course not. God would send a monster like that to Hell, or at least I would hope he would."

"What if he saw the error of his ways and repented for his sins?"

Timothy wiped his nose with his disheveled cuff. "You can't come back from something like that."

The pages of Jude's Bible flapped slowly behind his thumb as it dragged down the corner. "No Tim, you can come back, and that man did."

"Salvation for a Christian hunter?" Timothy asked cynically. "I'm pretty sure that goes against all the rules. You should check your facts."

"I have." Jude held up his Bible and gave it a shake. "About one-third of the New Testament is attributed to that very man; a ruthless persecutor of Christians." Timothy looked dumbfounded. "Through God's grace and mercy, Saul of Tarsus, an enemy of Christianity, was transformed and became an obedient disciple of Jesus. He changed his name and went on to become one of the most influential missionaries of the early Christian church. You might know him as St. Paul."

"Saint Paul?"

Jude nodded. "Yes, St. Paul."

Timothy looked down stunned. "I didn't know that."

"Still think you are too far gone for salvation?" Jude asked, but Timothy felt foolish for his ignorance and did not reply. "Still think Paul's testimony isn't relevant today?" Timothy shook his head. "God has a plan for every one of us. He loves us. He's heartbroken that any of his children would choose to go through life apart from him."

Timothy sobbed, holding his head in his hands. He replayed the vision of his mother, her invigorated face smiling at him. "My mom believed that. She tried to tell me, but I didn't listen."

"She loved you." Jude's words spurred more tears from Timothy. "She cherished the gifts of her children, and saw to it you were all baptized. She even named you after St. Paul's most cherished apprentice, Timothy."

Recounting these proofs of his mother's love was edifying, yet painful. "But none of us kept going to church after she died."

Jude explained again, "You might have abandoned the Lord, but he was always with you; Waiting for you to come home."

"If he was with me, why did he let Stephen die?" Timothy asked miserably. "Why did he let that happen?"

"It isn't always knowable, why things happen the way they do. We have free will to sin or resist sin. God does not prohibit us from choosing evil over His way." A car alarm in the parking lot began cycling through eight variations of ineffective chimes. "But I believe that the Lord takes every sinful action and finds some way to use it for good."

Timothy exhaled like a fresh punctured tire. "I thought getting out of prison would be different than this. I'm tired of spinning my wheels. I expected my life would finally change, but I'm stuck being the same loser I was before."

"You're not a loser." Jude assured Timothy. "Gaining your freedom was just an opportunity, not a guarantee of anything. If you want your life to change, you're going to have to take a serious look at how you're living it."

"Yeah, but-"

"It's up to you. No one is going to force you to do anything; you need to want to change on your own." Jude sounded nearly unsympathetic. "Free will, remember?"

"Yeah, I remember." Timothy took in Jude's candid message. Time slowed to a crawl while a string of lucid truths paraded through Timothy's consciousness. He thought about the volumes of shrewd advice imparted on him by his father over the years, and how fruitless it had all been. He thought about the strength and peace that his mother's faith granted her, even in her last moments. He thought about the hope he witnessed in Angelo's repentance, and was sure Angelo was doing better on the outside than he because of it. Timothy considered how his contempt for Jude's indelible spirit had given way to appreciation, then secretive envy. Timothy considered the handicap of his strong will, and how paired with his volatile rage it always led to disaster. He was no match for his own tendencies, but thankfully he had just acquired a game-changing revelation. . . "I can't do it." He proclaimed.

Jude looked puzzled. "Do what?"

"I can't do any of this on my own. I know that now." After he said it, his chest lifted. A calming clarity fell upon him as he happily surrendered his crushing vanity. "My mom knew it and tried to get me to see. She tried so hard to lead me in the right direction even when no one supported her. I get it now. I'm glad she never gave up." Timothy's chest expanded with rekindled hope. Reveling in the aftershock of his mother's enduring love, he knew that what he felt was right; what he felt was real. It wasn't something he could read about in a book or adequately communicate to another. The more he surrendered, the more he thirsted for what he had denied for so long. "I believe." He heard himself say.

Witnessing firsthand the touch of the Lord's grace brought tears to Jude's eyes. He blinked a few times and asked, "You're sure?"

"Yes, I'm sure." Timothy nodded. "I'm ready." He carefully pushed himself away from the wall and knelt on the steps, not caring about the pain in his bloodied knees.

"Oh, you don't have to-"

"I'm ready Brother Jude." Timothy clasped his hands together and bowed his head uncertain what to say. "Can you help me do this?"

Jude moved in front of Timothy and gently placed one hand on his shoulder and held the other palm up then closed his watery eyes. "Lord Jesus Christ, only son of the living God, have mercy on us sinners. In obedience to the Father, you died in our place so that all who repent and believe in you will have eternal life. You spared us from death. You are the good shepherd who lays down his life for his flock, rescuing those who have strayed and fallen into ditches." Tears rolled down Jude's face. "Today, your son Tim has-"

"Timothy. Call me Timothy."

Jude nodded, took a breath, and then proceeded, "Through the gifts of your Spirit, your son Timothy calls out to you, repentant and in need of your loving grace." Jude faintly squeezed Timothy's shoulder. "Just repeat after me. Don't say anything you don't really mean, or don't understand." Timothy nodded. "God, I am sorry that I have sinned against you. I humbly ask for your forgiveness. I believe in Jesus, your only son. I invite you back into my life. I know you have purposeful plans for me. I ask you to lead me so that I may always be obedient to your will." Timothy repeated each phrase with a quiet, repentant zeal. Jude concluded, "In Christ Jesus' name. Amen."

When done, Timothy opened his eyes and asked, "That's it? We're good?"

Jude smiled. "We're better than good, Timothy."

There wasn't a time Timothy could remember where he felt as sure about a decision in his life. Standing in the dank stairwell, covered in filth, he thanked God for saving him. It was a moment he would never forget as long as he lived.

Chapter 34

*O*ver the next three months Timothy adopted a curriculum of physical rehabilitation, life skills development and spiritual growth under Jude's guidance. The first step was going to reconciliation, something Timothy hadn't done since he was a boy. Jude offered support along the way and assured him there was nothing to worry about, and he was right. The elation Timothy experienced afterwards dwarfed any anxiety he had going beforehand. He thanked his mother for her insistence that he receive the sacrament despite the obstacle of his father.

Timothy received room and board at no cost in exchange for joining the St. Anthony staff, which he was thankful to do. The work placed him in the company of joyful people who brought out the best in him, and he wasn't required to wear a suit.

Every day, after preparing the morning meals, Timothy attended an hour-long bible study along with Sarah. The intensity of her crush softened, unable to compete with his newfound enthusiasm for the Lord. She too had returned home under Jude's guidance after years away from the church, but her coat of renewal had lost some of its original luster. She was happy for Timothy, but felt a twinge of resentment in losing her complaining partner to the other side. Timothy had always entertained her juvenile complaints about Jude's rules and guidelines, but now he seemed to find no faults with Jude and it annoyed her. Surprisingly, the more time Timothy spent studying scripture with Sarah, the more attractive she became to him. It was a combination of, "She knew me back when. . ." and sharing the experience of coming home after a long time away.

The Bible study sessions often included Timothy leaning over to Sarah in amazement and asking, "Did you know this was in here?" To which she would usually roll her eyes and remind him that she had spent twelve years in parochial school. The more he read, the more voracious his appetite for the Word became. The realization that everyone chronicled in the Bible wasn't perfect and condemnatory floored him. His journey through the Old Testament taught him that men and women of that time committed the same sins that men and women today fall victim to. He could relate to their struggles. People hadn't changed at all.

When the riots brought ruin to twelve square blocks of Old Town, many parishioners wailed over the damage sustained to St. Anthony. It was incomprehensible that God would let such a catastrophe displace an entire congregation. In the aftermath, the church emerged as a great pillar of support for the poorest residents of Old Town. St. Anthony now provided overnight shelter to homeless women and children in the newly constructed hall where the grade school once stood. The large kitchen now served nearly two-hundred meals a day to the hungry with support from local businesses. That was Jude's talent, soliciting donations to keep the kitchen stocked. Against incredible odds, he had always managed to bring in just enough to avoid a deficit. It was a lot of hard work to coordinate and manage, which is why he was happy to assign Timothy to meal services.

Working alongside Sarah and Miriam, Timothy was initially tasked with keeping a continuous supply of beans cooking on the stove. There were stations designated to sort, clean, soak and portion the beans running round the clock. The women cooked a never-ending supply of rice and whatever was donated during the week. The rice and beans were an inexpensive means to provide vital nutrients to those who might otherwise go hungry.

Not all of the rations were donated. About one-fourth of the beans were purchased from a local vendor at a greatly reduced rate. Jude kept an ongoing collection to fund the extra beans with the proceeds from recycled bottles and cans, monetary donations and whatever loose change he found on the street. At every opportunity, Jude trained Timothy in the art of bean conversion. "Table for how many?" Jude asked as he tossed a half-dollar across the kitchen to Timothy.

Timothy caught the coin and shouted back, "party of five!"

"Great!" Jude exclaimed. "You have really caught on. I need to put you to work pounding the pavement for new sponsors."

"The boy can count, whoopee!" Sarah added sarcastically, wondering why Jude had never considered her for the role.

"C'mon, go easy on the rookie will ya?" Timothy had lost his taste for sarcasm and teasing.

Jude ignored their sidebar and counted back twelve weeks in his head. "Every three months I spend a week canvassing the city, trying to find any businesses that might be willing to contribute towards the meal ministry. I don't see any reason why you couldn't do it."

"Really?" Timothy was astonished at Jude's trust in him. "But you'll give me the lowdown first, right?"

"Absolutely. Most people don't mind helping, they're just waiting to be asked. Some give damaged or defective products that would have been thrown away, other's give money. It's not hard, just requires some time and a thick hide."

"I've got a thick hide." Timothy held up his scarred hands. "I just hope it doesn't scare anyone off. Maybe Sarah should come with me."

Sarah snickered, "Sorry Tim, you're on your own."

"Call me Timothy, please."

Sarah nodded. "Sorry Timothy darling, you're still on your own."

"Don't worry. You two lovebirds will be venturing outside the kitchen together very soon." Miriam said snidely.

Timothy was quick to correct her. "Oh, we're not-"

"Our children over at St. Mary need instructors." Miriam ignored Timothy's correction. "So brush up. You start this Sunday."

"Sunday school? I can't. . . I mean, I don't-" In shock, Timothy could barely speak.

"I know. You are stupid about God." Miriam said frankly. "We need another body and so you will have to do." Miriam crossed herself. "Heaven help those children."

Sarah patted Timothy on the back. "It's not so bad. There's a book and lesson plan to follow. It's not like these classes haven't been taught forever and ever."

Jude looked around the kitchen. Looking over his crew, perfect in their imperfection, he thanked the Lord. "Great things are happening here at St. Anthony!" He announced to their hesitant ears. "We are blessed to serve him."

Chapter 35

*E*xcited to delegate his solicitation duties to Timothy, Jude was up extra early. In the dark, he made himself a cup of tea, pausing to determine the source of a soft whimpering. It was so faint that he nearly went about his way thinking it to be only ambient imagination. But then it sounded again, giving away its position above him on the third floor.

Jude climbed softly up the stairs and quietly rapped on Timothy's door. After a still moment, the door cracked open very slightly. "Oh, Brother Jude, it's you." Timothy coughed and sniffled to sound somewhat normal. "Is everything okay?"

"I was coming to ask you that very question." Jude said mildly.

Another still moment followed before Timothy finally peeled the door back, remaining in the shadows behind it. "Come on in."

Throughout his stay, Timothy had never attempted to rearrange the small room or apply his own style to the furnishings. Most long-term guests would inevitably introduce their creature comforts onto the property. Absence of this conduct usually meant the guest didn't intend to stick around very long. Jude hoped that was not the case with Timothy.

The two chairs where he and Timothy had shared many rich conversations were calling out to him to sit and council Timothy. He resisted their lure and instead stepped up to the dark windows to take in the panoramic skyline. "It'll be here soon."

"What will be here?" Timothy asked.

"Wind corralling time. It's almost here. As soon as the sun breaks over those factories there." Jude pointed, "It's a fresh start for everyone."

Timothy looked into the darkness but only saw fluttering neon and broken street lamps. "I've never heard of that before."

"When I was a kid, my Dad used to drink. He would beat the hell out of me and my two brothers whenever we'd get into trouble, which was just about every day."

"Um, are you supposed to be saying that in a church?"

"What, hell?" Jude looked distant. "Sometimes it just fits." Jude continued on. "My mom would protect us by sending us to bed early. Mama told us that as soon as the sun came up you got a fresh start. She said a person's evil nature took longer to wake up so you should get up early every morning and go out while people are at their best. 'Wind corralling', time she called it." Jude pictured her loving smile and soft skin. "She believed the morning air blew crisp with the uncorrupted spirit of goodwill."

"Do you believe that too?"

Darkness was giving way to an ashen haze down at the far end of town. "I believe God is merciful and forgiving. I believe there is good in all of us." Jude retreated from the window and sat down with Timothy trailing close behind. "What is upsetting you?"

Timothy squirmed a bit in his chair then spoke. "I was reading-" Tears formed again and he quickly wiped them. "I'm so sick of crying." Jude sat silent and waited for Timothy to compose himself. "I was reading the book of Acts and. . ." Timothy's voice quivered and he froze for a moment, desperately trying to not fall apart. Jude remained still, just listening. "I've been so wrong about everything. I didn't just deny God." Tears flowed freely. "I ridiculed him. I ridiculed those who follow him." For what seemed an eternity, Timothy sobbed quietly. Jude asked the Lord for the wisdom to minister to Timothy effectively as he sat quietly. "Brother Jude, I've done some really horrible things against God."

Jude finally spoke. "We've all done things we regret."

"I mean, really offensive stuff."

"The Lord has already forgiven you." Jude assured Timothy. "Sometimes the harder thing is forgiving yourself."

"I haven't been able to do that yet."

A small beam of sunlight shot across the room illuminating floating dust particles. "Wind corralling time." Jude said with a smile.

Timothy paid it no mind. "I've wasted so much time. How do I possibly fix that?"

"Be prudent with the time you have remaining." Jude answered plainly.

"There are people that I tried to convince, that they were delusional for following Jesus. They might change their minds someday because of me! I can't find all those people and tell them I was wrong. How do I make that right?"

"When you have faith - real faith - a lost soul spouting earthly arguments isn't going to crack your foundation. If anything, you walk away with stronger convictions. You may have acted as an instrument to strengthen someone's faith without even realizing it."

Timothy thought about it. "Like some kind of bizarro-world evangelist."

"Yeah, something like that." Jude smiled at the utterance. "But now you have a chance to share the good news in a more direct way."

"I don't have to go knocking on doors and stuff I hope."

"No." Jude shook his head. "Just living as Jesus instructed is testimony enough."

The compassionate treatment he had received from Jude since the first time they met came to mind. It was true. Had Jude come at him only with charismatic sermons, the truth would have become that much more clouded. Even when Timothy was rude and disrespectful, Jude's kindness never diminished. It made Timothy take notice of the quality of life he was missing. "I wanted to thank you for not giving up on me. I know it would have been really easy to do."

"As a disciple of Jesus, I have an obligation to share the good news. Especially with those who most need to hear it." Jude looked out the window. "Not everyone listens."

"I'm glad I did."

"Not everyone does." Jude muttered before rising up. "Ask the Lord to help you move on. Our past sins can either teach us or drag us down. You are holding onto it not Him." Jude took one more look at the rising sun then excused himself.

Chapter 36

*L*ess than a week had passed since Jude had entrusted Timothy with soliciting additional meal funding. With the aid of a copied registry of newly issued business licenses provided by one of Jude's numerous friends at city hall, Timothy had pinpointed his first candidate to approach. "Brother Jude!" Timothy called out as he descended the stairs like a cat with six legs. "Brother Jude, I got it!"

Jude had just come in from sorting bottles for recycling and it surprised him to hear his name. "What's going on?"

With a fist full of papers, Timothy waved Jude over to the kitchen counter. "Here. I've found the perfect one." Timothy flattened down a marked up hand-drawn grid. Among dozens of scratched out businesses, there was one circled, 'Tso Meat Company.' Timothy pointed to the name, then dragged his finger across to its Eastside address. "It's a little far from here, but I called and he gets a constant supply of meats. There would be scraps for us."

The slow nod from Jude was less than satisfying. His lips twisted and pursed. "I don't usually find that part of town fruitful. It's difficult to navigate Lei district with all those open markets."

Timothy pulled his St. Anthony necklace out of the top of his shirt. "We should be able to find our way with St. Anthony on our side!" Timothy said cheerfully but Jude was still reluctant to rejoice. "Tell you what, you come with me and we'll tackle this first one together."

"Sure." Jude agreed, still not as enthusiastically as Timothy hoped.

"Great, I've already got it mapped out. Our first bus leaves in fifteen. Get ready!"

Jude looked down at his attire and wondered what else there was to prepare. "Ready when you are."

"You'll see Brother Jude, this will be epic!" Timothy collected up his papers and scampered back up stairs.

Over the course of two hours and three buses, Jude and Timothy finally arrived in Lei District, located in the northeast corner of Old Town. It was just as dirty as the rest of Old Town, but had the added charm of butcher waste flowing through its gutters. Sketchy tables laden with raw meats and fish populated nearly every inch of the main boardwalk. Cheap, non-regulated and available to anyone with cash in hand, Lei District supplied both families and restaurants alike. The open market plots changed hands every month though an underground lottery system. It wasn't left to chance; you needed to put up some cash if you hoped to get anywhere close to the action. Happy Corner was the prime location, that's where the most money changed hands. Vendors paid as much as they could afford to jockey for a plot close by.

From the Happy Corner epicenter, markets and storefronts rippled outwards becoming less and less profitable. Tso Meat Company was four blocks away from the main action which meant sustainability but not necessarily profitability. One thing it had going for it was that the smell was slightly more tolerable, but only slightly. "Four fifty one." Timothy pointed at the modest red storefront littered with tables and tables of meat out front. Various butchered parts hung above the tables waiting for an owner. On one side was a fish market, just as cluttered, and on the other side was a produce market with a surplus of bruised zucchinis and squash.

Trailing Timothy slightly, Jude looked around the unfamiliar part of town taking it in. When he reached the meat display he asked Timothy, "You talked to this guy already?"

"Yeah, just briefly. It was kind of hard to understand him though." At that moment a short man in a blood-stained tank top came out of the shop holding a large bottle of wine in one hand and a cleaver in the other. He raised the bottle and shouted a salutation in Chinese to the crowd and took a big swig. He instantly spotted Timothy and Jude and made his way over to them. The man put down his bottle and cleaver so he could wipe his hands on his shirt. Timothy took a guess and extended his hand, "Mr. Tso?"

The man smiled and shook Timothy's hand. "Hello, we have good prices!" Mr. Tso pointed to the meats, picking up a good-sized roast and squeezing it he added, "Best quality!"

Timothy backed away from the roast. "Oh, we're not here to shop today. I'm Timothy. I called you on the phone earlier." Mr. Tso looked confused. "About donating some food to the St. Anthony meal ministry."

Mr. Tso laughed to buy some time, but then a look of recognition flashed over his face. "You wanted my garbage."

"Just whatever meat you can't sell; but it needs to be safe to eat." Timothy could see the glimmer of negotiation forming in Mr. Tso's eye. "You would be donating it to feed the poor."

"What does that mean?"

Timothy thought he had adequately spelled it out on the phone already. "It means you would give it to us free of charge."

Mr. Tso laughed. "Why?"

"Because, otherwise it would just go to waste."

Jude chimed in. "We are disciples of Jesus Christ. We follow his teachings which instruct us to help those in need." Mr. Tso became more serious at the mention of Jesus' name. "Timothy recognized that you may be in a position to help us feed the hungry. Can you help?" Years of experience taught Jude that directness was the only efficient way to solicit donations.

"Maybe. How much trouble will it be?"

"We can come by every two weeks." Timothy suggested but Mr. Tso's eyes grew wide. "Or just one a month."

"That is better."

"We'll only take what you don't need." Timothy assured Mr. Tso. "You are doing a great service to those less fortunate in Old Town." Timothy offered his extended hand to Mr. Tso to seal the deal.

Just as Mr. Tso raised his hand to shake with Timothy, an agitated voice erupted among the tables in the meat market. "You got a lot of nerve coming to my neck of the woods, Holy man!"

Timothy turned just in time to see an older man kick Jude's cane away and push him down to the ground. "Hey!" Timothy yelled at the man.

Jude landed hard but didn't try to get up. Instead, he held up his hand to Timothy and shouted, "Get back, this doesn't concern you." Timothy began to approach Jude but he yelled fiercely at him. "Get back!" This stunned Timothy. It was a side of Jude he hadn't seen before.

Jude's attacker stood over him and spat in his face and then taunted him. "How's the leg Jude?"

It was near impossible for Timothy to not come to Jude's aid. He shifted nervously waiting to pounce. "Leave him alone!" Timothy finally yelled to which Jude held up his hand again.

"What are you, the killer's newest errand boy?" Jude's attacker asked Timothy. Timothy looked very confused by the situation. The man laughed and looked down at Jude. "Oh, he doesn't know?" A wallet emerged from the man's back pocket. He unfolded it and held up a picture of a pretty young girl whose clothing and hair were from another decade.

"I wish there was a way to change things Felipe." Jude said wearily.

Mr. Tso went back into his store saying, "I don't want any trouble!"

Felipe held the picture up to Timothy. "Angela. My beautiful Angela. She was such a good girl." His eyes filled with tears. The wound was as fresh today as the day he lost her. "I was robbed!" The man picked up Mr. Tso's bottle of wine and poured it onto Jude's head. "Robbed by this pathetic drunk!" When the last drops of wine had fallen, Felipe angrily swung the bottle down on Jude's head, scattering it into a million pieces.

Blood gushed from Jude's head onto the pavement. It was too much for Timothy to sit by and watch. He charged Felipe, sending him into a group of his companions. Felipe's friends pulled him away saying, "Cool down Felipe, it's over!"

Timothy knelt down to help Jude. While being dragged away, Felipe ranted, "Eighteen months in the hole – you call that Justice! Burn in hell Jude! Burn in Hell murderer!"

Quickly, Timothy gathered up Jude's cane and got him to his feet. He performed a basic cleaning of Jude's head and face on the way to the bus stop. It hadn't quite been the epic success he had expected. Once settled in, the two said nothing until they switched buses. As they climbed aboard, Jude said, "The first job I ever had was delivering ice to the Lei District fish markets. I was young and cocky. I was finally making money and thought I was invincible. I had moved out of my parent's house and was so glad to be free of my father's wrath. I swore I'd never be like him. But I hadn't realized that I was already exactly like him in some ways. Little by little I had been seduced by alcohol. When I wasn't drinking I was thinking about my next drink." A tear fell down Jude's cheek. "I was too proud to do anything about it. And then one day I went sort of crazy. I drank more than usual even though I had to work. I knew it stupid, but I did it anyway." Jude turned from the window and faced Timothy. "I drove my delivery truck right over that girl and didn't even know it until people were beating on my windshield at the stoplight down the street."

Timothy felt sick listening to Jude's story. "Oh man."

"I don't know why I agreed to go down there. Of all the places for you to pick."

"I'm sorry."

Jude turned back to the window. "Forgiving yourself can be more complicated than you expect."

The two remained silent for the remainder of the ride back to St. Anthony, waiting for the miserable trip to end. Timothy was numb. He couldn't believe the Jude he knew was capable of such a horrible thing.

Upon arriving home, Jude grabbed his Bible and a tall glass of orange juice. He asked Timothy to grab a few bananas for him as well. Miriam entered the kitchen and immediately scolded Timothy, "Trouble follows you around like a swarm of gnats, boy!"

Jude lethargically waved his finger at her, and then beckoned Timothy to follow him upstairs. As they ascended, Jude asked Timothy, "Can you do me a favor?"

"Anything." Timothy said vigorously.

"I need to rest up. Can I crash in your room for the next day or so?"

"Sure, there's room."

Jude reached the door. "No, I need to be alone. I need you here outside on the landing standing guard." Jude opened the door.

"In case that guy comes looking for you?"

Jude turned his defeated face to Timothy. "No, in case I fold. Pray for me." Jude went in and shut the door.

Chapter 37

*F*or two days no one made any direct references to Jude being sequestered on the third floor. It was business as usual except with an underlying tension like that which a child feels when their parents are fighting in private. No one questioned Timothy's altered work schedule or Jude's absence; they all just picked up the slack and continued on.

Miriam kept a steady supply of tea and meals stocked outside the door. It was clear she had been through one of Jude's spells before, possibly more than once. On the second day, while retrieving Jude's spent dishes, she said to Timothy, "I'm sorry if you had a hard time hearing what I said to you the other day." The indication that he was thin-skinned was as close to an apology as Timothy would get. He diplomatically acknowledged her intent with a smile and a pat on her back, which made her spine rigid. "That's all I wanted to say." She declared before going back downstairs.

At the end of the second day, Jude emerged from Timothy's room looking renewed and optimistic. Freshly showered and in clean clothes, he appeared his usual self, minus the splatter of cuts on his head. The injury had healed to the point where they were not immediately obvious, unless you were looking him directly in the face. Timothy stood up to greet him, unsure of what was acceptable conversation. Smiling, Jude said, "Tomorrow, I'd like you to visit Skip Anderson, the produce manager at Henn Farms. He has helped us in the past, but can only do so seasonally. Now would be a good time to get dibs on bruised extras."

It was a welcome request since it established that they would not be discussing the Tso District incident anytime soon. "I need to go downtown and visit my PO in the morning, but I could go afterwards." Timothy only met with his probation officer, Ms. Unger, once following his release. Being a guest at St. Anthony provided him an added dose of leniency. She had not established any formal schedule of future meetings, considering Timothy to be a low risk tick in her case load. She only asked that he call if he ever planned a change in residence.

Jude looked worried. "You're not thinking of leaving are you?"

"No, not at all." Timothy assured him. "Ms. Unger got promoted or something and I'm getting someone new, that's all."

"Good." The answer was satisfying to Jude. "I've left everything just as it was." Jude pointed to the room. "I was thinking that maybe we could spruce things up with some new curtains or maybe a-"

"No, I'm fine. I don't need anything." Timothy found comfort in the simplicity of having few possessions. With just the necessary essentials he was content. "Thanks Brother Jude, but I have everything I need."

Slightly disappointed, Jude dropped it. "Okay, but if you ever need anything just let me know."

"You've been more than generous. Thank you."

Jude looked as if he wanted to say something but didn't know how. After an uncomfortable pause he said, "Are you excited about teaching today at St. Mary?"

The thought made Timothy's heart pound. "I'm a little nervous. I've never taught a class before."

"Pray for guidance beforehand."

"I need to pray that I don't throw up in front of everyone."

Jude smiled. "Follow the lesson plan. You'll do fine."

A joyous clamor erupted from the first floor. Hoots and praises to God abounded. "What's that?" Timothy wondered out loud.

"Let's go see."

Downstairs, everyone gathered around the janky piano. Miriam had one arm around a man in business attire, the other was holding up a piece of paper. As Jude and Timothy entered she shouted, "Halleluiah!" Everyone cheered.

The excitement dampened quickly as everyone noticed that Jude had entered the room. Out of respect, no one wanted to welcome him back for fear of calling attention to his absence. He walked over to Miriam and she handed him the paper. As he read it a broad smile came across his face. He read the last bit out loud, "The estate leaves ten-thousand dollars to St. Anthony church." Jude crossed himself and looked around at the silent crowd. "Well, don't stop celebrating on my account!" They all erupted into cheers again.

From the sidelines, Timothy observed the celebration solemnly. The memory of he and the boys blowing through ten-thousand dollars in one reckless Miami night soured his stomach. He recalled how important they felt cruising around in Bruno's flashy car. A mess of girls, partying, drinking and gambling that culminated with Fitch puking all over his suit. There was nothing to show for it but a mind-numbing hangover the following morning. Timothy felt sick as he tried to convert the Miami antics into dry beans.

A tap on his shoulder brought him back. "Hey, we have to get over to St. Mary." Sarah and her son Lucas had been waiting for him to come downstairs for some time. "Lucas and I have a load of recycling in the van, but there's still room for you."

"How's it going cotton ball head?" Lucas teased Timothy. The two had developed a thriving relationship on the edicts of adolescent absurdity. Sarah didn't have the sense to correct Lucas' off-color greeting, but it didn't matter. Timothy took no offense, and actually enjoyed making light of his appearance.

"I'd rather be a cotton ball head than a basketball head." Timothy held up his hands on each side of Lucas' head like he was taking measurements. "Look at the size of this noggin! How much grape jelly did you say it holds?"

Lucas laughed playfully. "We have a lot of recycling in the car so you might need to crush some of the cans before your big fluffy head will fit."

"Ugh, can we just go already?" Sarah had no patience for their horsing around.

Jude approached the trio and asked, "Sarah, do you have the workbooks?"

"They are already packed in the van." she replied.

Timothy added, "Lucas had to crush some aluminum cans to get them to fit, but they're secure." Lucas jabbed Timothy's arm impishly.

"Sounds like the students are in good hands." Jude said with a warm smile. It was pleasing to see the three of them getting along well. Not having a father, Lucas had grown very fond of Timothy since his arrival at St. Anthony. Jude knew the relationship was therapeutic for both of them.

The trio made their way two blocks up to St. Mary, an older, more grandiose property than St. Anthony. Its age afforded it a relaxed, sprawling layout with many structures in a neighborhood where residents were typically stacked. Its ample parking covered more square footage than most of the city's commercial buildings.

On the way over, in-between jokes with Lucas, Timothy made an internal plea to God to spare him from catastrophe. "Please guide me to be effective Lord." He begged. It wasn't until he was unpacking the books that he became aware of the fresh perspiration coating his body. It shook his confidence. "Just keep going." He told himself. HIs strategy was simple: follow the lesson plan. One foot in front of the other. Easy. He also knew he could lean on Sarah to do the heavy lifting. It would be over before he knew it.

"I'm in room four, you're in seven. Drop half of the books off in my room first." Sara commanded.

Timothy's heart dropped. "I thought we were teaching the same class?"

"No, you have your own class." Sarah wished he had paid closer attention.

"But-" Timothy began to panic. "I can't do this by myself!"

"It's kind of late to realize that now. There are kids waiting."

Timothy's face lost what little color it had. "Right."

Lucas floated the suggestion, "How about I go with Timothy and help him out?"

Before Sarah could answer, Timothy jumped on it. "Yes, basketball head comes with me."

The five-minute bell rang. "I don't care." Sarah was glad to get rid of the goofy duo. "Just don't do anything stupid."

Timothy gave Lucas half the books, "Put those in your mom's room then come on over." Lucas nodded and jogged off with the stack. "Don't run, you'll drop them!" Timothy heard himself yell out. He had never spoken to a child in such an adult manner before. It was an odd sensation that distracted him momentarily from his nervousness. It even caught Sarah's attention, but she opted not to tease him so soon before class.

A few minutes later the second bell rang. Timothy tried to get the children to all sit down and listen but his slight voice and soft, near fearful, presence was ineffective. Lucas let out a quick, sharp whistle and the whole class stopped cold. "This guy next to me is Mr. Clement. He's your teacher and you need to listen to him. Now sit down in your seats and pay attention." The kids instantly quieted down and scrambled to their seats and waited.

Timothy fumbled through the lesson guide, but it looked to be older than he. More than half of the pages were loose and in haphazard order. He took roll slowly, butchering more than half of the surnames. He then introduced himself and fumbled with the lesson plan. He was to cover the beatitudes, a subject he himself had only become familiar with recently. "Does anyone know what the beatitudes are?" He asked the blank faces before him. No one said a word. "Okay. Um, so I'm going to write them on the board."

With sweaty hands, Timothy spent several minutes scribbling the beatitudes on the blackboard in script that started off large but shrunk to microscopic lettering by the end of the line. Halfway through, one of the students called out, "Mr. Clemmy."

"It's Mr. Clement." Timothy corrected.

"We can't read handwriting." The student's concession made the rest of the kids burst out laughing. Lucas laughed along with them. It was easily the most interesting part of the lesson so far.

Timothy looked at the board and realized the young students couldn't possibly decipher his scribble. "I'll just read them to you then." Timothy pointed to the first illegible line. "Blessed are the poor in spirit, for theirs is the kingdom of heaven." Timothy looked back at the classroom expecting to see enthusiastic faces, but none of the kids were paying attention. "Does anyone want to tell me what they think that means?"

The hand of a small girl shot up. Jude pointed to her. "Um, it, um, means that you don't have no money." The whole class laughed again.

"Well, not exactly."

"This is too hard!" The little girl scolded Timothy. The rest of the class then joined in, complaining and getting more rowdy than ever.

Timothy looked over to Lucas to rein them in, but Lucas shrugged and said, "You're the teacher."

It was a situation that would have normally thrown Timothy completely off, but he remained calm. He didn't buckle and succumb to failure. Instead, his mind became very clear. Time slowed, allowing him to think through his recovery. He wiped the blackboard clean. He drew a large pair of glasses, his preferred starting point for MarGreat. As he filled in her features, the classroom quieted down, with the exception of a few random inquiries as to what he was doing. Timothy did not answer, allowing the suspense to subdue them even more. He added a speech bubble over MarGreat's head with the question, "Poor in spirit?" The question got the students talking amongst themselves, bickering over what is meant. Timothy then drew MarGreat's arms jetting up above her head with her hands clasping a hammer. The children gasped, sending suspicious whispers buzzing through the group. Finally, Timothy drew a piggy bank in front of her and another speech bubble, "How much spirit can I get for a buck?" Timothy turned towards the children and spoke the line in his best warbled MarGreat voice. The kids loved it and begged him to do it again, which he happily did. Once he had gained their attention, Timothy went on to explain the true meaning of the beatitude and they listened intently.

The exploit elevated Timothy to a whole new level of cool in Lucas' eyes. He watched with as much enthusiasm as the younger children as Timothy brought each beatitude comic to life. Lucas loved the silliness, the funny voice but mostly that it was his pal, cotton ball head, putting on the show. "What's her name?" Lucas asked. Immediately, all the children demanded to know as well.

"Her name is MarGreat." Timothy wrote her name on the board and stood back. The collection of smudged chalk drawings made him feel better than he had in ages. He thanked the Lord for allowing him to be effective.

Lucas raved to his mother about Timothy's teaching skills the whole way back to St. Anthony. Sarah didn't say much, but her expressions clearly communicated her skepticism. The situation made Timothy uncomfortable and he downplayed Lucas' praise several times. Sarah eventually changed the subject, "Do you need a ride to your PO's office tomorrow?"

"No, I got it covered." Timothy quickly replied. "I could use a ride to Henn Farms when I get back if you are around."

"I don't get it. Why don't you just let me take you to your PO check-in, and then after we'll go to the Henn Farms."

"It's something I like to do alone."

"You're weird." Sarah sensed being in a familiar place, where every relationship before had taken her. She was too enthusiastic and pushy, not respecting the slower pace at which Timothy lowered his guard. It made him withdraw and she felt slighted for her efforts. "I thought we were friends."

It wasn't anything Timothy was interested in discussing in front of Lucas. "We are. That's why I'm telling you I need to do it alone." Sarah didn't say anything. "So, can you take me to the Henn Farms when I get back?"

Sarah exhaled, unfulfilled. "I guess."

"Can I come?" Lucas pleaded.

Misdirecting her frustration, Sarah snapped at Lucas, "Don't be ridiculous, you'll still be in school!"

"Aw, man!"

Delivering a soft touch to her shoulder, Timothy tried to soften her disposition. "I appreciate your help."

Chapter 38

*D*espite her pouting the day before, Sarah had the van gassed up and waiting for Timothy as soon as he arrived back. Her mousy hair was pulled up in a palm tree ponytail on the top of her head, as it often was when she worked up a sweat in the kitchen. It was how Timothy liked her best, casual.

The two left early enough so there was no risk of running into traffic later in the afternoon. The store wasn't especially far, just buried in the most congested region of the city. The first half of the drive was quiet, neither of them having much to say. Sarah asked him about his morning appointment, but he gave a vague response and went back to staring out the window. She wasn't skilled at keeping any discussion afloat for long and Timothy wasn't helping. His mind was elsewhere wondering how Jude was doing. A jolt from a pothole brought his attention back to the ride. "Thanks for going with me. I appreciate it." Timothy said as genuinely as he could.

Sarah batted her eyes and said, "It's the least I can do for my son's hero." Timothy looked embarrassed. "Don't be bashful; he really thinks the world of you. I've never seen him look up to any of the guys I've-" Sarah rotated her hand in an assumptive motion, "ya know, guys I've known."

"He's a really good kid. You're blessed to have him."

Sarah laughed, "Listen to you – blessed. You're like a mini-Jude."

"I'm just saying. . ." Her patronizing tone made him self-conscious. "Not everyone is fortunate enough to even have kids."

"Well, let me tell you, there was a time I would have disagreed with you on the fortunate part." Sarah giggled inelegantly. "But yes, he has been-" Sara lowered her voice two octaves, "a mighty blessing." She laughed again but Timothy just half-smiled. "Don't be such a stiff!"

"I'm not!" Timothy protested.

"Ever since you came back to the church I can't have any fun with you anymore."

"That's not true."

"It is!" Sarah practically yelled. "It's like you are in a perpetual state of prayer or something." The truth was that he did actually spend most of his day in prayer, asking for guidance, acknowledging his blessings and praising God. He'd lost his taste for secular amusements and wanted nothing more than to serve the Lord as best he could through his second chance. "That's another reason I'm glad you and Lucas get along. At least you can let loose and have some fun with him."

Timothy found himself unexpectedly charmed by her rough-edged distresses. He couldn't fathom what it was about her that he found so alluring. She was visually and conversationally, uninteresting at best, but he was still captivated. "You know how it is. One day you wake up and find out there's a whole other world out there that you never saw before; like you have special glasses that allow you to see everything in a new way."

"I know. I'm just different than you."

"How so?"

"I'm not. . ." A surge of courage filled Sarah as she strained to explain. "When Brother Jude found me I was totally messed up. I had been in and out of rehab half a dozen times. As soon as I would get out and have a little freedom, I went right back to partying." Sharing her past with Timothy was refreshing. Up until now she had kept it scattered just enough to save Timothy from seeing the whole picture. "Then he asks me if I've ever heard about Jesus. My mom and dad never talked about Jesus. It wasn't like they didn't like Jesus; he just never came up in our house. So, after a couple of conversations I got it. I mean, I really understood it. The next thing I know, I stopped partying. I didn't care about it anymore. I felt like you do now – totally alive."

"That's awesome." Timothy was mesmerized.

"It was, for a while." Sarah continued. "I eventually moved on and got my own place. I got Lucas back. It was a good time for us." Her voice quieted. "And then one day I woke up and I got this feeling, just sort of hanging over me. I ignored it, but it kept on popping up. I knew deep down what it was." Sarah had reached the front of the store. She parked along the front curb and unlocked her door.

"Don't get out yet. Tell me more."

"After moving into my apartment I stopped doing things with my church friends. It started with me missing a few meetings and then before I knew it, I wasn't even going to church regularly. There was always something more important that would come up." Sarah opened her window. "It's so hot in here. Brother Jude shows up one day and tells me he's concerned. I tell him everything is fine, but I can tell he knows it isn't. He just knows. He can see right through me. You know why that is?"

Images of Felipe pouring wine over Jude's bleeding head raced back to Timothy. He didn't dare go there. "He wants the best for you and Lucas."

"Everybody's got something inside, deep down, that tries to own them. Everyone. Even Brother Jude."

"Maybe he-"

"That's how he knew I was partying again." She maintained. "We're fighting the same thing. It could have ended real badly for me if he hadn't called me out."

It was hard to deny, but Timothy still felt weird talking about Jude like this. "You're lucky to have him in your life."

"That's what I meant when I said we were different. I figured out that I'm not strong enough to fight off that part of me all the time. It catches up eventually. Praying helps, but I will always need someone to keep me straight. I don't understand why, if Jude and I have the same problem, he is able to resist so easily? Watching you guys is frustrating."

"Us guys?"

Sarah looked peeved. "You've been here a while and I've never heard you talk about gambling or betting on sports." The observation barely fazed Timothy. "People have told me things. I've heard about that wicked temper of yours, but it's hard to believe. I've never even heard you raise your voice."

If it were anyone else, all this poking around might have bothered him. "We're friends." Timothy reached over and took her soft hand into his rough, discolored, scared grasp. "We help each other."

"I need all the help I can get. I don't have any family left, like you."

It was an unexpected comment and Timothy wasn't sure what to say. "Sometimes it's better to have no family."

"What does that mean?"

"My family has disowned me. What's left of my family at least." Saying it out loud hurt his chest. "I can't say I didn't deserve it after what happened to my brother. But-"

This astounded Sarah. "Everyone in your family disowned you?"

"My two sisters and all the relatives."

"They wouldn't help you at all?" Sarah asked and Timothy shook his head. "I'm an only child, but I thought sibling bonds were tighter than that."

"My sisters aren't the kind of people who tolerate flaws or mistakes; especially ones that encroach on their social status. It's easier to just throw those parts away." Timothy looked away. "But only after you've milked the drama thoroughly."

Sarah winced. "That's terrible. Now they've lost two brothers. That must be hard for you"

"They never were very nice to me, even before the mess I made. Even so, I sort of expected them to cool down after a while and come around, but that never happened."

"They didn't talk to you at all after your brother died?"

"They were pretty brutal. Those jackals have always had to have someone on the outs at all times; someone to gossip about and conspire against. I really fed that beast with my screw up." All this talk of his sisters was sucking the life out of him. He shed himself of it and fixated on his uncanny attraction to Sarah. "I like talking with you." She smiled. "I like you."

Squeezing his hand in her clammy grip she warned him, "I'm not what you think I am."

Unable to restrain his enticement, Timothy leaned across and tenderly kissed Sarah's unsure lips then slinked back to his side of the vehicle. "I'll be there for you no matter what happens. You can depend on me."

"You know I'm a mess, right?" Sarah asked him.

"Aren't we all?" Timothy smiled. "I want to know all about you. Maybe we can go out Saturday and have a real date."

"You're sweet." Sarah sat back, and folded her arms. "But I can't. I have other plans."

"Then how about the following week?" His window of opportunity was slipping away, he needed to work fast. "I'll take you out for a good burger. No beans and rice, I promise." Sarah looked gloomy. "It'll be fun." He assured her but she didn't bite. Out of options, he pulled her halfway to him.

Hesitantly, she stared into his pleading eyes. Finally, she succumbed to his romantic gaze, "Fine, a date it is." Timothy instantly kissed her again. This time she grabbed his head and passionately kissed him back. Time stopped. Coming up for air, she grinned and confessed, "I've wanted to do that since you first arrived."

"It would have been different." Timothy reminded her. "I'm not the same guy who first walked in."

"I know." Her smile shriveled slightly.

Chapter 39

"Any minute now," Timothy whispered to himself, looking out over the dark morning skyline. It was how he started all of his days now, with a front-row seat to wind corralling time. His chair positioned front and center of the skyline view; he waited patiently, preparing for the new day. He had found no better way to clear his mind and offer himself to God's will.

Meditations, prayers and thanks flowed freely, unstructured, yet with purpose. Slowly, the golden seed would sprout on the edge of the horizon and convert his internal reflections into awe and praise as it bloomed into the morning sun. God had provided the gift of a new day to the people of his city once again. It was for everyone.

Once the morning's cold gray haze had draped the city, Timothy put on sweats and his running shoes and then hit the street. He had never been a runner before, but had increased his stamina quickly with daily morning jogs. The cool air felt good in his lungs and reminded him how alive he was.

Today, while roving the dingy city blocks, it finally hit him: this was his home. And as unlikely and undesirable as it seemed not long ago, it was now the only place he wished to be. He had become one of the many colorful souls claiming residency in Old Town. An appreciation of its character had developed in him, replacing his disdain for the perpetually renovating city.

The cranky Asian woman dumping an endless load of fish guts in the gutter had come to expect him on the route each morning but never returned his greetings. Still, he never ceased trying to draw a smile out of her. He wondered what her life was like and if Old Town held any common thread between them.

Timothy developed a taste for the bitter industrial scents that lingered in the morning air. They reminded him that the city was alive and constantly forging ahead. If there was progress, there was hope. As he proceeded along his favored route, he was joined, as usual, by a pack of stray dogs. They were harmless, but in numbers and varying sizes would freak an unsuspecting runner out. He had made the error of feeding scraps to them one morning, and the gesture was indelibly recorded in their brains. They always dropped away from him when he passed Franco's deli whose trash was irresistible.

People living on the street were a mixed bag. There were some regulars who smiled back and welcomed Timothy's morning salutation. Many kept to themselves, others solicited, while still others lashed out at Timothy's morning greetings with profane rebukes. He didn't mind. He could remember a time when he would have done the same.

Through trial and error he modified his morning route to minimize his exposure in rougher areas. No part of the city was completely secure, but some places offered more escape routes than others. Passing through Candle Street was the riskiest part of his run, but it was unavoidable. Today he found himself slowing to a stop on Candle Street, something he never did. A fresh sidewalk memorial drew his attention. The young victim's picture lay next to a bouquet of flowers and prayer candle. Jude closed his eyes and said a brief prayer for the young man's soul. After finishing, he heard a man thank him, and looked over to find a gang member giving him an approving nod. It wasn't the kind of person Timothy would normally interact with, but he respectfully nodded back before continuing his run. Jude's mother was right – folks did seem kinder first thing in the morning.

Coming back towards St. Anthony, he spotted a man on the street pleading in Spanish with a woman hanging out of a second-story window above. As Timothy got closer the woman disappeared from the window, and then emerged at the front door. She and the man embraced and kissed. As Timothy passed, he noticed a strong stench of alcohol; the woman became cross and slapped the man's face hard.

With St. Anthony in his sights, Timothy picked up his pace eager to get on with the day. An elderly woman on a ten-speed swerved past, nearly taking him out. On the back of her bicycle was a huge, overstuffed plastic bag packed with aluminum cans. She jetted her hand out as she wobbled away, offering a quick apology for the near collision. Timothy shouted out to her not to worry and have a great day. She gave him a quick thumbs-up, nearly losing control again.

"This town is alright" Timothy thought to himself as he reached home.

Chapter 40

"Just let me take a peek. One quick peek!" Lucas begged Timothy to tell him what was he had in the bag the whole way to St. Mary.

Timothy couldn't believe how quickly the week had gone by and that he was already teaching Sunday school again. "Sorry, you're just going to have to wait." He was up late reviewing the lesson plan and preparing his special study aids. The class gave him a new sensation beyond teaching; for the first time he experienced confidence devoid of arrogance. It was a welcome feeling.

A demure fusion of hot and cold emanated from Sarah. She and Timothy had stolen a few private moments over the week, but were taking it slow. She wasn't sure if getting what she wanted was really what she wanted. Pointing to the mysterious bag she asked, "Are you trying to show me up again? Everyone was talking about you last week."

"I'm just trying to do the best I can." It was the truth. Timothy had no ulterior motives. "I've got a lot of making up to do."

Sarah smirked, "Right."

Unlike the previous week, when he entered the classroom, most of his students were already seated and greeted him with excitement. They all beamed at him and he cheerfully told them that it was great to see them all. Lucas grabbed a chair up front next to Timothy and waited with equal anticipation for the lesson to begin. Timothy asked Lucas to take roll call while he taped large papers face down against the blackboard. The kids squirmed and strained to get a glimpse as roll proceeded. Once done, Timothy turned around and smiled. "Can anyone tell me what church is?" A few hands shot up. Timothy pointed to a young girl in the front, "You."

"God's house." She answered proudly.

Timothy nodded and smiled, "Yes, very good!" Looking out at the other students he asked, "And what do we do at church?"

This time Timothy pointed at a boy in the back, "It's where we all go to pray and worship God." Timothy nodded, and the boy added, "Sometimes people get married there and stuff like that too. Oh, and you get donuts afterwards." All the other kids giggled.

Timothy asked, "It is a pretty special place huh?" The kids agreed. "How do we behave in church? Like we do on the playground?"

"Noooo" the kids drawled in unison.

A fidgety girl shouted out of turn, "You have to sit still and not touch your brothers!"

Another said, "It super quiet like a library. You're not allowed to talk, except to God in your head."

"No running and no chewing gum." A voice called out from the back.

Joining the impromptu free-for-all, another boy declared, "I get in trouble if I have to go to the bathroom more than two times!" All the other kids laughed.

"Those are all very good answers." Timothy praised his students. "How else do we show respect while in church?"

A moment of silence passed while they thought. Finally a hand shot up. "We wear our nice clothes and brush our hair." A girl answered.

Timothy referred to his notes. "Is church the only place we're supposed to be good?" The class gave a resounding 'No!'

A girl in the front row who had been quiet the whole morning pointed at Timothy and squinted one eye shut, "God is everywhere, not just in church. He sees everything. You don't want to do anything that would embarrass you in front of him"

Timothy pointed back at the girl, squinted and said, "It's not polite to point at people" in his best MarGreat voice. The students erupted with excitement. "Okay, settle down. Shhh. . ." He instructed them.

He went over to the first paper he had taped faced down onto the blackboard and held the top of it until everyone had quieted down. He flipped it over and reaffixed it to the blackboard revealing MarGreat walking up to the doors of a church. The students remained quiet, waiting to see what would unfold in the next panel. Timothy flipped the next paper which showed Mar-Great bursting into the church and crying out, "Hey God, how's it going?" Timothy provided the accompanying voice and expressions.

"She can't talk like that in church!" The girl with pointy fingers exclaimed.

The next drawing featured several stern men and women in Sunday dress shushing Mar-Great. In perfect rhythm, Timothy revealed the next panel showing MarGreat appealing to the altar, "Can you believe how rude some people can be?" Again, Timothy provided MarGreat's twerpy warbled voice and the kids denounced MarGreat's audacious irreverence.

Already halfway across the blackboard, Timothy flipped the next panel showing a perturbed nun shaking her finger at MarGreat saying, "Young lady-"

Timothy revealed the next panel with MarGreat on her tip-toes shouting back, "Old Lady!" to the dumbfounded nun. A collection of gasps and giggles flooded the classroom.

Finally, Timothy revealed the last panel. MarGreat irate and informing the nun, "I'm having a private discussion, do you mind?"

"What do you think about MarGreat's behavior in church?" Timothy asked the class.

Immediately, a boy cried, "She's awful!"

"They should kick her out." Said another.

The pointer in the front remarked, "I like her pretty flower pin! Where did she get it?"

It was a minor detail Timothy had added to MarGreat at the last moment; a purple calla lily pendant adorning her shirt. It was his mother's favorite flower. "It was a gift from her mother." Timothy explained, having only thought of it a second before.

"Where is her Mom?" Another girl asked. "If she wasn't at church alone she would behave better."

The interest in MarGreat's backstory surprised Timothy. "Um, I think her Mom is on a work trip. Yep, her Mom travels a lot."

"And what about her Dad?"

It was getting complicated. "I'm pretty sure he's parking the car." Wanting to get back to the lesson material, Timothy asked, "Have any of you ever misbehaved in church?" The students looked around at each other, terrified to admit any wrongdoing. "Maybe just a little bit?"

The boy in the back spoke up. "I once had to use the bathroom three times." All of the kids cracked up.

For the remainder of the class Timothy shared MarGreat comics to help along the discussion on church etiquette. He, Lucas and the students were having such a good time that they were shocked when the bell rang. "Awwww. . ."

"I'll see you all next week." Timothy announced happily.

After the last students cleared out, Timothy began shoving the MarGreat panels into the wastepaper basket. Lucas stopped him, "What are you doing!"

"Cleaning up."

"You can't throw these away, they're great!"

Timothy laughed, "They're just to help me get through the class." He pointed to the rough lines on the paper. "I'm not very good."

At that moment Sarah entered the classroom teasing, "Well, aren't you Mr. Popular! All of my students are asking if you can teach my class too."

"He's really good!" Lucas told his Mom.

Timothy played it down, "I'm just following the lesson plan."

Sarah walked over to a comic on the board of MarGreat turning to a little girl in the pew next to her and saying, 'Last night my Dad made his famous meatloaf. It was so bad that my butt threw up!' Sarah shook her head, "Classy!"

Chapter 41

"You wanted to see me?" Timothy caught up to Jude in the main hall. Being summoned outside of his established routine didn't happen often, and it caused speculation to explode in his head.

A welcoming smile from Jude put Timothy at ease. "How is everything going Timothy?" He asked squarely.

"Great!" Timothy answered without hesitation. "Really great actually!" He expounded.

"I'm glad to hear that." Jude's gaze never broke. "How was your meeting with your new PO?"

Timothy's face was blank for a moment as he cleared away all of the other exciting things in his life to remember. "Oh yeah, it was fine." Jude remained silent, waiting for more details. "Routine stuff. I wasn't there too long. She doesn't want to see me unless I plan to move."

Jude's gaze intensified. "Have you had any feelings. . ." As he searched for the words, Timothy worried that Jude had found out about he and Sarah. ". . .urges to gamble?"

It was the last thing Timothy expected. "Gamble? No, not in the slightest. Not since. . . ya know."

An oscillating stare between each of Timothy's eyes and Jude appeared satisfied. "Okay. Let me know if that ever changes."

An uncomfortable nod from Timothy ended the subject. "Um, there was something I wanted to ask you." Jude listened attentively. "Would it be possible to get a small advance on my pay?" After the gambling question, there was no way to ask without also divulging his plans. "I asked Sarah out and need a little extra."

"Oh, wow!" Jude remarked, hardly surprised. There were few worse kept secrets. "Sure, I think we can arrange that."

"Thank you!" Greatly relieved, Timothy expressed his gratitude.

"Timothy." Jude brought his focus back. "It's important that you remember that everyone's spiritual journey is unique and develops at its own pace."

"I know."

Even with giving the abbreviated version, it was harder to say than Jude expected. "I just don't want to see you let down due to unrealistic expectations."

Timothy was unsure what Jude was digging at, but he wasn't interested in having the conversation. Disclosing his interest in Sarah was hard enough. "No need to worry Brother Jude."

Even Jude was ready to move the conversation along. "Father Connor tells me that you are doing a great job on Sundays."

"It's not just me. Lucas helps out."

"He's had three different parents tell him how much their kids love your class. They can't wait for Sunday to come." Jude patted Timothy's back. "Good work."

Sarah's criticism of his MarGreat classroom lesson had been hanging over Timothy's head. It was nice to hear the compliment. "I started drawing again to help with teaching the class. It makes it easier for me and the kids respond well."

"Wonderful!"

"There's this little girl I draw." It felt weird explaining MarGreat. Timothy decided Jude didn't need to know all the details about "Stevie the Great". "It helped me get through the beatitudes without totally croaking."

"Those who know great mercy will show great mercy."

Timothy wasn't sure what to say. "Anyway, it's been really great."

Chapter 42

S tepping off the curb, Timothy welcomed the perfect Friday night. The air was comfortable; not too cold, not too humid, and smelled better than usual. The walk to Sarah's apartment was a clean two block stint without any hazardous obstacles to plague him, even at dusk. For the first time since his job interview, Timothy donned non-casual attire. He even persuaded Miriam to trim his hair that afternoon. "Don't be nervous. Girls don't like nervous boys." She scolded him during the haircut, but he wasn't nervous. He was on cloud nine.

Armed with a bouquet of Miriam's best wild flowers and a wad of advanced pay, Timothy was ready to show Sarah that a relationship with him was not just possible, but in his mind, their destiny. As he strolled along he thought about his blossoming relationship with Lucas and how strong it had become. Surely she appreciated that. His resolve to support Sarah when tempted by her demons was strong as well. He couldn't relate to it yet, but if the temptation to gamble or fight did pursue him, he was confident he could overcome it with her support. They were both committed to the Lord, and they knew each other's strengths and weaknesses. Temptation didn't stand a chance, he thought.

Hiding the flowers behind his back, he proceeded up the manicured walkway to Sarah's front door. Along the way he asked the Lord to let his will be known. If a romance with Sarah was right, he was all in. If not, he'd try to persuade God to see things his way. He took a deep breath and then rang the bell. While waiting for her to answer, he noticed his white-haired reflection in the window but looked away. He wasn't going to obsess over his appearance. If she wanted him, she'd have to take him as he was - cotton-head, lobster claws and all. A moment passed and he rang the bell again. He waited another minute, but still there was no answer. He looked into the window and tried to see through the curtains, but couldn't make anything out of the shadows. "Maybe she's still dropping off Lucas." He thought. Sarah had planned for Lucas to spend the night at a friend's house. She wanted to shield him from whatever was brewing between her and Timothy until it felt right.

The shrill of squealing tires rang out in the alley behind Sarah's apartment. The complex had a dozen units, all tenants sharing the gravel paved alley in back for parking. More skidding tires trailed by echoes of female laughter peppered the evening air. The sound was familiar. Not the car, but Sarah's laughter.

Equably, Timothy walked the winding path leading to the back ally. Sarah's giggling grew louder as he traveled, mixed with the occasional automotive bravado that ate away at his cool.

He didn't see it at first when he stepped into the cluttered strip. It wasn't until Martin, the bartender at Cleo's, cackled that Timothy noticed the two of them in his car down at the end. Two of his wheels were up on the curb, leaving his muscle car unleveled. Again, Martin punched his engine and squealed the tires, leaving a black mark on the curb. Sarah's hysterical response was forced and unwarranted for the level of amusement he was providing.

Timothy marched down the center of the gravel road, heading straight for Martin's skewed car. Dusk had mercifully spared him until now from seeing Sarah sprawled across Martin's front seat, hanging on his neck, feeding his ego. The two of them acting like delinquent middle-school drop outs. Glaring at Timothy with bloodshot eyes, Martin took one last drag on his pungent clove cigarette, and flicked it in Timothy's direction with a smirk. The clove stench was quickly lost in a fusion of alcohol and other bad habits. Sarah was too bombed out of her mind to even notice Timothy's arrival.

And then it returned. That white hot mixture of adrenaline and hatred Timothy had parted ways with at the bottom of a dank stairwell. It had been a while, but it was back, and hadn't lost any potency. "Sarah!" Timothy barked.

Like a bobble-head doll, Sarah lifted her head off Martin's shoulder and clumsily followed the voice. Her dazed eyes floundered over him for a few seconds before she recognized Timothy. "Oh, you brought flowers, how cute!" Martin laughed at her patronizing tone. "Martin, this is Timmy, my date for the evening." The two of them sloppily snickered.

There had been many things Timothy had to deal with over the past few years that required tapping into strength he didn't know he had; keeping himself from beating Martin within an inch of his life was by far the hardest. "What are you doing Sarah?"

"I'm just having a little bit of fun." Her syrupy words mocked him. Then, she twisted the blade further, nipping at Martin's neck before saying, "Timmy is like God's number one cheer-leader." Martin cackled, showing his crooked, yellowed teeth. "He used to be fun, but now he just praises the Lord!" She uninhibitedly shouted out, "Amen brother!" Her slurred voice echoed throughout the parking lot, chased by Martin's laughter.

Her barbed tongue played with Timothy's head, redirecting his rage away from Martin and onto her. It wasn't just rage though. The painful sensation of betrayal, like that dished out by his awful sisters, kicked him in the gut hard. All of his pleas to the Lord to remain strong seemed to go unheard. How was it possible that minutes earlier he had declared himself Sarah's confidant, yet now he loathed her for her graphic infidelity? "Lord, give me strength." He prayed silently.

"Hooray for God! He made you so damn perfect!" Her diction was stiff with contempt.

After hearing her spiteful comment, Timothy's mind instantly cooled and all his hateful venom drained away. He remembered teaching the beatitudes during his first Sunday school class and the assurances they promised. 'Blessed are you when they insult you and utter every kind of evil against you because of Me.' He remembered it and looked with pity on Sarah. "Get out of the car Sarah. This isn't right."

Sarah turned to Martin. "See how good this one is? He wants to save me." All traces of laughter and fun had dissipated. She looked back at Timothy, "I tried to tell you, I need a real man, not a saint!"

The car lurched off the curb and back into the gravely alley, forcing Timothy to jump back. He pleaded with her, "Sarah, it doesn't have to be like this, you've got a choice!" Before she could respond, Martin's wheels screeched as they peeled away down the makeshift drag strip and dissolved into the city. When the dust cleared, Miriam's flowers lay trampled in the street between grooves of tire tread. Jude was right; his expectations had been over inflated. Timothy figured he had his answer from the Lord, and wasn't going to challenge it. He prayed for Sarah's safety, knowing he would never be able to protect her himself.

Chapter 43

As Jude reached out to shake Timothy's shoulder, it shocked him that Timothy's shirt was
drenched in sweat, but he put it out of his mind. Timothy stirred and rolled over. Jude shook
his other shoulder, equally sweaty. This time Timothy sat straight up and panted, shaking off the
remnants of a bad dream. "Come, I need your help." Jude quietly commanded.

Spending a minute to change his garments, Timothy could tell even this minor delay was
agonizing for Jude. He finished quickly and caught up with Jude who was already a quarter of
the way down the first flight. A mid-western woman's voice was fluttering up from the ground
floor, but Timothy could only make out a few words. "Who's that?" He asked, and wondered
what hour it was.

"She lives in the neighborhood. She has a son who goes to school with Lucas." Jude spoke
quietly, being frugal with his breath. An authoritative male voice backed with weeping met their
ears as well.

When they reached the entry hall, it stunned Timothy to find Lucas in a chair, bent over
and sobbing. A police officer and a woman he'd never seen before were also present. "Officer,
this is Timothy Clement. He is probably the closest thing to a father the boy has known." Jude
announced.

Lucas sprung from the chair and rushed Timothy, wrapping his arms tight around him.
Timothy wasn't expecting the arresting embrace and stammered before comforting the boy. "It's
going to be okay." He instinctively declared, not having the faintest idea what was going on.
Lucas didn't say anything, he just sobbed despondently against Timothy for a while. Eventually,
Jude peeled Lucas away from Timothy and led him outside for some fresh air.

The police officer took Timothy aside and asked, "I understand you were acquainted with
the juvenile's mother?" Timothy nodded. "She was found unresponsive this morning about two
blocks from here. The medics were unable to resuscitate her. I'm sorry for your loss."

"Found unresponsive?" Timothy's head was spinning. "I just saw her." He looked at the wall
clock which read three-twenty. "Less than nine hours ago. Are you sure?"

The officer nodded. "My partner and I took the call." Lowering his voice he continued, "She's
had a history of problems."

"I know." Timothy was numb with shock. None of it seemed real. "What happened?"

"It will be a few weeks before the toxicology screening comes back, but based on the para-
phernalia we found at the scene, preliminary assessment is an overdose." Reflexively, the officer
paused to let Timothy digest what he said. Delivering this news never got easier.

"She was with someone." Timothy blurted out. "Maybe that creep can fill in the blanks."

"We've picked up a person of interest based on information provide here." The officer dubiously added, "It's unlikely he'll be charged. Being a bad influence isn't a criminal offense."

"How much does the boy know?"

"Technically, she died of heart failure. That's what has been communicated to him. He was spending the night at a friend's house." He pointed to the woman on the other side of the room. "Father is unknown. There is no next of kin. He insisted we take him here." The officer handed Timothy a folded up paper bundle.

Timothy opened up the tattered wad. In Sarah's handwriting were instructions for Lucas's care if anything were to happen to her. Several members of the St. Anthony staff were listed as suitable candidates for legal guardianship, including Jude, Miriam and to his surprise, himself. "Seems like she saw this coming." Timothy said as the first wave of grief fractured his numbness. He turned away from the officer, not wanting to share the intimately painful moment with a stranger. From behind, he heard Jude and Lucas come back in and approach.

Lucas tapped on Timothy's shoulder prompting him to turn around and poorly disguise his grief with a half-smile. "I don't want to go with child services." His face was extraordinarily puffy and red from crying. "Mom said to go to you if I ever needed anything. She always said you were a good man."

"Your mom was very special to me." The young man's despair reminded him of living through the loss his own mother. He remembered being left to the wolves afterwards. He didn't wish that on anyone. "If it is okay with Brother Jude, I'd like to become your guardian." Lucas nodded at the idea. Timothy held the boy's chin forward and looked him square in the eye. "Don't let all this fool you. Your mother was a wonderful woman. Sometimes bad things happen to good people, and we don't ever know why."

"God rest her soul." Jude wept. "You are welcome here. Both of you are welcome here as long as you want."

The officer interrupted. "That is nice of you to step up Mr. Clement, but in light of your past record I'm afraid you don't meet the qualifications." Disappointment filled the room.

"It is I who will be his guardian." Jude announced. The officer looked up and back between Timothy and Jude not buying the convenient last minute switch. "Sarah requested me didn't she?" Jude pointed to the paper in Timothy's hands.

Realizing that even with Timothy's criminal record it was the boys best shot, the officer agreed. "I'll notate it on the report." No one else was going to take in a stray teenager.

Jude whispered in Timothy's ear, "Sarah's counting on you - Dad."

Chapter 44

*T*here are many highs and lows that come with instant parenthood. Inundated with missed opportunities, unrealistic expectations and hormones, Timothy struggled at first to stay afloat. He reached out to Jude, but Jude was of no help. He reminded Timothy that he had no children of his own, and hence no secret wisdom. He delivered the news with a smile and an encouraging confidence in Timothy's abilities. Timothy muddled on, better than he expected. Through trial and error and much practice, he settled into a comfortable rhythm and eventually life was as good as ever at St. Anthony.

Under the wing of Timothy's empathy, Lucas pressed on. The sting of his loss softened more each day. The two shared the unwanted comprehension of life without a mother. It was that understanding that built up trust between them, and strengthened their bond.

As guardians go, few were more qualified to nurture Lucas than Timothy. His allegiances to Sarah, and the Lord, compelled him to provide Lucas the best life possible. He treated his new responsibilities seriously, knowing them to be a great blessing. He did what he could to ensure Lucas was on the right path and living life to the fullest. Caring for Lucas was not work, but one of his greatest pleasures so far.

Additionally, Lucas's model behavior made the transition easier for everyone. Timothy never had to get after him to do his chores, complete his homework or remember his manners. It wasn't uncommon to find Lucas holed up with a book, or his Bible, in all corners of St. Anthony. Early on, Timothy had to persuade Lucas to go outside with his friends; he knew returning to a normal routine was crucial for healing. In time, Lucas loosened up and did go back to his normal teenage life, complete with drama, ephemeral independence and a proclivity for pretty girls.

Raising Lucas was a double-blessing. It also provided Timothy with a peek at what might have been; a taste of what his peers were experiencing outside of Old Town. He knew he didn't deserve it. He was especially thankful for the sensations that surfaced while he interacted with Lucas; sensations he hadn't experienced since Stephen's death. It was like he was a father-brother hybrid, blessed beyond measure to experience both.

Every afternoon after Lucas got home from school he'd badger Timothy to draw him a Mar-Great comic. Today was no different. "Whatcha got for me today?" Lucas hounded as he burst into the room.

"Hello to you too!"

Lucas donned his best British accent, "Hello, hello, good to see you sir. Might I be privy to your latest etching?"

The amount of energy Lucas brought into a room astounded Timothy. "Whatever happened to a simple hello?"

An imaginary horse filled Lucas' bowed legs, "Enough with the pleasantries." His eyes narrowed like an old western bandit. "Now where's the stuff Clement? Don't play stupid with me or your horse gets it!"

It wasn't his style, but Timothy had learned how to play his part in these silly scenes Lucas invented. He held up his hands and said, "Now don't do anything rash. I hid it."

"Where is it hombre?"

"I guess I got no choice but to tell you now." Timothy wiped imaginary sweat from his forehead. "It's in your homework! There, I told you! Finish your homework and you'll find it."

"Oh come on, that isn't fair!" Lucas broke character and whined.

"What can I say? Don't come to a gunfight with an invisible horse."

Giggling, Lucas rushed Timothy and put him in a headlock. Timothy lifted Lucas' scrawny body, still holding tight to his neck, still giggling profusely. "Put me down cotton head!" Lucas protested.

Lucas' grip slipped. Timothy hoisted him onto his shoulders horizontally and then spun him around like a professional wrestler, the two of them laughing so hard they could barely breathe. "Give up?"

"Never!"

The two collapsed ungracefully onto the floor. Timothy grabbed his stomach and yelled, "Ouch!"

"What's the matter?"

"I've had a sixteen year old on my shoulders, that's what's the matter." Timothy laughed while trying to catch his breath. "I guess I'm not as young as I used to be. Pulled a muscle or something."

A playful smug expression crept over Lucas' face, "So, you admit defeat – old man!"

Timothy pointed to Lucas' book bag, "Homework."

"I finished it on the bus."

"Then why-" Timothy fought for another breath. "Why didn't you just say so?"

"How much fun would that be?" Lucas snickered. "Now, how about that MarGreat comic?"

Timothy groaned aloud. "Over there." He pointed to his well-worn Bible. "Matthew 6:16"

Lucas snatched up the Bible and opened it up to the scripture. A folded half-sheet of paper held the spot. Before removing the paper, Lucas read the passage, "When you fast, do not look gloomy like the hypocrites. They neglect their appearance, so that they may appear to others to be fasting." Then Lucas extracted the paper and opened it.

This was Timothy's favorite part of the day; watching Lucas' intent expression dissolve into joy after reading a new MarGreat comic. A sequence of frames showed MarGreat's cheeks bursting as she shovels in her school lunch without taking a breath. Then finishes by sucking down her milk in one sip, then plops back, bloated, and exhausted. Looking on with dumbfounded expressions, her classmates are stunned by the lunch inhalation they've just witnessed. MarGreat notices all the judgmental eyes on her and asks, "What? Haven't you ever fasted before? That's a new record for me!"

Chapter 45

"So much has changed." Miriam sighed as she and Jude waited for Timothy and Lucas to join them downstairs at the piano.

Jude nodded. "Life goes on."

Once a month, the St. Anthony staff got together to remember Sarah by singing her favorite hymn, Amazing Grace. The piano's wooden finish was unevenly worn, and many of its keys had soured, but Miriam could still manage to bang the melody out of the schlocky upright with her arthritic fingers. "I worry about that boy." She confided in Jude.

"No need to worry. Timothy is doing a fine job caring for him."

"I meant Timothy." Miriam's permanent scowl itched. "He still ain't over her. He walks around all distracted like, and he don't eat like he used to."

He couldn't disagree, but Jude didn't wish to feed her anxiety. "He just needs more time."

"I remember you saying that about Sarah once."

The phantom of Sarah's fruity, paint thinner breath tickled his memory. "This isn't like that." He hoped. "Nothing tears a young man up like heartbreak."

"Here they are now." Miriam stabbed the keys with introductory bars, drawing a dozen milling bodies near. Timothy and Lucas merged with the others around the piano and lent their voices to the memorial. Always the performer, Lucas belted out the hymn with gusto. Although the piano faltered, and the hodgepodge chorus couldn't agree on a key, to Timothy's ears there was no sweeter harmony than their collective remembrance.

Before the last chord had fully faded, Miriam shifted tempo and led the group in a birthday song for Lucas. The scent of candles filled the room as a chocolate cake with seventeen candles was brought in from the kitchen. Lucas was very moved by their celebration, so much that he required some assistance to extinguish all the candles. When the song ended Timothy gave him a hearty hug and said, "You didn't think we'd forget your birthday did you?"

Collecting hugs and kisses from everyone assembled, Lucas thanked them all profusely. Jude presented him with a small box. "What's this?" He asked.

"Go on and open it." Everyone urged.

With all eyes on him, Lucas slowly unboxed the present. Resting on a bed of synthetic cotton was a necklace with a St. Anthony pendant attached. "Like yours!" Lucas exclaimed to Timothy. His unsteady hands fumbled to open the clasp.

Miriam took the necklace from him and unhitched it. Like an old pro, she reached up and affixed it around his neck in one motion. "There you go." She stepped back and smiled. "Splendid.

Now who wants cake?" Miriam turned to Timothy and poked his ribs. "I'm bringing you two slices young man!"

Timothy ignored the comment and stole Lucas away, leading him over to a side table. From the table drawer he produced a rectangular shirt box decorated with crooked ribbon. "This is a little something from me." He handed it to Lucas.

Lucas' eyes widened as he felt the object's weight. "I don't think there are clothes in here." He ripped away the ribbon and lifted off the top of the box. "Cool!" He shouted, attracting looks from the others. Inside was a repurposed Sunday school three-ring binder. A pair of glasses was drawn on the strips of masking tape which concealed the original cover. The lesson plan inside had been replaced with a collection of MarGreat comics specially created for Lucas. Some were old favorites and some never seen.

"I hope you like it."

"Are you kidding me? I love it!" Lucas flipped through the pages wearing a huge grin.

Giving a tug on the corner, Timothy suggested, "You should put this away for now." He spotted Jude's straining neck angled in their direction from across the room. "Now is a time to celebrate."

Lucas nodded and returned the book to its box. "Thanks for everything." The gift would become Lucas' most prized possession. "I don't know where I'd be right now if it weren't for you."

Timothy patted Lucas on the back. "You are very welcome."

Chapter 46

*E*aster break had arrived and with it an abundance of shenanigans around the church. The sounds of laughter reverberated through the grounds, something Miriam in particular took great delight in. Time had filed down her barbed temperament. She gladly filled the role of surrogate mother to both Timothy and Lucas, doing whatever she could to ease their trauma. It pleased her to see them interact playfully with each other. She was sure Sarah was smiling down on them.

The St. Anthony necklace hadn't left Lucas' neck in two months. He slept, showered and lived every moment with it on, usually displaying it outside his shirt collar despite Timothy's recommendation not to.

With his new responsibilities, Timothy didn't get much time to spend with Jude anymore. Only when Lucas was out with his friends, and Timothy was able to slow down and enjoy a moment of peace in Miriam's garden, did he realize how much he missed their conversations. He thanked the Lord daily for the blessing of their friendship. Just as Jude had professed, it seemed the Lord had a plan for him after all.

"Hello Timothy." Jude's greeting yanked Timothy from his daydream.

Planting himself in Miriam's flower garden was one of Timothy's favorite ways to spend what little free time he had. The warm weather and floral aroma always whisked his thoughts away. "Brother Jude, I was just thinking about you."

"Good thoughts I hope." Timothy smiled. "I imagine you have a great deal on your mind these days." Jude pointed to the vacancy next to Timothy, "Do you mind?"

"Please, sit."

Jude winced as he settled in next to Timothy. "My knee is stiff. It acts up when we have beautiful weather like this."

Timothy nodded, "Perfect day."

Pointing to the stacks of colorful planters nearby, Jude recalled, "There was a broom closet right over there once, at the far end of a hallway. When I first came to St. Anthony I was part of the custodial crew. I always hated having to make that long walk by myself. I knew when I got to that closet it would be dark and gloomy. Only one way in or out. No chance of running into a friendly face." Jude looked around at the stunning flowers thriving around them. "I never would have imagined something as beautiful as this garden could occupy the same spot."

"Was this whole place very different before the riots?"

Slowing pivoting his head, Jude's memory projected what had once been there. "Yes." Spending a moment more reminiscing, he outlined the school footprint with his finger. "There's a void. This was once a home to playful chatter. I miss it."

It was hard for Timothy to imagine St. Anthony any better than it was. "Well, I like it here."

"When something goes away and leaves a space, anything can fill it; good or bad. This kitchen of ours is a good filler." Jude looked at Timothy. "Same thing happens inside of people. When life takes a chunk out of us, we can either fill that hole with something good or something bad. Do you know what I mean?"

It was obvious what Jude was saying. "I'm not doing anything I shouldn't be."

"Miriam says you've been running more errands than usual."

"That's true, I have." Jude was quiet, waiting for further explanation. "I've got some things to take care of."

"She says you've been keeping a stash of money in your room." Jude said as unthreateningly as possible.

Surprisingly, Timothy did not get upset. "That's true as well. But I promise you Brother Jude, I am not gambling."

"This isn't just about you now." Jude lectured. "You've committed to the welfare of that boy. The last thing he needs is another person in his life losing control."

"I know." Timothy replied confidently. "I'm not gambling."

From inside, Lucas's voice rang out calling for Timothy. "I hope for his sake that's the case." Jude finished.

Lucas ran out back and grabbed Timothy's hand. He pulled on it until Timothy stood up. "You won, you won Timothy!"

"Whoa, slow down."

"You won!" Lucas shouted as if Timothy was a dolt. "You got the grand prize!"

"For what?"

The mention of grand prize made Jude uneasy. "What are you talking about?" He dreaded hearing more.

Lucas let out a free-spirited hoot. "I entered one of the MarGreat comics you gave me on my birthday in an online contest. It won first place!" Lucas pulled again on Timothy's arm. "Come on, let's go to the library and I'll show you."

"The library?" Jude asked.

"They got Internet there." Lucas explained.

"Hold on." Timothy wanted to make clear to Jude he had nothing to do with it. "I never agreed to entering any contest."

"I told you they were great!" Lucas delighted, ignoring Timothy's reprimand. "Let's go!"

"You two go ahead, I'm going to rest my knee."

The Old Town library was less than a block away. Not looking back, Lucas and Timothy scampered off. With adrenaline surging through their veins, they flew through the street and were running up the library steps in minutes.

Once through the front doors, Lucas grabbed an open terminal and logged on to the website. "Here, check it out." He panted.

Over Lucas' shoulder, Timothy saw the words, 'Winner Announced!' flashing. Directly below was his MarGreat comic titled, 'The Bully'.

"I love this one!" Lucas exclaimed in a hush.

In the comic, MarGreat arrives home from school. Her father asks how her day was and she cries out, "Terrible!" Her father asks what happened and MarGreat shouts, "I was bullied!" After more coaxing, MarGreat divulges that it was a French foreign exchange student who bullied her. Her father asks, "What did she do to you?" MarGreat tells how the girl pestered her all day long. MarGreat is so grief-stricken she can't say any more. "You can tell me anything." Her dad assures her. Finally she musters up the courage and blurts out, "She asked me to be her friend!" The phone rings and father answers it. "Yes Mr. Principal I understand." Sternly asks Margreat, "Did you happen to take that little French girls lunch money today?" MarGreat smiles, "Just a little loan between friends."

It was strange to see his private sketches out in public like this. "I can't believe anyone else likes MarGreat."

"She's hilarious!" Lucas scrolled down the page to the comments section. "Lots of people like her, see?" There were hundreds of comments, mostly positive. Pointing to a particularly vulgar critique Lucas added, "There are always some twelve-year-olds who aren't happy unless your comic takes place during the robotic zombie apocalypse. Don't let it get you down."

Then Timothy noticed for the first time the cash prize award. "Ten thousand bucks?"

"I know, isn't that great!" Lucas couldn't hide his excitement. "What are you going to do with it?"

It struck Timothy that he had involuntarily been made steward of funds he would have clearly mismanaged in the past. The Lord was merciful and gave him an opportunity to do what was right. He remembered the man who left the same amount to St. Anthony in his will, but dismissed the possibility. He knew his thirsty ego would be too enticed by the glory. Instead, right there on the spot Timothy decided to put the money away for when Lucas turned eighteen. He was a good kid and deserved a break entering adulthood. He could use it for school, to start his own business, or whatever. "I think we should celebrate. How about some ice cream?"

"Excellent!" Lucas agreed and then closed the web session.

As they approached the library exit, Timothy slowed, "Hold up, I'm going to use the men's room first."

"Okay, I'll be over there." Lucas pointed to a chair near the book return chute before Timothy scuttled away. After sitting down, Lucas observed a mother and her young daughter returning their books. The mother looked exhausted. Her daughter nestled up to her side and squeezed close. The weariness on the woman's face transformed into a reassuring glow. The daughter's contentment made Lucas long for his mother. She wasn't a perfect mother, but she loved him wholly, just like the woman in front of him. He said a quiet prayer and waited for Timothy to return.

Chapter 47

"*H*e isn't here right now. Can I take a message?" Jude asked, mildly annoyed as the call-waiting tone beeped. "Can- can you hold for a sec?" Pressing the receiver once, he answered. "St. Anthony, may I help you?" Jude's forehead crinkled as he listening to the caller, "What? No." He squared off a stack of small square papers on his desk. "I'm not at liberty to give out that kind of information." He paused. "No, absolutely not. I'm sorry; I have to go now." Jude hung up the receiver and sighed. The phone rang again. "Hello?" Jude's irritation was less repressed. "Oh! So sorry, I forgot you were on hold. Let me take down your name and number and pass it along." Jude scribbled on another small square sheet of paper and added it to the pile. "Very well, goodbye."

The familiar sound of Timothy and Lucas arriving home murmured outside Jude's office. Following a playful exchange with Miriam, the two entered Jude's office carrying several grocery bags full of canned goods. "Check it out! This month's canned food drive is off to an early start." Lucas announced.

"Some aren't even dented. Mr. Angston really pulled through this time." Timothy added.

Jude briefly showed his approval of the collection. "Great. Put them over there." Jude pointed to a table in the corner. Once Timothy freed his hands of the bags, Jude thrust the stack of small papers to him. "Here."

"What's this?"

"Apparently, you are some kind of a celebrity." Jude eased back down into his chair, looking stiff and inflexible as ever. "Reporters, television producers, publishers, they're all in that pile. Your silly girl comic is quite the sensation."

Surprised, Timothy asked Lucas, "How many contests did you enter?"

"Just one!" The attention shocked Lucas as well. "Looks like MarGreat might be going viral."

"What?" Jude was uncomfortable with all of it. "Is that legal?"

Lucas' wheels were spinning. "It's a good thing. I think."

Restlessly, Jude told Timothy, "One guy was trying to track down Ms. Unger, your old probation officer. I don't know how they ever got her name."

The mention of Ms. Unger dampened whatever enthusiasm Timothy had for MarGreat's popularity. "I'm just the same old Timothy Clement. There's nothing to tell these people." He crumpled the wad of messages in his hand.

"No, Timothy. You're going about this all wrong." Lucas took the papers from him. "People are only digging around because you haven't given them anything."

"I don't have anything to give them!"

"Not yet, but we'll fix that." Lucas assured him. "Finish up whatever you've got to do around here and then we'll go down to the library."

It wasn't making Timothy feel any better. "I don't want to go researching how to answer these annoying calls."

"We're not." Lucas smiled. "We're going to build a website."

Part III

Seventy Eight Times

If we are unfaithful
he remains faithful,
for he cannot deny himself. – 2 Timothy 2:13

Chapter 48

The more Timothy tried to downplay it, the greater MarGreat's popularity flared up; like his modesty was gasoline. Very quickly, life changed for Timothy, and accordingly for Lucas and St. Anthony. Initially, Timothy gave a few local interviews, mostly to get Lucas to stop pestering him. Those appearances attracted larger markets and from there, his visibility snowballed to a national level nearly overnight.

The website Lucas created was getting thousands of visits daily. The rapid growth required Timothy to invest in a personal computer for Lucas to manage the site, and do homework of course. Timothy was clueless when it came to technology. He thankfully entrusted the website, e-mail, and community content to Lucas. It did cut down on calls and uninvited visits to St. Anthony, but not completely. Lucas helped Timothy scan and upload new MarGreat comics to the site every week. He also printed out all of Timothy's new email messages every Tuesday since the computer screen gave Timothy headaches. The email address attracted fair-weather friends from his previous life requesting freebies, but he never replied. Occasionally, a celebrity, or more likely, someone impersonating a celebrity, would drop a kind note. The best perk he received in his email box was from Customs Agent Hosnic, the very same one who flew back from Peru with him. Hosnic complimented Timothy on getting his life together and said he was a good role model to others who had made mistakes. He told Timothy to call if he ever needed anything. Timothy kept the message as a reminder that he had changed.

It was another perfect day for relaxing in Miriam's garden. Timothy was reading his latest batch of email messages enjoying the floral aromas. Jude sat nearby, having just finished warning him about the dangers of gambling for the millionth time. It was becoming harder to not be offended by Jude's 'concern', but Timothy knew he had no license to complain. "Brother Jude, what does syndication mean?" He asked.

"It means an author's work is published in several different periodicals or newspapers. Sort of like those magazines and newspapers are subscribing to the author's work. The author's content might be distributed daily, weekly or monthly."

Timothy read the email in his hand again. "That's a good thing then, right?"

Jude nodded. "It can be lucrative." Timothy passed the correspondence to Jude. He read it, nodding as he made his way through it. "Wow, eight papers." He remarked with raised eyebrows. Halfway through the email he grumbled, "This can't be right, that is a lot to pay for one of your comics." Hunching forward, his finger began leading his eye. "That's per each paper!" His voice squeaked, and he read faster. "Insurance, housing allowance, car allowance. . ." Jude pulled the paper even closer to his face.

"I don't even have a car."

"Oh my!" Jude exclaimed towards the bottom. "The sign-on bonus would buy you a car."

The offer made Timothy nervous. It was either part of God's plan for him, or a destructive distraction. He couldn't tell. "I don't know what to do Brother Jude. It feels way out of my league."

"Perhaps your league has changed." Jude answered.

"I haven't changed!" Timothy protested.

Jude smiled, "That's not what I said." Timothy looked frustrated. "But, I'd disagree. I think you have changed, for the better." Jude shook the email in his hand. "This isn't your garden variety job offer. It might be worthwhile to take them up on a meeting." Jude passed the email back to Timothy.

Timothy thought about it. It couldn't hurt to take a closer look. "Lucas has been doing all of the complicated stuff for me. I just like to draw MarGreat. But he's seventeen and this is more serious than managing a website. I need help. Can you go down there with me?"

"Of course!" It delighted Jude that Timothy wanted to involve him. It allowed him to keep a close eye on Timothy.

"It says Luric Syndicate will cover all transportation and lodging expenses for me and my representation." Timothy looked at Jude. "I'll give them a call today."

The comics editor at Luric Syndicate was more aggressive and fast talking than Timothy was accustomed to. Timothy explained that he and Jude would like to visit their offices in two weeks. A handful of masterfully crafted quips and ego-strokes whizzed by and suddenly Timothy found himself agreeing to a meeting in two days. Their first class tickets were reserved before the brief conversation even ended. Timothy stood by the phone and wondered what just happened.

Jude didn't get too perturbed with Timothy. He knew it was his lack of negotiation skills that necessitated his presence at the meeting in the first place. It wasn't so bad, he welcomed the impromptu escape.

Located in the heart of an expansive upscale metropolis, The Luric Syndicate building was synonymous with the area's rich history. Passed down to generation after generation of Luric sons, it had consistently prospered, swallowing up its competitors in the process. Only Fluto Media Solutions posed a serious threat to their market share. With an equally impressive history, Fluto kept Luric Syndicate on their toes.

A swank town car shuttled Timothy and Jude from the hotel to Luric Syndicate headquarters. For the second time, Timothy was clad in one of Jude's suits. He promised to return it in pristine condition this time. "You look better in that than me!" Jude complimented him. "Very slimming."

The smooth elevator ride to the fortieth floor provided a spectacular view of the cityscape, and theatrical fountains below. The vantage point provided a blunt contrast to the view of Old Town from Timothy's third floor loft.

A quartet of young executives intercepted Timothy and Jude once they were inside. Two trendy young men with identical haircuts and tie-less suits, a whimsical fashionista with candy-apple red hair, and an apathetic ghoul with coin-sized plugs in her earlobes complimenting the assortment of piercings in her face. Timothy offered a handshake to the first young man, but he recoiled when he saw the scars on Timothy's hand. "Oh, I'm just getting over a cold. Don't want to spread my germs." The man lied while making evident faces to his colleagues. Timothy shelved his hands into his pockets and offered smiles all around instead. The four executives rattled off their avant-garde names and titles so fast he didn't have time to understand any of them.

The dreary one slinked over to Timothy and pulled his hand out of his pocket, completely disregarding his personal space. "So cool. Do you think they could, like, do this to my hands too?" Timothy pulled his hand away and buried it again in his pocket, taking note of the tattoos peeking out from every border of clothing. The girl's phone chimed, and she lost interest.

Once tagged with visitor badges, the pretentious executives ushered them though a seemingly endless series of plush carpeted hallways festooned with modern art and unintelligible sculptures. The executives took turns becoming preoccupied with the chirping of their electronic gadgets during the stroll.

Finally they reached a grand conference room with an ornate spread of hors d'oeuvres on the table; fine cheeses, fruits, meats and breads. The room's permanent bar stocked any beverage one could desire. Timothy and Jude were offered its spoils, but no one else was eating so they politely declined, for the time being. The redhead escorted them to reserved seats at the head of the table. Timothy noticed she was now wearing a name tag which read, 'Qui'ai Z. – Modernization Analyst'. It made him question his intelligence. Was this how the rest of the world lived?

An older, silver-haired gentleman entered the conference room with his young female assistant. "Mr. Clement, I'm Benito Prouville. We spoke on the phone." It was the first person who looked to be over the age of twenty-one they had encountered since arriving. "It is such a pleasure to have you as our guest today!" The other four executives started showing respect only after the man's exaggerated interest in Timothy.

One of the twin boys pawed Timothy's lapel. "I just love this throwback getup. You must, like, spend all your Saturdays combing retro boutiques. Am I right?" The boy's phone chirped, sending him sliding into a chair, furiously composing a message with his thumbs.

Timothy looked to Jude, thoroughly confused. "What?"

"Your hair is super cool too." The other boy bounced his hand off Timothy's overgrown fuzz. "How often do you tone it?"

Timothy swatted the intrusive hand away. "Keep to yourself pal."

Benito let out a contrived laugh, "You'll have to excuse Dalton and Kobe, it's their job to stay on top of the latest social trends."

"Shall we get on with business?" Jude suggested, wanting to spare Timothy from any additional culture shock.

"Excellent! I can see why Mr. Clement butters your bread! Smart man." Benito used every opportunity to stroke Timothy's ego. The young assistant lowered the in-ceiling projector. "I won't beat around the bush, your little girl Margie is a sensation."

"MarGreat." Timothy corrected him.

"MarGreat, yes of course." Benito didn't skip a beat. "We here at Luric Syndicate, the largest distributor of syndicated comics, believe we can leverage MarGreat's rising popularity to the fullest. The window of opportunity is there, but you only get one chance. We're your chance to take this momentum to the next level."

So far, it sounded okay to Timothy. The assistant had placed a legal sized binder containing a contract in front of Jude. Timothy felt stressed. He got up and took some crackers and cheese from the platter. Everyone was silent. He looked at their dumbfounded expressions, "Go on."

A presentation appeared on the screen titled, 'Clement Test Mods 2274'. "You've no doubt reviewed the generous offer included in our first letter. Those figures are based on models extrapolated using our proprietary data analysis algorithms. We have the most talented social research teams on staff. They specialize in knowing what is cool and what is not." The slideshow advanced to a busy graph with the sub-title, 'Focus Group M 10-24' across the bottom. "Our databases are unmatched in the industry. This helps us accomplish two things: Minimizing our risk, and maximize our content provider's profits. It's a win-win formula."

"What are you saying?" It was indecipherable to Timothy.

"Dalton, please show Mr. Clement your findings."

Dalton put down his phone and beckoned for the slideshow remote. "Basically, little girls are out. The market is too saturated. Teenage boys have yet to peak." The slideshow advanced to a test image of MarGreat in pants and shorter hair. "We tested this prototype of MarGreat as a tomboy, but it tanked. Then we just turned her completely into a teenage boy." Next slide showed a pimply teenager looking unhappy. "Reaction was better but-"

"What is this?" Timothy interrupted. "You can't change MarGreat to a boy!"

It was an old tactic at Luric; reach for all the cookies and see what you could get away with after being smacked. "That's what I said." Benito played good cop. "Sometimes these programs come up with kooky ideas. MarGreat is all girl."

"Thank you!" Timothy was pacified, for the moment.

The slideshow advanced rapidly through several male iterations of MarGreat, finally stopping on Timothy's rendition. "Fine, she's a girl." Dalton pouted as his thumbs pried away from his phone. "You're going to have to wake up and see that we know what people want better than you."

Seeing his work bastardized on the screen stirred Timothy's temper. "I know that visits to our website have been doubling nearly every week."

"Yeah, and how are you going to monetize that?" Dalton grabbed the remote again. "Look at this chart. Do you see how much you're leaving on the table by including all this church stuff? Not everyone wants to read that gibberish. We print secular comics for a reason – broad appeal, broad sales! It doesn't' take a rocket scientist."

"It's my comic. What I say goes."

Jude spoke up, "Actually, this contract designates full creative control to Luric Syndicate and their subsidiaries."

While Timothy tried to understand what Jude said, Dalton pressed on, "The gender and the God references aren't the biggest problem. It's these." The slideshow advanced, revealing MarGreat without her glasses. "Glasses aren't cool. Kids hate them."

All Timothy could see was Stevie the Great. "No."

"Don't be a moron!" Dalton sassed, reclining back in his chair. "You'll never get another chance like this. You think this is the first feisty girl comic to come through here?" He sped through the slides to a graph. "Look at the data! The numbers don't lie."

Timothy rose from his seat and Benito tried to salvage his intellectual property takeover. "Be reasonable Mr. Clement. They're just a pair of glasses."

What should have been a great step forward had turned sour. Timothy had had it with their hardball tactics. He appealed once more to their sensibilities, "I'm asking for the last time, please don't remove MarGreat's glasses."

Benito coldly replied, "Glasses don't sell."

"God, some people are so dumb!" Dalton cried out as he texted on his phone. "Sign the contract, take the money and buy some clothes manufactured in the last hundred years, genius!" Timothy snapped. He marched over to Dalton, ripped the phone out of his hands and smashed it against Dalton's head. "What the hell man! That phone costs me six-hundred bucks!" Blood leaked down his face.

"Let's go." Timothy instructed Jude as he calculated how many beans the phone could have bought.

On their way to the elevator, Dalton shouted out, "You're through! I'm going to call the cops and sue you!"

Benito tried to get them to stay, but it was a lost cause. Dalton came after them, but Benito pushed him back forcefully. The elevator doors closed. "Luric Syndicate roughs up MarGreat creator. Imagine that headline dummy. Go wash up."

In the elevator Timothy frantically checked Jude's suit for any frays or tears. "I'm sorry Brother Jude. I lost it back there. I know there's no excuse."

A broad smile beamed on Jude's face. "I'm very proud of you Timothy. A lesser man would have sold out."

"But I-"

"He deserved it." Jude looked the suit over. "Clean as a whistle." Jude could see the worry and disappointment on Timothy's face. "Has God not been good to you?"

Timothy thought about where he was just a little over a year ago and could barely recognize himself. "Yes. He saved me from myself when I didn't even deserve it. He blessed me with friendship, family and the opportunity to offer penance."

The elevator doors opened. To Jude's surprise, the town car was still waiting. "Blessed is he whose hope is in the Lord his God."

Not wasting a minute, Timothy and Jude flew home at the first opportunity. The polluted haze of the Old Town skyline as they descended was a comforting sight. "I can't wait to see Lucas." Timothy told Jude. "I hope he's not too disappointed. He really wanted this to happen." The dread of letting Lucas down couldn't compete with Timothy's longing to be back home again.

As the car pulled up to St. Anthony, Lucas and Miriam were waiting on the curb. "Did you do it?" Lucas cried out as soon as Timothy exited the car. He hoped he could ease into it and not get ambushed.

"Sorry Lucas, it just didn't work out." Jude broke the news for him.

Lucas and Miriam rejoiced exuberantly, "Hooray!"

"I don't think you understood Brother Jude. We didn't reach an agreement." Timothy explained.

Still jumping around with excitement, Lucas handed Timothy a printed email from Fluto Media Solutions. "They sent it today. It has everything Luric Syndicate offered and more! You retain full rights and creative control, plus you'll be syndicated in thirty-six newspapers!"

The Fluto Media Solutions proposal easily met with approval from Timothy and Jude. The large hand on Timothy's life jumped to the waiting hour. Timothy could never have imagined the magnitude of the Lord's plan.

The syndicated comic, religious themes intact, struck a nerve with a public tired of crusades to eradicate God from culture. They welcomed the unabashed tribute to the Lord and his teachings. Unavoidably, the column equally angered those who did not fear God.

Love of the comic grew and syndication expanded. Soon it was the most syndicated comic in the United States and Canada. Then MarGreat spread to South America and Europe. At first, Timothy had a hard time adjusting to professional life. Jude stumbled upon several thousand dollars in un-cashed checks in Timothy's wardrobe and had to assist him in opening a bank account. Timothy continued to live a very modest life at St. Anthony despite the ample wave of income. He split his pay each month between savings, a fund for Lucas and the remainder was given to St. Anthony to fund the shelter. His automotive allowance provided a practical van for the church to use, fuel and maintenance. Against Timothy's wishes, Jude surprised him with a beautiful wooden writing desk in the loft and new chair. He thanked him but thought it was too much.

Eventually, the day came when Lucas reached adulthood. Huddled around the piano, St. Anthony celebrated the eighteenth birthday of their favorite son. It was bitter-sweet for Lucas. He loved being at St. Anthony and appreciated all they had done for him, but the itch to spread his wings had begun to tingle. "Come with me." Timothy led Lucas out back to Miriam's garden. "Have a seat with me." From his coat he removed two envelopes, one thick and one thin. He gave the thick one to Lucas, "Open it up."

Inside, Lucas found ten-thousand dollars in cash. "What the heck? Timothy, what is this?"

"It's the prize money from the contest. I kept it safe for you." Lucas' eyes were still bugging out. "It was you who entered the contest, so it rightfully belongs to you."

"I've never see so much money!"

"I know you'll be responsible with it." Timothy passed the thin envelope to Lucas. "This is a gift from me."

Paranoid of attracting attention, Lucas bundled up the cash and jammed it under his arm. He then opened the thin envelope. It was a cashier's check. The amount eclipsed the cash more than a dozen times over. Lucas didn't know what to say.

"I didn't know how interest works when I stashed the cash, but this should make up for it." Timothy thought about Sarah and all she would have wanted for Lucas. "You can go to school, or invent something, or whatever you want." Lucas was too emotional to say anything. He just leaned sideways and rested his head on Timothy's shoulder. No one had ever been so generous with him. "You can depend on me." Timothy remembered saying those same words to Sarah. "But you'll be fine no matter what happens. You're smart, you're honest, and God is first in your life. A man like me might fail you, but He won't."

Chapter 49

*N*ot since Sunday school ended had Timothy been back to St. Mary. The momentum of Mar-Great had placed his attentions elsewhere, but today he made a special trip and was now staring at the shadowed grill, examining his conscience once again.

The partition slid aside. Timothy made the sign of the cross and began, "Bless me father, for I have sinned. It has been over a year since my last confession." He paused for strength. "I've not always been truthful. I've had impure thoughts. I've had fits of rage."

A moment of silence passed and the priest asked, "Is that all?"

"No." A dull pain throbbed in Timothy's belly. "I haven't been able to forgive my sisters."

"Why is that?"

He had never thought about the reason, just the inability. "They have always treated me badly. I think I might hate them."

"Have you always had these strong feelings against them?"

Timothy thought back. "No, not always."

"But you say they have always wronged you." The priest inquired.

"Yes."

"Have their hearts changed?"

"No."

The priest paused. "You know their nature. You know they haven't changed. So, why are you expecting to be treated different by them now?"

The question stumped Timothy. "I just sort of figured they'd come around by now."

"Because you've changed?"

"Maybe." Timothy muttered.

"You don't have any influence over their behavior. All you can do is control your own actions. Right now, your actions are vengeful and unforgiving. How can that motivate change in them?" The priest wasn't giving the answers Timothy had counted on. "How can you ask the Father for forgiveness, when you are unwilling to forgive those who have wronged you?"

"It's not like they asked to be forgiven."

"And they probably never will. That doesn't mean you shouldn't forgive them and pray for them." The sound of rustling pages came through the partition. "Then Peter approaching asked him, 'Lord, if my brother sins against me, how often must I forgive him? As many as seven times?' Jesus answered, 'I say to you, not seven times, but seventy-seven times.'" The Bible clapped shut. "If you do not forgive others, then your Father will not forgive your transgressions." The priest waited patiently before asking, "Do you understand son?" He didn't answer.

A woman's voice broke the silence, "Bless me Father, for I have sinned. It has been six months since my last confession."

"Please excuse me." Fr. Connor exited the confessional just in time to catch a glimpse of Timothy exiting out the main doors.

Chapter 50

*T*he sound of breaking glass trailed by Miriam's scream tore Timothy from his sketches. He flew downstairs calling out, asking if she was okay but she didn't answer. When he reached the bottom, a familiar voice said, "It would be a shame in anything happened to this place". It was Bruno and his muscle, Raspy, both looking slimy as ever. Miriam was up against the wall, clearly terrified. Two window panes lay shattered at her feet.

"Get the hell out of here!"

"Oh God, what happened to you?" Bruno chuckled and lowered his sunglasses to get a better look at Timothy's head and hands. "Is someone filming a monster movie?" Raspy laughed at the uninspired joke.

"I said get out!" Timothy didn't want them anywhere near St. Anthony. "You've got no business here!"

Raspy shattered another window with his tire iron. Miriam yelped. "What's the matter, you don't play no more?" He hissed.

Timothy stood paralyzed. He didn't want St. Anthony paying for his past debts. "What do you want?"

"It ain't what I want, it's what Mr. Rex wants – the money you still owe him." It embarrassed Timothy to have the conversation in front of Miriam. "With interest and penalties, we're talking a quarter-mill, which we know you can afford now." Miriam gasped at the figure. Bruno smiled arrogantly, "You didn't know this one was the patron saint of doubling-down?"

"That's enough!"

"Bring the cash in two days to the bridge that leads out of this pit; Five-thirty sharp. There'll be a green hotel van parked halfway across with its emergency lights blinking. Mr. Rex and I will be waiting to settle your account." Bruno shook his fist at Timothy. "Come alone, or don't bother coming at all."

Raspy added, "And if you don't show, it's going to be worse than the riots around here."

Shaken by the commotion, Jude came in asking, "What is going on in here?"

Raspy laughed, "Ask your boy. We were just leaving" He then bumped Jude with his burly shoulder as they exited, sending him to the ground.

Jude became furious, cursing and threatening like a guard dog, but Bruno and Raspy simply snickered as they slipped away. It surprised Timothy that Jude could still scrap like that. He rushed to help him up with Miriam right behind him. "Settle down, they're gone."

"I will not settle down!" Jude hollered and he got to his feet. "I warned you about sliding back." Months of suppressed intuition and suspicion boiled over. "You think we don't notice you disappear during the week without explanation? You get summoned by your PO and have nothing to say about it." Miriam tried to calm Jude down but he waved her off. "I didn't pry. I gave you many opportunities to let me help, but you shut me out. And now this!" Jude pointed to the mess of glass on the floor.

Timothy hated seeing Jude like this. "Brother Jude, I'm not gambling anymore. I swear!"

Jude peered into Timothy's eyes as if looking for someone he used to know. "Do you owe those thugs money?"

"No. I mean-"

"A quarter-million they said." Miriam sniffled, heartbroken.

Timothy desperately tried to explain, "It's not like-"

"Enough with the lies!" Jude barked. "You've selfishly put us in danger. I won't have it." Turning his back to Timothy, he did what he never wanted to do. "The boy is an adult now; it's time you both moved on. I'd like you out by the end of the month." Taking a broom and dustpan from the closet, Jude began cleaning up the glass.

Inconsolable, Miriam scowled at Timothy, "How could you do this?" She cried.

There wasn't enough money in the world to buy back what he had lost. Timothy hustled upstairs and dug though his desk. Tossing aside piles of papers, he searched desperately though the clutter. Amid the mess he spotted it and thanked God. He folded the paper and headed for the phone.

Chapter 51

*T*he business day was ending. "Thank you for waiting." The female bank agent handed the five and a half pound bundle to Timothy. "It's all there, large bills, as you requested." Timothy didn't recount it; he just stuffed it into his backpack. "Would you like one of our financial advisors to contact you tomorrow Mr. Clement?" It was the second time in his life he had been asked the question. Again, he declined. "Is there anything else I can do for you?"

"Can you please call me a cab?"

The girl pointed across the lobby. "Have a seat over there. A hospitality clerk will alert you when your car has arrived."

Timothy sat across from a brawny man in a garish purple suit. While he waited, he didn't obsess over the mess back at St. Anthony in the slightest. He was at peace with it. After today, he was confident it would all blow over and he'd never have to deal with Bruno or Mr. Rex again. Instead, Father Connor's words tumbled around his head, burdening him.

"Mr. Clement, your cab is here." Timothy got up. The beefy fellow across from him rose as well. Timothy was sure it was one of Mr. Rex's associates.

Timothy loaded himself into the back seat and instructed the driver, "Drop me at the bridge." They pulled away, leaving the muscular shadow behind. Timothy stirred his bony frame in the seat, trying to get comfortable. "No need to take the scenic route." He snapped at the dawdling driver.

Ten minutes later Timothy knocked on the plastic partition. "This is good." He paid the fare and exited directly in front of the pedestrian walkway. He slung his bag over his shoulder while cars whizzed by on their way out of the city. An eerie feeling crept up as he gravitated into the mouth of the pathway. The last time he walked this path he was coming from the other direction and he never completed the journey. He reached into his neckline and pulled out his St. Anthony necklace, letting it fall on top of his clothes. Lucas would approve, he thought.

There was moderate foot traffic on the path. As he progressed, the green hotel van passed him and pulled over some distance ahead. Reciting every prayer he could recall, Timothy plotted up the bridge towards the flashing emergency lights. A clammy nervousness daubed the insides of his clothes, reminding him that success was the only acceptable outcome. As he got closer to the van, Timothy whispered, "Jesus Christ, only son of God, have mercy on us sinners."

The side panel door slid open inviting him in. He slowed down and struggled to count heads through the tinted glass. He was pretty sure Raspy was driving. It looked like Bruno and Mr. Rex were the only occupants in back. "Need a lift, pal?" He heard Bruno call out to him.

The backpack slid off Timothy's shoulder down to his hand and he climbed inside. "Blessings." He greeted the wayward souls with an obedient nod.

"What?" Bruno asked incredulously. "Stop fooling around!"

Mr. Rex chuckled and pointed to the St. Anthony necklace on display, "No, I think he's really into this stuff."

Bruno shook his head, "This guy was ready to take my head off two days ago. I don't think so."

"It's true, your treatment of my friends did make me angry." Timothy confessed. "But I have forgiven you."

Mr. Rex laughed again, "You hear that, he's forgiven you! We're one big happy family now!" He slapped Bruno's knee. "Bruno said you'd be hard to recognize, but this is too good!"

"Alright, enough with this. You got the money?" Bruno snapped.

"I always keep my word." Timothy lifted the backpack and began to carefully unzip it. Bruno snatched the whole thing away from him. Timothy looked at Mr. Rex, "Has anyone ever talked to you about Jesus?"

"I should have seen that coming!" Mr. Rex scoffed. "First time in the joint a chaplain tried feeding me that boloney. He tells me I can get to heaven if I just believe in Jesus and repeat a bunch of words after him. He says there ain't nothing I can do to be kicked out of Heaven after that. I said what he told me, but only for the early release points. When we were done, he said I was in!"

"It didn't count." Timothy said tenderly.

The unaffected response to his tired story bothered Mr. Rex, "Of course it did. The guy was a chaplain for Christ's sake!"

"Only if you had said those words with a sincere heart would they have brought you salvation and life everlasting. The path you chose leads to death." Timothy spoke as if letting down a good friend. "I'm sorry."

"It's all here." Bruno broke the tension. "Let's dump this chump."

"You don't know that. God will be the one to judge me, not you." It was Timothy's wholesomeness that pushed Mr. Rex to dig for a rationalization of his choices. "No one is perfect."

"You're right; judgment day will come for all of us." Timothy said sorrowfully. "Those who sincerely tried to live by God's commandments will be remembered. Those who repent will be forgiven. How do you think you'll fare?" Timothy let the question hang. "You shall worship the Lord your God and Him only shall you serve."

"Kid, it's not like I'm paying homage to the Greek god Apollo." Mr. Rex snickered, trying to lighten the conversation.

"Who then is being glorified when you run a laundry gambling den in the Apollo Business Center?" The statement removed the confident smile from Mr. Rex's face. "You're right, you don't worship Apollo. You worship a different god - Money."

"I like money; who doesn't. You're just sore that you bet more than you should have and had to use the sucker exit. Plenty of losers have lost their shirts gambling in my 'poor-man's' casino, and I don't feel sorry for one of them."

"The problem with false gods is that they pull you away from the one true God." Mr. Rex was irresistibly hooked into the conversation. "You find it easier to ignore his laws. Thou shalt not steal suddenly doesn't apply to you anymore. Your god, money, says it's okay to plunder Peruvian antiquities as long as the pay is good."

"If I didn't fence those artifacts, someone else would have."

Bruno fidgeted impatiently, "Can we go now?"

"We're having an adult conversation here." Mr. Rex reprimanded Bruno. A trend of disrespect had been forming for some time. He could sense Bruno staking out his shoes. "We'll go when I'm good and ready!"

"Talk of salvation makes those who disrespect authority uncomfortable." Timothy preyed on Mr. Rex's insecurities. "They are loyal only to themselves, they reject God's rules."

"It's called survival of the fittest. That's why I've got this-" Bruno held up the backpack. "And you've got Jesus."

Mr. Rex took the backpack from Bruno. "Actually, you don't got this." Distain seethed from Bruno's once cocky eyes. "Maybe if you learned to keep your mouth shut you might amount to more than just my errand boy." Mr. Rex began to re-count the money.

"Even the most respectable man will falter. Jesus is the only one whom you can always depend on."

"Give it a rest, church boy!" Bruno disregarded the advice he had just been given.

"The Lord will never bear false witness against you." Timothy said to Mr. Rex. "You don't have to worry about him plotting against you. He would never try to kill you. He wants you to live."

"What the hell are you saying?" Bruno was slow to pick up on the insinuation. "You accusing me of lying about Mr. Rex? You think I would kill him? That's not my style."

"You killed my friend Steve without a second thought."

"Steve who?" Bruno spat.

"The man living in the box car." Bruno's face lit up. "The one you shot with the gun you tricked my kid brother into handling."

Bruno laughed, "I can't believe you know his name. He was a Jesus freak like you. He didn't beg for his life, he just prayed and prayed. I did that loser a favor putting him out of his misery."

"Survival of the fittest?" Timothy asked Bruno. "Lying about others to get what you want. Killing them if they get in your way."

Mr. Rex was no longer counting money. He was staring intently at Timothy. "You give this moron too much credit. I'm the one who told him to bring the gun to your brother." Mr. Rex watched the serenity in Timothy's eyes wane. "Things don't always go as planned. Both of you piglets were supposed to die, but somehow you lucked out." Bruno laughed watching Timothy learn the harsh truth. "I bet you're plum out of forgiveness now, aren't you?"

"Judgment day is coming sooner than you think." Timothy held onto his St. Anthony medallion. "It's still not too late to repent."

"I'll repent in hell." Mr. Rex sneered. "Get him out of here."

The van door slid open. Raspy grabbed Timothy by his shirt and roughly tossed him out onto the sidewalk. Bruno leaned over to get a good look. Timothy's shirt was hiked up revealing tape and wires on his lower back. "What the-"

Before they knew what happened, Bruno, Mr. Rex, and Raspy found themselves cuffed and faced down on the ground. The prattle of law enforcement and flashing lights exploded around them. It was impressive to see them work.

Reaching out to Hosnic had been a game changer. Within hours of his call, the Feds had drawn up a plan to apprehend Mr. Rex and Bruno. Timothy would make the delivery on the bridge as expected, but there would be an audience.

By the beams of headlamps, technicians worked to remove the wires and tape from Timothy's body. The Feds snatched up the recording device and drove away before the real cleanup began. For having succeeded, Timothy didn't feel great. All the excitement was overwhelming. "Excuse me." He stepped away from the technician and sat on the curb. He stomach throbbed with pain and he was sweating again.

"You're dead Clement!" Bruno shouted as he was loaded into a nearby police cruiser.

Timothy turned to look, then felt the pavement against his cheek. A fading voice yelled, "We need a doctor!"

Chapter 52

"Again, please." Miriam nodded, and with weary eyes began playing Amazing Grace from the beginning for Timothy. Like a doting father, Jude hovered nearby Timothy, pulling the edges of his blanket every so often to ensure his gaunt legs weren't cold. Miriam could no longer sing soundly, so she stammered out a hum instead. Lucas had fallen asleep upstairs before the ambulance delivered Timothy home leaving the three of them together, almost like old times.

"The doctor said there is no reason for you to be in the hospital." Jude wiped his eyes. "There isn't anything they can do for you, but you knew that didn't you?" Timothy nodded. "I know I said some things before, but you and Lucas are welcome to stay as long as you like."

"Thank you." Timothy whispered. "I was telling the truth when I said I wasn't gambling."

Jude regretted that he ever had the nasty exchange with Timothy. "I wish you had told me about the tumors."

"My doc thinks it was caused by what freed me - mold. Not that he can prove it." Sucking in a deep breath, Timothy continued, "I didn't want you to worry. It was easier to lie about going to see my PO than to explain my treatments."

"You didn't need to lie." Jude said sadly.

"It was the only thing I lied to you about." Timothy coughed. "I almost came clean after Miriam found my doctor money, but I couldn't do it."

Miriam apologized, "I'm sorry for snooping. I was worried you were getting into trouble."

Delicately reaching for her hand he said, "You don't need to apologize for caring about me."

"So what happens now?" Jude asked.

Timothy scratched his head. "There's something I could use your help with. I need you to get the word out that we're having a party here at St. Anthony in one month. A big wonderful party they won't want to miss. On me."

Miriam asked, "What is the occasion?"

"I'll be making two announcements. That's all everyone needs to know."

Work began the very next day, despite protests from Jude and Miriam that he wasn't well enough yet. "No time to lose." Timothy reminded them. He had enough MarGreat comics in his stockpile to put drawing on hold for the time being without missing any deadlines. He labored day and night, tying up the phone line with back-to-back calls. Early on, Jude was sucked into the frenzied project, often disappearing behind closed doors, only to reappear without divulging any details. The announcements remained a mystery to all but Timothy and Jude.

Miriam and Lucas were getting a little fed up with all the secrecy. Timothy and Jude spent three and a half weeks meeting privately. Often they would travel downtown together, files under their arms, and not return until evening. The intrigue was maddening.

"I've got another set for you to review." Timothy told Lucas. The prior week, Timothy had him rate MarGreat logos for two hours straight. After the first fifteen minutes, his head spun and all Lucas could see were football heads and glasses.

Timothy hired a wedding coordinator to help plan the party. A constant parade of vendors visited St. Anthony with samples, cameras, and measuring tape. It was hard for Miriam to stand by and watch another woman flourish in her stomping ground, but she knew the outcome would be grand. "I don't want you to do anything but relax and enjoy yourself." Timothy told Miriam. "I want you to attend the party, not throw it."

The day before the party, a team of men in overalls arrived and packed up everything in the hall into a truck; serving stations, furniture, the piano, all of it was loaded into a white truck. Then another team arrived to scrub and polish the floor. Finally, an army of workers came through, setting up tables, chairs, decorations and a temporary parquet dance floor in the center of the room. The St. Anthony hall was hardly recognizable.

Later in the evening, Timothy, Lucas, Jude and Miriam all enjoyed some late night hot cocoa under the stars in Miriam's garden. Lucas exhausted his repertoire of favorite impressions, leaving everyone in stitches. Jude regaled everyone with his humorous account of the first time Sarah served a meal for a hundred guests and ended up passing out cookies. Miriam gave a concise history on every section of flowers in her garden: when they were planted, why she chose the variety, and in whose memory they were planted. Even Jude did not know the flowers were a living memorial. Finally, everyone joined hands, and Timothy led them in an Our Father, finishing with a resounding, "Amen!"

Light flecks of water tickled their faces. The moon had become obscured by boisterous clouds. "We should go in." Miriam suggested, collecting up their cups.

"I hope this clears up before tomorrow night." Lucas stuck out his tongue to catch a few drops.

Timothy assured them, "Don't worry, the party will be great no matter what." He followed them inside.

Chapter 53

Miriam finished brushing her teeth and rinsed. Leaning into the vanity she studied her eyes in the mirror, gently tugging and pushing the aged contours of her skin. It didn't seem so long ago that it was firm and blemish free. Her body had put up a fight, but there was no denying what hour she was living in. She marveled that despite the years, she felt the same inside as when she was a girl. It was still her.

There was a knock at her door. She cinched her robe taut, took another look at herself in the mirror before answering. When she opened the door, a large silver department store box lay at her slippers with a card bearing her name. She looked both directions, but no one was there. She felt a pang of childlike excitement as she brought the gift inside and laid it on her bed. Delicately, she opened the envelope and extracted the card from the foil lined interior. On the card's face was a simple, elegant watercolor painting of a rose. Miriam's unsteady fingers opened it. Romans 15:1 was written in Timothy's handwriting, 'We who are strong ought to put up with the failings of the weak and not to please ourselves.' On the opposite side he wrote, "Dear Miriam, this does not come close to repaying all of the kindness you have shown me. I look forward to seeing you in this tonight. Love, Timothy"

Sliding the cardboard seal aside, Miriam opened the lid of the box. Inside was a beaded lace and chiffon evening gown with matching shoes. She gasped as she removed it from its casing. Never had she owned such an extravagant garment. "Oh my. . ." she breathily exclaimed as she held the dress up to her body in front of the mirror. With her free hand she gathered her brown locks and twisted them up onto the top of her head like a bun. It was hard for her to believe the reflection was her own. "Thank you." She whispered, overcome with emotion.

Above the patter of raindrops, Miriam heard another knock at the door. When she answered, there was a young woman outside she had never seen before holding a plastic carrying case. "Are you Miriam?" The girl asked.

"Yes." Miriam answered apprehensively.

"Mr. Clement sent me to do your hair and makeup for the party. May I come in?"

Miriam embraced the strange woman and squeezed her tight; it was the last thing she expected. "Bless you Timothy, bless you!" She cried.

The main hall looked like a grand ballroom with balloons and streamers suspended from the ceiling. A dozen banquet tables, dressed with thick table cloths, full course dinnerware, lace napkins and bright floral centerpieces bordered the hall. "How much longer?" Timothy asked Lucas as he peeked out the window at the empty wet parking lot wondering if anyone would show.

"Guests aren't due for another fifteen minutes. Relax Timothy." Lucas smiled and straightened Timothy's bow tie. "This is going to be great!"

Jude came over and rubbed Timothy's back. "Everything is set. Tonight will be a night to remember."

A clap of thunder rattled above. Timothy studied the parking lot again. "I hope so."

Just then four, then five cars entered through the gate. The valet company sprang into action, giving tickets and escorting with umbrellas. "Get ready, they're coming!" Lucas shouted and ran out to greet the incoming guests. The steady stream of arrivals continued, until the parking lot was nearly full.

Parishioners from St. Anthony and St. Mary alike showed up in droves. All of the city's elected officials were in attendance as were many of Old Town's prominent business professionals. Folks ate and danced and celebrated with vigor completely forgetting about the storm outside.

Timothy continually walked around and greeted everyone who showed, listening to their stories and jokes attentively. He was so captivated by his guests that he hadn't even remembered to eat. At the height of his jubilation the lights dimmed three times, signaling the time for his announcement had come. Lucas and Jude guided him to a podium at the edge of the dance floor.

Timothy cleared his throat. "I hope everyone is having a great time." The guests hooted and applauded. Timothy took the opportunity to adjust the microphone so he could lean further forward onto the podium for support. The fatigue of celebration was setting in. "Most of you know me because of my comic strip, MarGreat. It's a lot of fun to create, and I'm glad people seem to like it. But, there is more to MarGreat than humorous, youthful misunderstandings." Timothy took a drink of water. "Not very long ago I was lost. Not just lost, I was delusional. I was sure that I had all the answers, but had nothing to show for it. It was a painful way to live." Timothy looked out at all his guests, and his anxiety disappeared. "The Lord still loved me even though I had abandoned him. He gave me another chance. Through Brother Jude's persistence. . ." Timothy grazed Jude's shoulder with the tips of his fingers. "I was led back home. I saw the world in a whole new way. It was like I had put on a new pair of glasses." Behind him, a banner unfurled showing a pair of MarGreat's iconic sketched glasses. "There are all kinds of glasses one can choose to wear. There are glasses that shield you from the sun, glasses that are used for reading." Timothy pointed to the banner. "These glasses treat near-sightedness. They allow us to see far ahead. They allow us to see our next generation. They show a self-professed tolerant world that is less tolerant of our Christian faith. They show our educational institutions infiltrated by those who do not fear the Lord." A flicker of lightning flashed through the hall. "But there is more. These glasses also show us hope. They show perseverance. They show us strength in our faith." A second banner unfurled with a picture of MarGreat along with the words, 'MarGreat Scholarship Fund' printed on it. "Beginning today, right now, the Margreat Scholarship Fund will provide tuition and school supplies to struggling families seeking a faith based education for their children. Additionally, a quarter million dollars in collegiate scholarships will be awarded through Christian essay contests and comic strip competitions." Everyone stood and applauded for several minutes. Timothy appreciated the sentiment, but was anxious to get to his next announcement. "There is one more-" The applause did not die down. "Please." Timothy waved his hands. "There is one more announcement. Please take your seats."

Little by little then guests took their seats and quieted down. Jude brought Timothy a fresh glass of water and told him, "You're doing great!"

"As most everyone here knows, St. Anthony suffered a significant blow during the riots." Timothy coughed hard. "Excuse me." He wiped his mouth on his sleeve. "From the rubble sprang the city's largest hunger ministry, serving three-hundred meals a day. Soliciting the help of local businesses and parishioners like you; Brother Jude has done an amazing job of managing this program." The group broke into a round of applause for Brother Jude. Timothy dragged him forward. "The Lord had a plan and Brother Jude listened!" Timothy bellowed, causing the guests to cheer louder. Lucas and Miriam hugged Jude on each side. "But there's something missing. Someone told me St. Anthony once resonated with the playful chatter of students." Timothy pointed to the ground. "Right where we are celebrating, in this very hall, students once sat in classes. Thankfully, our brothers and sisters at St. Mary have taken them in, but wouldn't it be great to teach the next generation here?"

Timothy stepped back to allow Jude access to the podium. "Good evening. I have spent the past month sequestered with Mr. Clement, trying to answer a question he hasn't ceased asking me: What is missing at St. Anthony. It's a difficult question. It's a question whose answer should responsibly come from our pastor, but we have none. I wasn't sure how we could restore it to its previous form without losing the kitchen and meal ministry." A wide banner unfurled from the ceiling showing an artist rendition of a renovated St. Anthony complete with a new school, chapel, hall and parking lot. "After analyzing several architectural proposals, this is what we came up with." Lots of conversation broke out. "Father Connor from St. Mary has provided much input in selecting this design. Unfortunately, he could not be here tonight due to a prior engagement. It's still pending approval, but with the generous donation from Mr. Clement, our chances are very good." Jude turned to bring Timothy up and recognize him, but he didn't see him anywhere. Jude finished with more encouraging words for the partygoers, and the action picked right back up.

Slumped back in his writing chair, Timothy covered his legs with a blanket and observed the storm from his panoramic view. He hoped everyone downstairs was still having a good time. It was the best party he had ever been to. It was worth it just to see Jude, with storm-greased knees, getting down on the dance floor with Miriam. The storm's intensity had swelled several times throughout of the celebration, building up to the tempest it was now. Timothy's frail body absorbed the flashes and sonic rumblings with awe. The last time he experienced a storm like this was on the bridge.

On his desk were neat stacks of documents separated into finances, legal documents, personal papers and MarGreat comics. Timothy looked through the legal stack and removed a blue binder. Stuck to the front of it was a note reading, 'Mr. Clement, I've made the changes you requested.' He opened the folder and reviewed the contents briefly, stopping to write, 'Romans 14:8' on the cover. He then sealed it shut with packing tape and put it inside a larger manila envelope, sealing it with tape as well. He took a business card from his dresser drawer and wrote, 'Read me.' on the back of it. He then taped it face down onto the package with clear tape. Not wanting to fall sleep yet, Timothy watched nature's fury well into the night, finally falling asleep in the chair.

Hours later, the door to the loft opened slowly. "Hey cotton ball head, I hope you weren't having too good of a dream." It was Lucas and Jude.

"I'm up."

"I told you he'd be up." Jude said to Lucas.

"Great party." Lucas smiled, his lips still stained with blue frosting. "You're the coolest guy in Old Town now."

The visit surprised Timothy. "What are you still doing up?"

Lucas laughed, "We went to bed last night after the party. Jude said we were going to do something special early today."

Timothy had no point of reference for terms like, 'today' and 'last night'. "What time is it?" He asked.

"It's just about wind corralling time." Jude answered. "I thought it was time Lucas got to experience it."

"Experience what?" Lucas asked.

Jude smiled, "You'll see."

Timothy nodded, "That would be nice. I'd like that." He told Lucas, "Pull up a chair."

Lucas and Jude sat beside Timothy and looked out into the wet darkness. "Storm seems to have settled itself." Jude said. "This is the kind of rain that's good for-"

"Catching lobsters." Timothy joked.

Lucas twisted, "I don't get it?"

Jude moved on without pause, "This is the kind of storm that cleans away all the dirt and grime. A big storm is good to have now and then."

Timothy fidgeted with pursed lips, trying to get comfortable. He looked frail and tired; just a hint of his former self. Jude slid a pillow behind his back which seemed to offer some relief. Lucas turned away, not wanting to see him this way. They all sat quietly for several minutes before Timothy announced, "Here it comes. It always starts over there." Timothy's emaciated arm rose up and pointed.

"What are we looking at?" Lucas asked, straining to see.

"You know how wonderful it is to sing hymns with Miriam?" Lucas nodded; it was one of his favorite activities. "She never fails to lift our spirits and fill the hall with beautiful praise even though that piano is a wreck." Timothy watched a budding shard of sunlight cut through the drizzle. "Much like that piano, good things can come from imperfect people."

They watched as the sun climbed over Old Town, not intimidated by the rain. It punched holes in the grey sky wherever it pleased. Even when out of direct sight, there was no questioning its presence. Darkness didn't stand a chance.

Jude gave Lucas the skinny on wind corralling time, sparing no intimate details of his tough childhood. Lucas fell right into step, observing the living city's awakening, but hadn't fully bought off on the theory. "Hey Timothy, do you really think everyone has some good in them?" Timothy nodded, not taking his gaze from the skyline. "Even your rotten sisters?"

The question broke Timothy from his watch. An expression, like he had just smelt spoiled milk soured his face. "Come here. I'll tell you exactly what I think my sisters have in them." Lucas bent over and Timothy whispered in his ear.

"Dear Lord, forgive what curses are whispered under your roof." Jude prayed aloud and turned away, not wanting to hear any part of it.

The door opened. It was Father Connor. "I got your message."

"Thank you for coming Father." Timothy said. Jude and Lucas greeted his as well, but were very surprised he was there. "Can you guys give us a few minutes?" Timothy asked Jude.

"Of course." Jude tried his best not to wonder what Timothy planned to discuss with Father Connor. "Lucas, let's go down to the kitchen and make breakfast."

"One second." Timothy lifted the manila envelope off his desk and handed it to Jude. "Don't open this until the time is right." He said ominously.

"What's in there?" Lucas asked innocently.

"Don't worry; I've got something for you too." Timothy shuffled through the MarGreat stack and removed a comic strip. In it, MarGreat is sent to the principal's office. When she arrives, he pulls out a chessboard and tells her it's her turn. He asks her what she did this time and she says, 'Apparently, Mrs. Teacher has already forgiven me seventy-seven times.'

"Cool." Lucas began to read it as soon as it hits his hands.

"Why don't you take that downstairs and read it." Timothy suggests.

"Okay." Lucas rolled the comic up loosely. "Thanks again for the awesome party. It was so much fun."

Timothy's eyes moistened. "I'm really glad we could do that."

248

Chapter 54

*L*ucas was on his second serving of eggs when Jude returned from the washroom. "Maybe you should slow down with the tea Brother Jude." He teased.

"Respect your elders." Jude countered as he fired up the kettle. He enjoyed Lucas' playful nature.

They both stopped and listened. Above them, Father Connor had begun his descent with slow, heavy strides. "Do you think we can go back up now?" Lucas asked.

"Not yet." Jude joined him at the table and waited for Father Connor to reach the bottom. It seemed to take an eternity, but he finally entered the kitchen with his hands full.

Coming over to them, he delicately announced, "Timothy has returned home." Jude's face collapsed into tears. Father Connor put his hand on Jude's shoulder and said, "You did real good Brother Jude, real well."

Lucas covered his face and cried. "No, we just saw him."

Father Connor laid Timothy's tattered, marked-up Bible on the table next to Lucas. "He loved you very much." Without another word, Father Connor exited out into the rain.

Jude and Lucas huddled together, crying into each other's arms. "Tell me it isn't true." Miriam cried from the doorway. Her eye's dripping black trails through the remnants of last night's makeup. "Oh God, tell me it isn't true!" She wailed.

Chapter 55

*B*alancing her latte' on top of a stack of candy colored soft-core drivel, Elizabeth waited impatiently to purchase the books her superficial friends had been toting around as accessories for the past month. She had an extensive collection of unread tomes at home that had fallen out of vogue. Trashy novels, diet crazes, relationship advice and a slew of self-help mumbo jumbo. She subconsciously believed that keeping up with trends would keep aging at bay. All the books in the world weren't going to change the fact that she was old, and trumped by a whole new generation of bimbos. The window to get by on cutesy mannerisms was closed.

The checkout line snaked around, leaving her facing a display of MarGreat books and merchandise. She had become aware of Timothy's success through her penchant for pop culture but would never read the comics or let anyone know that they shared the same bloodline. The intoxication of banishment surpassed the benefits of having a celebrity in the family. As the line progressed past the display, she diverted her view from it defiantly.

"Next in line." The college student with craggy hair manning the furthest register called out. Elizabeth sauntered past the other checkout windows and noticed the covers of her favorite weekly periodicals all featured stories about Timothy's death. She stopped and stared in disbelief.

"What did he do to his hair?" She asked herself. "Serves him right."

"Miss, I can help you over here."

She jostled her merchandise, splashing drops of coffee on her blouse. "God! I heard you the first time!" She reprimanded the teller.

Moments later, Elizabeth was furiously scouring the stains with a wet towel inside her car. As she scrubbed, she got to thinking about Timothy's passing and what was in it for her. She dialed her older sister Victoria and put the phone on speaker. Victoria answered with, "What!"

"Oh my God, you're such a spaz!" Elizabeth squealed. "Have you heard the news?"

"I don't care that he's dead. I don't want to waste my breath on him."

"Me neither, but I was thinking-" The car horn honked beneath her scrubbing. "Oh, sorry. He probably had a bunch of money. There's no wife or kids to leave it to. Maybe there's something for us. I'm sure he felt guilty, as he should have, for what he did to Stephen." Only the sound of Victoria's student playing piano came through the receiver. "I think I'm going to go to the funeral."

"Whatever. You're stupid." Victoria said coldly. "He's not my brother."

Elizabeth didn't flinch at the harsh words. It was how they did things. "I'll let you know if he left you anything."

"One, they don't hand out money at a funeral, moron. Two, whatever money he had I'm sure he gave to the church that brainwashed him. That's what losers do; screw up, find Jesus, and give away all their stuff - rinse and repeat."

Elizabeth thought about it. "I'm still going to check it out."

"Whatever." The phone went dead.

Chapter 56

*F*or seven days the rain fell. Sometimes whipping into a storm, other times a steady drizzle, but never ceasing. The tenor bell in Timothy's loft tolled. Father Connor performed the Requiem Mass in the packed hall where just a week earlier much of the same crowd had been celebrating.

Following the mass, Timothy's casket was taken to the cemetery. Father Connor blessed the grave and asked that Timothy's soul rest in peace. The soft muddy ground didn't deter anyone from paying their graveside respects, except Elizabeth, who watched from the comfort of her car window. Observing people of faith praying together brought back memories of her mother, which she swiftly stifled.

Afterwards, everyone came back to St. Anthony to celebrate Timothy's life, share stories of his time with them and console one another. Tables of food and flowers filled the hall where they reminisced. The sky grew restless and billowed more thunder while grieving voices murmured to the score of large raindrops pelting the church. The week's activities left Jude drained, emotionally and physically. He excused himself from a cluster of mourners, needing a fresh cup of tea. The cup in his hands kept them from quivering. As his spoon rang against the inside of the cup, a familiar voice comforted him, "My condolences, Brother Jude." It was Dr. Martin.

He looked different. Jude realized he had never seen the doctor in anything but hospital garb. "Thank you." Then it caught his eye. Around Dr. Martin's neck, resting on his tie, was a thin silver necklace with a small cross dangling from it.

Seeing Jude's eye on his chest, Dr. Martin said, "Don't get all excited Brother Jude."

Jude smiled. There wasn't anything he needed to say about it. "I'm glad you came by. Timothy appreciated all you did for him after the accident."

Dr. Martin nodded and paused. "Likewise." He looked at his watch. "I've got to get going. If you're ever in the neighborhood, come by. We'll do lunch. Like old times."

"I'd like that." Jude shook his hand.

Slipping in unnoticed, Elizabeth meandered through the crowd, eavesdropping on their conversations. She wondered how church people could lie so easily. She knew the real Timothy, and he wasn't at all whom they described. Timothy Clement didn't help people pay their utilities, support school sports programs or donate bus passes. "Ew!" She said to herself at the thought of public transportation.

"Miss Miriam, there's someone here for you." The young girl whispered in Miriam's ear. She excused herself and grabbed an umbrella, before traveling through her garden to the main building. Inside, a delivery man waited for her, holding a large cellophane-windowed box. "I'm Miriam." She announced.

Ruffled fabric pressed against the box window. "Your cleaning is done. Where would you like it?" The man asked.

"Follow me." Miriam led him down the hall towards her room.

Along the way, she heard Lucas call out, "Miss Miriam!"

"Just a moment Lucas!" She yelled back, and then continued escorting the delivery man to her quarters. Once inside, she opened her closet revealing an already cleared space on the top shelf. "Up there is fine."

The man cautioned her, "Okay, but be careful not to fall when you take it down next time." Miriam didn't worry. There would never be another occasion worthy of its wearing as far as she was concerned.

Miriam thanked the man and caught up with Lucas in the kitchen. He was drinking a glass of water, staring out the window at the storm. "I know he's in a better place, but I still miss him." He told her.

"Me too." She rubbed his back. "Shall we?" Lucas nodded.

Heads turned as Lucas entered the hall, pushing the janky piano with Miriam in tow. Once situated, Miriam closed her eyes and privately thanked God for blessing St. Anthony with Timothy's brief stay. Then, like she had done so many times before, she stretched her fingers to the familiar chord positions of "Amazing Grace" and hammered down. A rich, full tone boomed throughout the hall. She gasped and pulled away. She turned to Lucas, but he just shrugged. Unbeknownst to anyone, Timothy had arranged a complete overhaul of the instrument's innards prior to his departure. Miriam began again, this time happily surrendering to the blissful sound. Everyone joined in; good, bad and even worse voices, singing a stretch of hymns that gushed from Miriam's fingertips untamed.

When the music finally quieted, Elizabeth couldn't believe that she had sat through it all. Since childhood she had always proclaimed that church music wasn't her 'thing', but today it captivated her and calmed her nerves. She hastily credited the peaceful spell to the hypnotic patter of rain outside.

Lucas's youth, and tight integration with the day's events aroused Elizabeth's interest. It seemed everyone present had made a concerted effort to comfort and extend assistance to him. Elizabeth moved to the table of food knowing it would be easier to overhear Lucas reminisce from that position. A cocoon of ever-changing supporters surrounded Lucas at all times; their verbal sentiments frequently mirroring each other, as there are only so many words one can use to console a foundling. Lucas sat between Jude and Miriam, soaking up the security of their presence.

Elizabeth was busy, privately criticizing the disproportionate number of sweets on the table, when she heard Brother Jude utter the word, 'Dad'. The mean streak Elizabeth had been holding in all day twitched. It had been an annoying series of let downs. Her fantasy of Timothy rotting away, miserable and alone, was left unfulfilled. She gritted her teeth as anger wormed inside her. She cursed the injustice of the day's commemoration. Timothy didn't deserve anyone's pity; he didn't deserve a second chance; and he definitely didn't deserve anyone's love. "Were you his son?" Her sugary, counterfeit inquiry stopped the conversation.

Lucas turned to her, "Well-" A loud crash of thunder accompanied by a flash of lightning rolled over St. Anthony, inciting weather commentary throughout the room.

When the rustling settled, Miriam proclaimed, "Timothy was as fine a father as anyone could wish for!"

Everyone vigorously affirmed Miriam's sentiment. A lather of approbations bubbled over the entire room. The new wave of reverence unleashed fury deep within Elizabeth. She slinked back, not wishing to know anything more about Timothy. She wished she had listened to Victoria. Another flash of lighting illuminated the room signaling to Elizabeth it was time to leave. As she approached the exit, the door opened and the cranky Asian woman from Timothy's jogging route entered. Her hands were full with two trays of fish, complete with the heads. "Oh gross!" Elizabeth rudely exclaimed and covered her mouth. The woman returned an equally offensive remark, but in her native tongue. Elizabeth frowned and batted her eyelids waiting for the woman to free up the exit path, but she didn't. Then the woman's face lit up, and she put the trays of fish down on the floor. Stretching out her index finger she drew circles in front of Elizabeth's face and nodded. "Do you mind?" Elizabeth asked, but the woman kept circling and pointing at her face.

Miriam came over and picked up the trays of fish while Lucas tried to gently lead the woman further inside, but she refused. She pointed to Elizabeth and then to a picture of Timothy on a nearby wreath. Finally, she yanked on Lucas' tie and pointed at her own eyes. Lucas nodded, not understanding what she was so worked up about. That appeared to satisfy her. She walked off and caught up with Miriam and the fish.

Completely repulsed, Elizabeth rushed for the exit. As she passed by him, Lucas realized what the Asian woman was trying to say. "Oh, you're-" he stopped himself. Elizabeth shot him a vile look and pushed open the door. "It was nice of you to pay your respects." He muttered.

Holding the door, she turned back and hissed, "He didn't deserve any respect."

"Then why did you come?" Elizabeth glared at Lucas, detesting his docile expression. The rain hammered the cobblestones behind her while she thought about it. She was unable to come up with a suitable answer so she debated what insults to unleash on him instead. "He told me what you did to him." Lucas said before she could answer.

This infuriated Elizabeth. She stepped back in and shoved him hard. "You didn't know him!" Her blistering shouts drew attention from everyone. "Whatever he told you was a lie!" She sneered at the judgmental faces around her. "He was a loser, get over it!"

"Timothy Clement was an honest man." Lucas declared confidently as she unraveled. "I am more certain of it now than ever."

Consumed with hatred, Elizabeth crept into Lucas's space and slurred, "What lies did he tell you?"

"He said you-" Lucas stopped, wondering if there was any point in telling her.

"What!" She snarled. "What did he say?"

Lucas replied solemnly, "He said you threw him out." Elizabeth's face went limp. "He said you threw him away like a piece of trash when he needed you most. That's what he said." Elizabeth stared blankly at Lucas for a moment. He thought she might cry, but she didn't. Instead, her scowl reappeared. She turned and ran out, not looking back.

Lucas followed her outside and watched her run out past the overhang into the storm. Ten yards out, she slipped on the wet cobblestones, falling forward onto her knees, ripping holes in her nylons. Lucas sprang from the doorway to help, but she yelled, "Leave me alone!" the moment she saw him.

His thoughts drifted back to the morning of Timothy's passing. He remembered the anticipation he felt while watching the sunrise with Jude and Timothy. Lucas took a deep breath and yelled into the storm, "He forgave you!"

She staggered to her feet and shook her head, "How would you know, you little creep? You're not even his real son!" Having inflicted her final insult, she turned and limped away, unmoved.

Jude arrived and stood by his side. Lucas's tears mingled with raindrops as soon as they fell, keeping anyone from knowing how hurtful Elizabeth's words had been. "I know because he whispered it to me the day he died. It was the last thing he ever said to me." He said, but she was already out of earshot.

Chapter 57

*T*he cab ride downtown was quiet. Miriam and Lucas gazed out their windows while Jude twiddled the card in his hands. The words "Read me" were still visible on the back of it beneath transparent tape. The blue sky was sunny and clear, the air was pleasant, and Jude's knees were stiff.

The driver dropped them off in front of a posh brick building. A metal sign out front read, 'Benjamin Goretti, Attorney'. The three went inside, and after checking in with his assistant, sat down in the lobby and waited to be seen. Miriam looked around the lobby and asked, "Where are the others?"

Jude looked at his watch. "Perhaps they are already inside."

The dividing door opened and a short portly man with thinning hair came over and greeted the three with handshakes, "Good morning. I'm Benjamin Goretti, Timothy's attorney and executor. You must be Jude and young Lucas." He remarked, shaking their hands.

Jude tried to peek past the door. "Is everyone else back there already?"

"It's a very short list of beneficiaries." He said wryly. "Please come back." Turning to Miriam, he said, "Make yourself comfortable. I won't keep them too long." She sat back down in the rolled arm leather chair and waited.

For the next twenty minutes, Mr. Goretti outlined Timothy's final wishes. The total value of his estate was far higher than Jude or Lucas imagined. All future rights to the MarGreat comic, likeness and merchandise were to be transferred to Lucas. In addition, Timothy left Lucas a trust that would allow him to live a very comfortable life and pursue whatever dreams he wished. Next, Mr. Goretti passed to Lucas Timothy's well-worn Bible. The weight of the book in his hands pulled Lucas' heartstrings. The vestige of Timothy's salvation journey was Lucas's most cherished inheritance. Finally, Mr. Goretti handed Jude a weighty shoe box with the letter, "S" written on its top. "What is this?" Jude asked.

"Mr. Clement didn't indicate the contents." Mr. Goretti handed Jude a pair of scissors to break the seal.

Inside the box Jude found an oxidized railroad spike with, "Matthew 25:35" painted along its length. Also in the box was a handwritten note from Timothy asking that the spike be mounted on a wall in the meal ministry kitchen. Jude looked again at the lid unable to discern what the "S" stood for.

All other assets and existing MarGreat royalties had been left to Jude along with a sealed envelope. He opened it up and silently read the handwritten note. Tears fell as he read the contents. In it he thanked Jude for all he had done for him, especially leading him back to the Lord.

He also requested that Miriam be well cared for. And finally, he made a small request which Jude would need Miriam's help to fulfill.

The men emerged from the office, and with teary faces and embraced Miriam. They thanked Mr. Goretti before heading back to St. Anthony. In the cab Miriam asked, "Everything taken care of?"

"Almost." Jude looked at her exhausted face; the puffy residue of sorrow clung to her visage. He took her hand. "I'm going to need you to do some gardening."

Above the urban din, birds chirped, the wind gusted, and the lost residents of Old Town persevered.

Epilogue

*T*ime moved on, and the emptiness at St. Anthony became less prominent. The task of realizing Jude's vision of a restored St. Anthony kept everyone busy, and distracted them from their hurt. It was a labor of love that united the community, and kept Lucas from straying too far from Jude and Miriam. Every time Lucas was close to completing a project, either Jude or Miriam would assign another. The progress filled Jude with mixed emotions. On one hand it was wonderful to witness the grounds transforming into the artist rendition hanging on his wall, but the completion of the venture held an uncertain future for Lucas at St. Anthony. The clues from casual conversation told Jude he shouldn't expect Lucas to stick around forever. For now, Jude and Miriam persuaded him to move into the belltower loft for the remainder of the construction. He agreed, but didn't get too comfortable; preserving the state Timothy had left it in.

A new plot of soil was tilled in Miriam's garden where she planted purple calla lily bulbs, tending to them regularly. In a few months the delicate buds began to break through earth and rise up. As they bloomed, Miriam was surprised to discover a single white lily pushing its way up among the purple perennials. Lucas immediately took to calling it, 'cotton ball head'. The garden became Lucas' favorite place to unwind, meditate and pray. Sometimes he felt like Timothy was right beside him, comforting him. The memory of Elizabeth's demented tirade still disturbed him. He could only imagine what Timothy must have gone through. Lucas included her in his daily prayers, and hoped that she would come to know the Lord someday. Never again did she attempt to contact anyone at St. Anthony.

Samuel Fitz, the Comic editor at Fluto Media Solutions, checked in with Lucas every few weeks trying to convince him to sell MarGreat, so she could live on at the hands of another artist. Lucas never declined outright. Instead, he always told him he would need to stew on it more.

The completion of the renovation also weighed heavily on Lucas. He had the means to do whatever he wanted, but didn't know what the Lord had in store for him. Nothing felt permanent any more.

"Lucas!" Miriam called from downstairs.

He popped his head out of his doorway. "Yes?"

"Can you please come down here?" Then she added, "dress appropriately!"

That meant he'd be interacting with yet another vendor, contractor or city official. He threw on a pair of shoes, tucked in his shirt, and scampered downstairs. To his surprise, a beautiful young woman was downstairs talking with Miriam. Her shiny hair and aroma of her sweet perfume were intoxicating to him. "Hi, I'm Lucas." He shook the girl's hand nervously, not even paying a glance to Miriam.

"Sharon Rojas" she smiled, equally betrothed. Her soft, innocent voice returned the introduction.

Miriam didn't feel slighted, she found his infatuation sweet. "Sharon is the newest member of our teaching staff. She'll be joining us as soon as construction of the school is complete." Miriam imagined Timothy looking down on them. "It is a great blessing to have her!"

Lucas nodded in agreement, "So, you teach, huh?"

"I'm going to finish out the year at St. Agnes."

"Never heard of it."

"It's a school that specializes in helping girls with behavioral issues." She explained.

Lucas blurted out, "How could someone as sweet as you teach bratty girls?" He immediately felt foolish for the outburst. "I mean-"

"Lucas!" Miriam exclaimed, trying to keep the hopeless bumbling boy from making a bigger mess.

Sharon giggled, "It's okay, I get that a lot."

"It is a very respectable thing, looking after those young ladies." Miriam complimented her.

Lucas clammed up and could only manage to nod in agreement. Sharon divulged, "I was kind of a handful myself, when I was younger. Other teachers get frustrated and walk out, but I understand these girls and can relate to them."

"Well, we are very pleased you accepted our offer." Miriam said.

Sharon extended her hand to Lucas, "It was very nice to meet you Lucas."

His heart thumped hard. After an awkward pause, he grabbed her hand and shook it harder than he should have. "Yes, it was." Lucas stammered, "I mean it was a pleasure meeting you too. I look forward to seeing you around here, um, like when you start teaching and stuff."

Sharon giggled as Miriam pulled her away towards the door, saving Lucas from any further embarrassment. He watched her feminine profile slip outside with Miriam and noticed that he felt fantastic. He couldn't remember when he had ever felt so good.

Then it hit him. He raced up to the loft as fast as his feet could take him, skipping every-other step along the way. Plopping down at the drawing desk, he retrieved a fresh sheet of sketch paper, and a sharp pencil. He began furiously marking, smudging, and dotting the paper. The exaggerated frame and bell of a schoolhouse took shape. In bubbly letters a sign read, 'St. Jude's Academy for Ill-mannered Girls.'

Lucas sat back and smiled at the drawing, admiring the possibilities. He then drew a nun with glasses and a traditional habit, writing on the board. Behind her, unruly students were throwing paper airplanes, passing notes and making ridiculous faces. "This is great!" He said to himself.

More and more panels flowed from his pencil, detailing the rambunctious girls' failed attempts to sabotage their seemingly naive teacher. Fire alarm, stink bombs, pizza delivery! Each time, the clever nun outwitted them, seemingly by accident.

For hours, Lucas feverishly scrawled panel after panel. With each new strip, the school, the girls, and the teacher became better defined. Finally, Lucas stopped and looked at the comic in his hands. The strip began with scissors slipping out of the nun's hand and puncturing a whoopee cushion on her chair. She exclaims, "Whoops!" and the two scheming girls responsible sulk. One of the girls says to the other, "I thought you said it was a whoopee cushion, not a whoops cushion!"

Lucas twirled the pencil around his fingers, recalling how Timothy used to spend hours at the very same desk creating MarGreat comics. Up until now, Lucas hadn't felt comfortable sitting at the desk or opening any of the drawers.

Tearing off a new sheet, he began another comic. In this one, the crafty nun traveled up a winding road with a bouquet of flowers in her hands. She then passed through iron gates and arrived at a headstone that read, 'Mom'. The nun placed the flowers on the marker, in the process giving a glimpse of a calla lily pendant. Finishing with a kiss to the headstone, she said, "Hope you have a good work trip Mom."

Lucas picked up the phone and dialed Samuel Fitz. Mr. Fitz answered, "Lucas, what a pleasant surprise. I was just talking about you. What's going on?"

"Mr. Fitz, I have an idea. . ."

CPSIA information can be obtained
at www.ICGtesting.com
Printed in the USA
BVHW080350190120
569937BV00005B/82